P9-CRM-040

Celebrating the Church Year
with Young Children

Celebrating the Church Year with Young Children

Joan Halmo

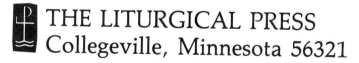
THE LITURGICAL PRESS
Collegeville, Minnesota 56321

Editing, design, and layout by Donald A. Molloy.

Cover design, section and chapter pages by Don Bruno.

Line illustrations by Sharon Pulvermacher.

Photos by Michael Pomedli.

Children's art indicated by page numbers: Angela Hodgson, 121; Annika Hodgson, 92, 104; Kristin Hodgson, 111; Chantal LaPlante, 30, 46, 71, 90; Stefan LaPlante, 13, 31, 49, 83; Stephen Pomedli, 27, 45, 74; Rachel Pomedli, all remaining art, and musical compositions, 37, 45, 125.

Music Notation by John J. Dominik

Published by *The Liturgical Press*
   The Liturgical Press, Collegeville, Minnesota, U.S.A. 56321—ISBN 0-8146-1580-5

Manufactured in the United States of America.

Library of Congress Cataloging-in-Publication Data

Halmo, Joan
Celebrating the church year with young children / Joan Halmo.
         p.   cm.
Bibliography: p.
ISBN 0-8146-1580-5
1. Christian education — Home training. 2. Family — Religious life.
3. Christian education of children. 4. Catholic Church — Education.
5. Church year. I. Title
BV1590.H35   1988
249-dc19   88-25994
                  CIP

DEDICATION

*To my parents
and
to Michael, Rachel, and Stephen*

CONTENTS

ACKNOWLEDGMENTS

Special thanks to the families who have engaged in the celebrations and activities described in this book, and who have offered insightful comments; to the children who have allowed us to glimpse their spiritual vision as expressed in their art and music; to Sharon Pulvermacher, not only for her sensitive illustrations and for expert culinary advice, but also for her companionship in the birthing of this book; to Bernard La Plante, for meticulous conversion of all measures into metric equivalents; to those who have sung the music with me—Al Gerwing, Margaret Boatz, Doris Murphy, the children who have prayed the psalms and songs, and particularly Ursula Hodgson, who was often telephoned at midnight to hear a musical interval; to Andrew Britz, O.S.B., and Frank Henderson for reading the manuscript and for their valuable suggestions; to the Ursuline Sisters of Bruno, Saskatchewan, for their active support of the preschool catechetical dimensions of this project; to the Saskatoon Chapter of the Knights of Columbus for a financial contribution to assist in the completion of the publication; to my sister Donalda and her daughters Kathryn and Barbara for proofreading time, recipe testing, and various forms of rescue service; to my father and mother for years of encouragement, inspiration and generous help; to my children, Rachel and Stephen, for patience during many months of "book time;" and most of all, to my husband Michael, partner in shaping our family's faith journey and wonderful editorial assistant whose untiring care has helped make this book a reality.

Introduction

Reflections on Faith Formation of the Young Child

Some years ago, when our daughter was approaching her second birthday, my husband and I began to look ahead to the time when we would share with her our deeply cherished traditions of liturgical spirituality. I began to collect books of prayer and domestic liturgical customs. Many of the books predated the 1960s and were no longer entirely pertinent because of cultural and liturgical changes which have taken place. A number of publications from the 1970s and '80s left gaps in concepts and information for parents. Generally, these more recent books concentrated on only one liturgical season (usually on the preparatory time rather than the season of celebration); these books hardly ever established priorities among Sundays, feasts, and seasons; and they were usually "how-to" rather than "why" books, bypassing the theological/scriptural/liturgical underpinnings of the Church year.

Drawing on my background in liturgy and my in-service training as a mother, I put together various ideas for the domestic celebration of liturgical times. Other families in our city borrowed some of the concepts and went on to form "family groups." The latter now include numerous families who meet regularly to support and assist one another in Christian formation of, and celebration with, their children.

Recently, the work of the eminent catechist of preschool children, Sofia Cavalletti, has greatly enriched my understanding of the spirituality of the very young child. Within months of reading Cavalletti's *The Religious Potential of the Child* (New York: Paulist Press, 1983), I was privileged to participate in a course given by her international team in Toronto during the summer of 1986. Although Cavalletti's primary concern is catechesis, and my interest is the faith environment of the home, many aspects of her work have brought inspiration and new impetus to mine, and her wisdom and long experience have been a beacon to my own family and to others with whom I have shared her book.

Cavalletti's background in the Montessori educational philosophy held special interest for our family because by the time Cavalletti's book came to my at-

tention, our daughter was completing her second year in Montessori preschool. With the writings of both Cavalletti and Maria Montessori in hand, my husband and I were beginning to see for ourselves the remarkable capacities of the very young child, the preschooler. We had noted particularly in our child and in her little friends many of the following characteristics of early childhood which Montessori had described decades ago: a sense of purpose and constancy in children's work/play as they discover their environment and seek to master the universe; a kind of innate yearning for order, repetition, and regularity in their work and in rhythms of living; a great capacity for concentration and silence, for complete immersion in tasks or subjects of deep interest to them; and, of course, a remarkable sense of wonder and delight in all things! Like many parents, we witnessed with awe our child's spontaneous absorption of the environment, language, and culture as if through a process of sensorial osmosis. All that the child sees, hears, touches, smells, and tastes becomes part of its ever-expanding consciousness.

As we prayed with our young child and did various religious/liturgical activities with her, one of our

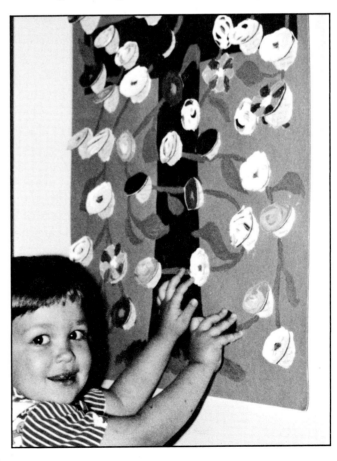

parental intuitions seemed to be confirmed: children, even at a very young age, have a wonderful capacity for the spiritual. Our observations found concurrence and affirmation in the writings of Cavalletti, who attributes to the young child an openness and ease in its relationship to God, a spiritual directness akin to a mystical gift.[1]* With Cavalletti, we saw these surprising and deeply touching characteristics in the preschool child who is presented the gospel and led into liturgical and prayer experiences: a great and peaceful joy in relationship with God; the possession of mysterious knowledge, often of deep theological truths which the child has not been told (many parents can attest to this, we have discovered); an ability to grasp the invisible, beyond the veil of signs and symbols; a capacity for prayer, remarkable for its qualities of spontaneous praise and thanks, and for its duration; and finally—as psychology also tells us—the need of the child for an unconditional, abiding, global love, which is answerable only by infinite love.[2]

And specifically, as we prayed and celebrated the liturgical year with our young child, what else did we discover? Over five years, and with a second child joining the family scene, we made the following observations:

> (1) The liturgical year, with its rituals and symbols, its Scripture and song, is an inexhaustible source of spirituality and faith formation both for young children and for their families.

> (2) The gospel, in small selected sections, can be given to even a very young child (three years or so), for instance, such parts as the Good Shepherd parable, other gospel parables, and some of the stories of Jesus' life and mission.

> (3) Little children *can* pray, and they do so in many ways, often in ways which are unlike adult prayer. Children might express their spiritual response in movement, dance, or silence. When they do speak in prayer, they tend to do so with few words, usually in the spirit of gratitude and praise rather than intercession.

> (4) Domestic resources and family activities—music and dance, arts and crafts, the enjoyment of nature, the preparation and sharing

of food—all these can unabashedly be part of celebrating faith and can help the little child experience the breadth of Christian living. Moreover, these very sensorial aspects of life can provide the child with the sounds, the colors, the tastes, and the aura of the days and the seasons which we call our liturgical year.

(5) The nature and needs of the child limit the scope of early faith formation. Not all of Christianity need be imparted to a preschooler! For the very young child, presenting the essentials is sufficient. It is part of the Montessori philosophy of education to divide complex matters or actions into manageable segments for the child to master one by one; the basics are given first and in such a way that they need never be retaught, only added to as the child is able to comprehend more fully. Applying this educational principle, we can begin by reiterating for religion what psychology and human wisdom have already taught us, namely, that for the child, the essential thing is to know love. Spiritually, "one thing necessary" is all that the child needs in its earliest years—to delight in love, especially the love of the persons who surround the child and the love of God who is ultimate love. The home specializes, as it were, in providing the experience of love and in celebrating it. If the home environment for the early years of the child's life is more properly suited to the discovery and enjoyment of God's love than to catechesis in the formal sense, then parents should capitalize on this possibility. In doing so, many families will feel liberated from their anxiety about teaching their little ones formal religion. The family need not concern itself about filling the young child's mind with elements of moral or dogmatic formation. The latter aspects will follow as the child reaches an age more suitable for this kind of development.

(6) Faith formation is more than a seasonal effort, more than a periodic attempt to share faith vision and values. To celebrate only the great feasts and seasons is an approach insufficiently rooted in the child's—and the family's—experience of time. It seems very important to respect the natural progression of human and religious experience, beginning, as the young child

* All footnotes appear on pp. 157–58.

2

does, by perceiving fragmentary moments, then moving on gradually to larger blocks of time. First, there is the day with its rhythms of light and darkness, its rituals and meals, its joys, sorrows, work, rest, play, hellos, and good-byes. Then, for Christians, there is the week crowned by the week's first day, the Sunday, which gathers up all these events and infuses them with the light of the paschal mystery of Jesus the Lord (paschal mystery refers to Christ's passion, death, and resurrection collectively, the central event of Jesus' life). Next, there is the annual paschal cycle, that is, the Paschal Three Days, with its overflow into Eastertime and its preparatory time of Lent, altogether an extended immersion in the paschal mystery and intense articulation of what we live each day and celebrate each Sunday. And then, finally, because there is Pasch, there is also joyful remembering in the seasons of Christmas and Advent of the Lord's coming among us.

(7) The Christian formation of the child begins much earlier than does an explicit faith-sharing. The very attitudes, values, and lifestyle of a home are being absorbed by the child long before the parent and child are able to converse about them. We have concluded that perhaps people who are planning to be parents ought to consciously organize their style of living, their home's spiritual and attitudinal environment, as early and as carefully as they purchase baby clothes and decorate a nursery space. It is not a question of producing religious "superbabies" who have had moral and doctrinal information imparted to them from flash cards from early infancy, but rather of creating a milieu in which Christian living and celebrating are gently "caught" rather than actively taught (see Appendix A).

Above: Sunday Eucharist; age 5.

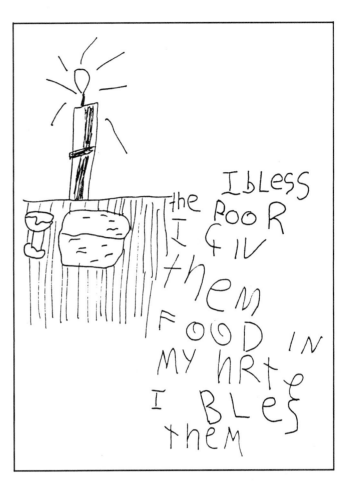

Family: Locus of Ritual and Celebration

Learning to pray, to worship the Lord—the home is where it all begins! We know that, of course; we have said it and heard it said, but have we taken it seriously enough to let it challenge and alter the way we live as family?

The basic, the first, the most important task for a household in the enterprise of faith formation of its little ones is to be a religious home, a home which treasures and fosters the religious dimension of life. Religious home in the sense intended here means one that responds to "the human need to concur on a set of symbols and rituals which create order, give identity, and provide motivation," as Gail Ramshaw Schmidt writes.[3] Does the family share meals in common? Are there household rituals, moments together that regularly and reliably happen? Is there respect for the wonder of life? Is there time for poetry, art, music, the enjoyment of nature? Does the family face and embrace pain or the death of loved ones? In a word, does the household stand open to the whole mystery of life as it presents itself in the unfolding of every day?

Openness to the mystery of life is not highly prized in our society, for we are besieged by busy-ness and overinvolvement; we are absorbed by the world of daily care. Yet, as the philosopher Josef Pieper writes, the rational "useful" world which preoccupies us is but a partial environment for our humanity; we need to be able to transcend the purely pragmatic, the visible and verifiable, and embrace the whole as marvel, as gift.[4] Encountering that gift, the mystery of life, we can choose to leave behind temporarily the workaday world of labor and practicality, and enter into the "uselessness" of festivity, laughter, extravagance, and absence of calculation. Actually, for the little child, not yet bound by the constraints of workaday necessity, the "useless" world is ever at hand as a natural home. Indeed, the child is often more capable than the adult of a receptive attitude, of enjoyment, of wonder. Could it be that the child within the household unit is the teacher in openness to mystery, in respectful stance before the gift of life?

To celebrate is to break out of the ordinary routine and enter that free and freeing space which we call festivity. Each family needs to set aside time for celebration: at the moments of births and birthdays, journeying and homecoming, goals achieved, anniversaries reached, occasions large and small in the fabric of life. All family members, even the youngest, can in some way share the many apsects of festivity: by planning and preparing, dressing up in special clothes, welcoming and gathering, sharing stories and memories, listening and speaking, singing, laughing and playing games, expressing affection and affirmation, giving and forgiving, setting the table, eating together, participating in symbolic actions like cake-cutting, exchanging gifts, and so on. All these activities which are part of our celebration as family and extended family invite the young child to express what it already knows is essential: to revel in the gifts of being and loving, to wonder, to rejoice!

It is within the rhythm of daily living and within family relationships, then, that we learn many of the gestures and rituals that are integral to the public worship we call liturgy. Of all the domestic rituals which form us as family and teach us about community, none is as powerful as meal. The centrality of meal seems to become ever clearer within the family as infants grow to toddlerhood and take their place at the household table. Day by day, the table is where we gather not only to nurture our physical life but also to reach out to one another, tell our day's stories, remember the past, and look ahead; we share food from bowls and also the food of community, human communing. The domestic table is the basic sacrament for the child and for the household. We learn gradually at the family table what is done at the Eucharistic table of the larger family, the Church.

Beginning explicit faith sharing

There are specific prayer and liturgical activities a family can do for and with its little ones in their earliest years.

As soon as parents begin hanging charming mobiles near their baby's crib they could consider which icon or classical representation of Jesus (or Jesus and Mary) might also be there. Even when children are small, parents might draw their attention to the figure of Jesus (and his mother). Parents might also procure a fine religious work for their home, such as a cross or a reprint of a religious painting or a small sculpture—something which can occupy a prominent place in the home and which can serve as the child(ren)'s introduction to the world of sacred art. Needless to say, cheap representations and plastic figurines cannot be considered the optimum choice for the formation of anyone's faith, least of all the impressionable little child.

Simple prayers and gestures can be used in the presence of the very young. The time-honored parental blessing of the child, with roots in the Jewish tradition, can be done regularly with children of all ages. A gesture of the parent's hand on the child's head, or, if desired, the tracing of the cross on the child's forehead, can accompany a simple blessing such as:

May God bless you, N_____;

or a more extended blessing such as that from Numbers 6:24-26:

May the Lord bless you and keep you,
May the Lord let his face shine on you
and be gracious to you.
May the Lord uncover his face to you
and bring you peace.

At our home, the latter has served as a good-night blessing for our children since their babyhood and also as a good-bye wish prayed by anyone waving farewell to departing family or friends.

Table prayers are, of course, an excellent time for children to begin learning community prayer. A traditional table grace or a song of thanks (such as Song

36 or 37 in Appendix C) or a seasonal song may serve as both a moment of remembering God, the source of all, and as a time of family com-union in prayer. (Suggestions for seasonal prayers and songs are offered in each of the chapters of this book.)

The family can have a prayer corner in its home where anyone, adult or child, may come for moments of reflection. The space might be in the family's primary living area, ideally a quiet and generally undisturbed spot, or in a separate room (we use our formal living/dining area as a prayer place), or even in a corner of the child's bedroom. In the prayer area, there could be a religious representation (an icon or a small statue of the Good Shepherd or a cross), a candle (if adults will be handling it), and a Bible. The space could be used as well for any gathering of the family for formal prayer. Even though tiny children will not necessarily frequent the space as a prayer area, they will become aware of its existence and its importance for the adults around them.

If a family finds that it can pray communally on a regular basis, it may wish to gather in the morning or after the evening meal or before bedtime for a short prayer time. The prayer may well follow the structure of the Liturgy of the Hours, the Church's official prayer. An abbreviated form designed for the presence/participation of young children follows:

Proclamation of God's Word in the Assembly; age 6½.

Call to Prayer: (Leader) Come let us worship the Lord,
(All) Let us praise his goodness and love!

Psalm: for example, Psalm 116 [117], A psalm of praise
(Song 38 in Appendix C)

Scripture Reading: a gospel passage, selected verses from the Sunday's gospel (list given in Appendix B)

Canticle: for morning, Song of Zechariah *(Benedictus),* see p. 153
for evening, Song of Mary *(Magnificat),* see p. 140

Intercessions: short, and structured in the manner of presenting people and their needs before the Lord

Our Father

Blessing: (Leader) The Lord bless and keep us all in his love.
(All) Amen.

Further suggestions for opening prayers, psalms, canticles, and other songs are found in all chapters of this book under the heading "Resources . . . ," and musical scores are found in Appendix C.

The more formal prayers suggested above need, of course, to be part of a fabric of prayer in the home, part of an ease in speaking of and speaking to the Lord. Such informal prayer or spiritual conversation frequently arises from everyday experiences. A beautiful morning? We are grateful to God for this gift, we enjoy! God gives us wonderful things for our happiness? We sing, clap, dance! Something sad befalls us? We accept it as best we can, embracing one another. Someone is ill or dies? We know the Lord, the Good Shepherd, cares for that person and for each of us in our need.

**Keeping the liturgical cycle
in the home**

Finally, we come to the celebration of the liturgical year in the home. It is my experience that the sacred rhythms of the week and the year can provide an admirable way of initiating the child into the celebration and enjoyment of belonging to the Lord. Furthermore, the theological richness of the feasts and seasons is so vast that our repeated keeping of these times continues to give us the formation (and eventually the *in*formation) which defines us as Christian. What we love and celebrate and value, we become!

Many parents have said to me, "But I don't really understand the liturgical cycle very well." In this book I provide an overview of each of the major feasts and seasons of the Church year. In doing so, I touch on historical roots and some subsequent developments affecting how we celebrate a given liturgical time; by allusion to scriptural and liturgical texts and often to patristic writings of early centuries, I try to capture the original spirit of each liturgical feast or season. Much more can be written, of course; for those who want to delve more deeply into the subject of the liturgical year, a brief bibliography is included (see Appendix D).

The liturgical order of this book is not usual, in the sense that I do not commence with Advent and proceed chronologically through the Church year. Instead, I set out the Church's major feasts and seasons in the order they evolved historically, for that *historical order of development reveals theological priorities*. First, there is paschal mystery, celebrated weekly on Sunday and annually in the paschal cycle, and then there is the Christmas cycle. I sometimes suggest to parents that if they have only a limited amount of energy for liturgical endeavors with their children, they can best use it to celebrate the Sunday worthily. If they can manage a second liturgical-year commitment, the choice should fall to the Paschal Three Days, and so on, in the sequence set out on the following pages.

Parish: the Wider Church at Worship

After the household has done all it can for the religious and liturgical formation of its little ones, there remains the parish's role in the faith formation of children. How are children incorporated into the liturgical life of the parish? How are they ensured a positive experience of the wider community at worship? And how are the home and parish to be linked to provide a similar and mutually supportive liturgical emphasis?

First of all, to ask the question of the child's place in parish liturgy is to face the issue of whether the child is an "object of catechesis" or "subject of worship," as Robert Hamma delineates it.[5] The perspective which sees the child as object of catechesis, Hamma calls the cognitive approach. This view emphasizes faith as a conscious commitment, liturgy as word-oriented and orderly, catechesis as a systematic presentation of the content of faith, and liturgical formation as learning to know the mystery signified in liturgy. The vision of the child as subject of worship is, by contrast, an experiential approach. Here, faith is an orientation toward God and thus is more developmental and active than rational, liturgy is more symbolic and ritualized, catechesis is a discovery of the Christian mystery through parables and story, and liturgical formation is participation in the mystery for the sake of personal transformation.

In the Vatican's *Directory for Masses with Children*, a landmark document published in 1973, the experiential approach prevails. Children are primarily subjects of worship. They, like the rest of the baptized believers at worship, are called to full and active participation in the liturgy, even though they cannot as yet comprehend the entire meaning of what they do. They are invited to share in worship with their whole being, their whole persons involved in a very sensorial way. They, like adults, are addressed by the symbols and gestures and surroundings of liturgical celebration—light, water, Word, the bread, the cup, movement and decor and music.

When parish liturgies are being prepared, how does the planning committee take account of the children celebrating in the assembly? Are the planners concerned about how the spirit, milieu, and prayer of this community can touch the children—the experiential approach? Or are they concerned about whether children are "*understanding* liturgy on their own level"—the rational approach?

There is a strong penchant in many places to slant the liturgy toward instruction of children, to regard them as objects of catechesis. Sometimes this is done by adapting the Scripture readings and homily to them, at the expense of the entire community. More often, it is done by removal of children from the full assembly to their own "Liturgy of the Word." How quickly the latter leans toward instruction is evident, for example, from the "lesson leaflets" provided for the children; or from the terminology of adults, who call the children's gatherings "catechism" or "liturgy classes."

Parishes often set up programs and practices without sufficient study of underlying issues and principles; and in regard to children at worship, I believe this is happening today. The question to be asked by parish liturgy planners is not simply, "What can we do to attract families with young children?" but "How do we lead our whole assembly, old and young, to active and full participation in the liturgy?" The latter is the more difficult question and much harder to answer in liturgical practice. Later in this book, in the section on the Sunday (see p. 15), I propose several areas where parishes can contribute more creatively to the long-term liturgical development of children.

In the *Directory for Masses with Children*, celebrations in which children are present in the assembly are considered to be the norm (celebrations primarily with children present are to prepare and enable the children to enter more fully into worship with the whole community). In this book the family or household will be regarded as the normative unit at liturgy.

Parents need to know something about liturgy. Children are generally with their parents at Sunday Eucharist and together with them celebrate the feasts and seasons; therefore parents can use information to prepare their children for special aspects of liturgy during the Church year. Some parents may also be on the parish's liturgy planning committee and can effectively work for good celebrations which help build up the faith in all of us. My remarks on parish liturgy in each section of this book are offered in the hope that liturgy be richer for children and their families in the midst of the assembly of God's people.

Notes on Resources

Following each discussion of liturgical feasts and seasons, I sketch some possibilities for family prayer and activities under the heading "Resources. . . ." Each of the resource sections proceeds with its own logic and with some order of priority within itself, according to the character of each season; the sections are therefore not parallel one to another. A note on the contents of the resource sections follows below.

Prayers, spoken and sung

Since this book emphasizes liturgical formation, most of the prayer forms, texts, and songs presented here originate in liturgical sources. The selection is necessarily limited, but sufficient, I think, for use with young children, for whom repetition of text and music is extremely important. For further prayers, blessings, and so on, the household might invest in a book such as Gabe Huck's *A Book of Family Prayer* (New York: Seabury Press, 1979) or Edward Hays' *Prayers for the Domestic Church* (Easton, Kansas: Forest of Peace Books, 1979) or the small volume from the Canadian Conference of Catholic Bishops, *Family Book of Prayer* (Ottawa, 1983).

Formal common prayer should not replace moments of individual prayer lest children think of prayer exclusively as words derived from a source outside their own language and experience. I do propose some brief passages from our tradition in the hope that their vocabulary and spirit can be formative in the prayer and spirituality of the child and the family.

The question of inclusive language arises when one addresses the topic of early formation in faith. In this book, I have deliberately chosen to give liturgical and scriptural texts in translations currently used in liturgy. In many church communions, parents are presently the ones who will lay foundations for the regular use of inclusive language by their children in the future. As a beginning, for example, parents can ensure that their children grow up with a rich set of images for God. Through praying the psalms and other scriptural passages with their families, parents can enable children to discover that God is both mother and father; that God is nurturer, healer, gentle and strong one. Current literature on inclusive language can give families more ideas on how to continue supporting this broader consciousness.

In choosing/composing the music for this book, I try to represent the spirit of the Church's major feasts and seasons. The psalms are those traditionally linked with the particular seasons in the liturgy and can be used at morning/evening prayer. By including only one stanza of each psalm and only selected verses of the canticles, I relinquish my purist tendencies as musician and liturgist and affirm that for the young child, few prescribed words are preferable to many.

The refrains, acclamations, and songs, many original and published here for the first time, can be used at common prayer or at meals or at other times. A number of the settings are based on the pentatonic scale, especially on the *mi-sol-la* intervals, which the composer Zoltan Kodaly identified as the first and easiest for children to learn.[6] Many of the music selections in this book came into being simply because there were no similar sung texts accessible to young children. *If fine liturgical antiphons, psalms, and songs are in use in one's parish, it is preferable to choose those for home use* in order to reinforce and unify children's experience of the Church's feasts and seasons.

In regard to music listening, I make only passing allusions to some selections traditionally associated with the feasts and seasons of the Church year. There is a good deal of other recorded liturgical music from which families can choose. In general, I always encourage the young child's exposure to the great classics of sacred music, especially those which are liturgically/scripturally based, e.g., Gregorian chant, the works of Handel and J.S. Bach, and so on. A list of contemporary liturgical music recordings would include the music of the ecumenical community of Taizé—children quite easily learn the Taizé repertoire because of its litany structure—and of groups such as the St. Louis Jesuits and Weston Priory.

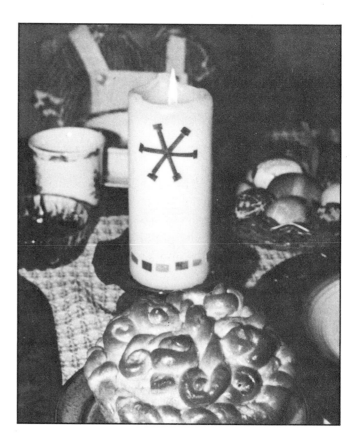

Activities, crafts, foods

Various activities have been incorporated into each chapter, with some initial reluctance on my part! My hope is that by deepening its understanding of the spirit of a feast or season, each family can create its own pattern of activities and collect its own recipes appropriate to the interests, the customs, and the ethnic roots of that family. Friends have convinced me that resource sections in this book will serve a useful purpose, and with that in mind, I share descriptions of activities which our household has found enriching.

In proposing activities, I try to emphasize simple ways of honoring other persons and of appreciating the natural world. In the choice of arts and crafts, I try to keep in mind the limitations of very young children in some projects; in others, I assume the ability of a slightly older preschooler or the presence of a helping adult. Generally, the materials required for craft projects are inexpensive; frequently, household items can be used as substitutes for commercially available materials.

As for recipes in a liturgical book . . . well, food has always been theological in our tradition! Not only do we eat and drink of the Lord as our central act of common worship, the Eucharist, but we have for cen-

Above: The household paschal candle and braided bread.

turies set our domestic tables with the food of the Church's liturgical seasons: the pretzels of Lent, the dyed eggs and rising breads of Easter, the beautiful breads of Christmas, of Bethlehem, which means "house of bread." (Breads, incidentally, so important a staple food, are often the carriers of the liturgical season in our tradition; this accounts for the preponderance of bread and baking recipes in this book.)

The recipes reflect some of the domestic customs which have grown up wherever Church is, and they represent some of the favorites of my family and friends; other households may already have their own "liturgical foods." As far as possible, I try to be conscious of nutritional value and simple procedures in the few recipes suggested, largely for the children who ideally will be not only the eaters but also the helpers in preparing food for the feasts and seasons. Liturgical gourmets will be pleased to find a far more extensive array of recipes for the Church year in the publication by Evelyn Birge Vitz, *A Continual Feast* (New York: Harper and Row, and Toronto: Fitzhenry and Whiteside Ltd., 1985).

A Flexible Agenda

Throughout the book, I sketch a range of possibilities which each family can adapt to its own "personality" as family and to its own needs. There is no fixed formula which will yield a correct result. So if your family is less interested in crafts than in the great outdoors, expand on the nature activities for a particular season. If you are not a singer but a great storyteller, why not make up some children's stories related to the liturgical seasons?

Not everything suggested in these pages can be done by any one family in a given year. Indeed, not everything should be done! Cavalletti maintains that for the little child, oversaturation in religious formation is less desirable than sparseness.[7] Hunger and yearning are better than overfeeding; a little less is more!

It is important to remember that in households with little children, flexibility is the saving virtue. Parents propose an agenda, and life with children presents an agenda—not always the same one. By doing what we can in the best way, we accept the reality of our pilgrim state, our human condition, our incompleteness on our journey! In the end, our lives lived out in love are our liturgy.

Sunday entrance procession with cross, lighted candles, and the Book of God's Word; age 6.

9

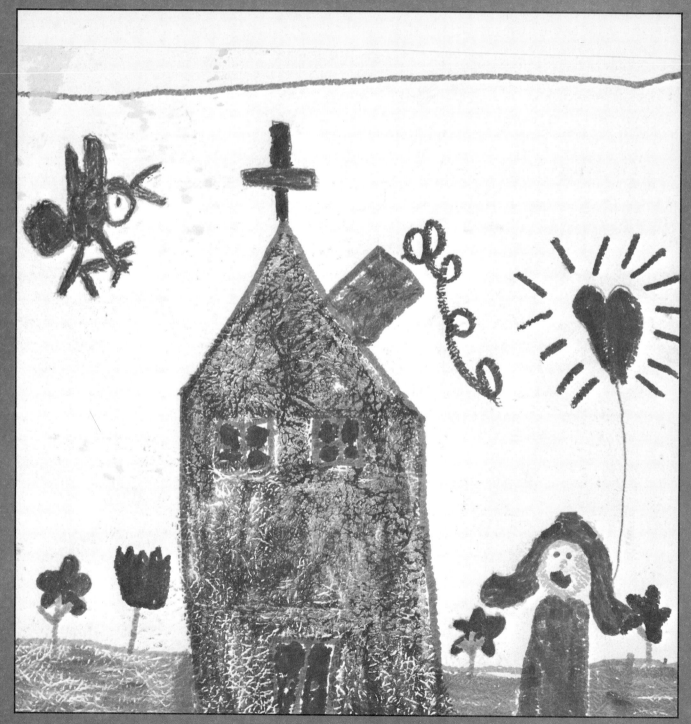

Going with joy to the house of God; age 5½.

Lord Has Made!"

Chapter 1   Sunday

SUNDAY

Procession of gifts at the Eucharist; age 6.

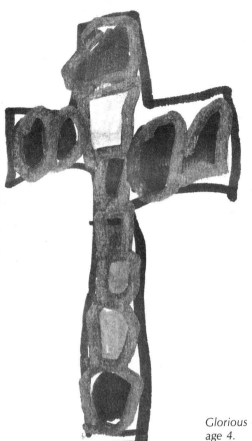

Glorious cross; age 4.

Origins and Spirit of Sunday

Sunday is our original feast day, the first Easter celebration, and the heart of the liturgical year. We know that at the very beginning of the Church's life there was Christianity without the great feasts and seasons we now consider to be major, but there has never been a Christianity without the Sunday! We can discover a great deal about Sunday's significance by examining the names traditionally given to Sunday.

According to the Christian Scriptures, Jesus Christ rose from the dead on the third day, and thereafter his followers came together weekly on that day for common worship (1 Cor 16:2; Acts 20:7). The author of Revelation calls this day of Jesus' resurrection "the Lord's Day" (Rev 1:10). The latter designation is significant because it is linked to a specific scriptural name for the Eucharist, that is, "the Lord's Supper" (1 Cor 11:20). Both the Lord's Day and the Lord's Supper are described by the term *kyriake* (in Greek, literally "Lordy"), which is used in only two contexts in the Christian Scriptures: those pertaining to the "Lord-y" day and the "Lord-y" supper. This scriptural connection witnesses to a fundamental stance on the part of the early Church, that the Lord's Day (the Sunday) and the Lord's Supper (the Eucharist) belong together. It is on the Lord's Day that Christians gather to share the Lord's Supper. And the Supper, the Eucharistic gathering, is what makes the Lord's Day!

In the mid-second century, Justin, a lay philosopher and catechist, writes a description of the celebration of the Lord's Day:

> On the day which is called Sun-day, all, whether they live in the town or in the country, gather in the same place. Then the Memoirs of the Apostles or the Writings of the Prophets are read for as long as time allows. When the reader has finished, the president speaks, exhorting us to live by these noble teachings. Then we rise all together and pray. Then, as we said earlier, when the prayer is finished, bread, wine and water are brought. The president then prays and gives thanks as well as he can. And all the people reply with the acclamation: Amen! After this the eucharists are distributed and shared out to everyone, and the deacons are sent to take them to those who are absent.[1]

So on the weekly resurrection day, the Lord's Day, the Christian community gathers together to share the Eucharist, and in this event recognizes the Lord Jesus, Risen One. This is a familiar pattern of events recalling the resurrection appearances of Jesus. The Lord reveals himself at the breaking of the bread (Luke 24:28-35). His followers, baptized into his death and alive with his risen life, seek him with longing, seek the Word which makes their hearts burn within them, seek his bread and cup. The Christian community *needs* the Sunday, the Lord's Day, and the Lord's Supper. It is as the fourth-century martyrs of Abitina declared: "We cannot live without the Sunday!"[2]

Another important name given the Lord's Day in the early Church is "the eighth day." The present age moves in cycles of seven days but the Lord's Day, the eighth day, bursts the bondage of time and realizes the final age among us. It is a divine gift, this eighth day, not of mortal making, not an ordinary reckoning of time. The eighth day is replete with the presence of the Risen Christ and is the true home of those baptized into him. There is always a strong link between the eighth day and baptism. The Church Fathers sometimes likened baptism to Jewish circumcision, which took place on the eighth day, or to the rescue from the flood, when Noah was the eighth person saved. The understanding of the eighth day as kingdom-already-present even found its way into architectural

13

forms such as the octagonal baptistry building and baptismal font.

For the Jewish people, the day they called "the first day of the week" commemorated and honored God's creation in a special way. On that day, God shattered the darkness with his Word "Let there be light" (Gen 1:3). Because the Lord's Day coincided with the Jewish "first day of the week," it would be natural for Christians who see Christ as the "new creation" (2 Cor 5:17) and as true light of the world to incorporate this entire theological complex into their Sunday. As Justin wrote: "We hold this meeting of us all on Sun-day because it is the first day, the day when God transformed matter and darkness and created the world, and also because it was on this same day that Jesus Christ, our Saviour, rose from the dead."[3] The Lord's Day, then, is when Christians praise God for the wonders of creation, both the first creation and the new creation in Christ.

When Justin refers to "the day of the sun" in the passage above, he is using the planetary terminology current in the second-century Roman Empire. The day which Jewish people called "the first day of the week" and which Christians called "the Lord's Day, the eighth day," was commonly known as the sun-day. Just as the general populace honored the sun deity on this day, Christians came to see the sun-day as a time to honor Christ their Risen Sun. Christ is the light who enlightens his own (John 1:4f.; 2 Cor 4:4-6; Heb 1:3; 1 John 1:5f.); and in anticipation of his coming again in glory, Christians for centuries have prayed facing the east, source of the rising sun.

Near the end of the fourth century, Jerome gives us a classic summary of the meaning of Sunday:

> The Lord's day, the day of the resurrection, the day of Christians: that is our day. It is called the Lord's day because on it the Lord ascended victoriously to the Father. When pagans speak of it as the day of the sun, we gladly agree, for on this day the light of the world, the sun of justice, arose and salvation is hidden in the shelter of his wings.[4]

All these aspects of Sunday—day of resurrection and of Eucharistic rejoicing, the eighth day, day of the new creation, day of the risen sun—eventually came to be attributed as well to the Church's most ancient season, the fifty-day Eastertime; hence the annual fifty days acquired the collective name "the great Sunday." Both the weekly Sunday and the Easter fifty-day Sunday were considered a gift of the kingdom, a taste of alleluia-time in this present age. Because during both

these times that the Church knew itself to be in possession of the fullness of risen life, there was on Sunday and during the "the great Sunday" the singing of the Easter song "Alleluia"; and during these liturgical times there was neither fasting nor kneeling.

The Jewish Sabbath elements which later became attached to the weekly Sunday celebration were not present at its origin. The early Church considered the Sabbath law fulfilled in Christ; that is, a daily life of holiness in Christ was the keeping of the Sabbath. Interestingly, there are second-century Christian representations of the Ten Commandments which show the Sabbath commandment absent. The real Sabbath is Jesus himself (Matt 12:8; Col 2:16-17).

Only in the time of Constantine, in the fourth century, was Sunday set aside by law as a day free from usual business. Actually the Church's attitude to this legislation was first to ignore it and later to react negatively against it. A day of idleness in the midst of a non-Christian society could provide all kinds of alluring temptations for the young Church. Gradually, the Church came to emphasize the keeping holy of the Sunday as a replacement of the Jewish Sabbath. Finally, by the sixth century, the Sabbath commandment of the Decalogue became part of the Church's explanation of why Christians rested from work on Sunday.

In our day, the context of an increasingly pluralistic society puts new strains on the way Christians have for many centuries been accustomed to keeping the Sunday, both as a day of worship and also as a day of rest and rejuvenation. There is an important task at hand for the Church as a whole and for families and individuals as well, that is, to reassess for today the meaning of the Lord's Day.

A recent pastoral statement by the Canadian Conference of Catholic Bishops reminds Christians of their calling to live in the full spirit of the Sunday. Participating in the Eucharistic celebration is the highlight of the Lord's Day, but it is also the source of a new outlook on life which can manifest itself on this very day. In the words of the statement, "[The Christian] belief in the dignity of the human person as the image of God calls us to make a special effort on this day to identify areas where we have let human values be replaced by material aspirations in our own personal lives or in the life of society around us. As followers of Christ, who calls all people by name, we should try, especially on Sunday, to be more fully ourselves as persons and to pursue those activities which make society more human."[5] Ideally, then, Sunday can be a day of peace, presence to others, playfulness, and the praise of God.

Sunday in the Parish

Every Sunday in the parish is a celebration of the Pasch of Jesus Christ, the passing from death to life of both the Lord and his people. Every Sunday is the gift of the kingdom here present, the breaking-in of eternity into our lives, the taste of the Promised Land where milk and honey flow, the place of the Risen Lord and Shepherd. Every Sunday is Easter, and Easter is every Sunday!

The Lord's Day, according to the Second Vatican Council, is indeed the original feast day and is the heart of the liturgical year. We live our daily Christian rhythms of life on the strength not of an annual feast or season but of the Sunday festivity of the Risen Lord. In the parish, then, the real centerpieces of the year's celebrations are or ought to be the Sunday Eucharistic liturgies (the term "Eucharist," from the Greek *eucharistia*—giving thanks, will be used for the most part in this book in preference to "Mass," as the former designation articulates more accurately the very purpose for which the Church gathers on the Sunday).

In practice, quite often the Sundays outside the boundaries of liturgical seasons tend to be celebrated in a humdrum way and lack the zest and commitment elicited from us by festal times such as Easter or Christmas, or even their respective preparatory periods of Lent and Advent. We seem to have lost some of the excitement of the ancient Christians who exclaimed that they could not live without the Sunday!

For the parish—for its ministers and liturgical planners—deepening the appreciation of the Sunday means that preparation and catechesis for this day should be given the same serious attention as for liturgies of the festal seasons. It means that the assembly is aware more and more of its Sunday liturgy as an Easter celebration and of itself as an Easter people, with the proclaimers of the Word, powerful and prayerful; the musicians, rehearsed and spiritually uplifting; the Eucharistic ministers and welcomers, gracious, personable, warm; the presider, full of God's Word and full of the spirit of *eucharistia*, giving thanks with the assembly gathered for the paschal prayer of the Sunday.

In some places, it is in vogue to plan Sunday Eucharist around themes or motifs extracted from the scriptural readings or from some civic holiday or cause. The liturgy should not and may not remain aloof from genuine social concerns, but the way to address current social issues at the Sunday Eucharist is through the homily and the intercessions, and also through the active presence of parish social justice groups. Assigning themes to the Sunday Eucharist can erode the resurrectional festive character of the day, and can narrow the focus of a day which celebrates "the mystery of Christ in all its fullness."[6]

In many of our parishes today an urgent issue confronts families with young children: Do the children belong *in* or *out* of the worshiping assembly? In some places, it seems to be fashionable in pastoral care to set up a program providing young children with an alternate Liturgy of the Word or even other activities to occupy the space of the whole Sunday Mass.

Some of these programs are well grounded in liturgical practice and may indeed be fostering in the child a better appreciation of the Word of God.[7] Some of these programs, on the other hand, appear to be little more than drawing and coloring exercises, as the following anecdote suggests. A priest friend, assisting with Easter Sunday Eucharist in another parish, was visibly puzzled when announcing the prewritten directive that all children should proceed to the basement, where they would meet the Risen Lord. At the earliest opportune moment, the teenaged acolyte quietly reassured the perplexed priest that the announcement simply meant that the children were to go downstairs and color!

Whether the separate children's liturgy is excellent or mediocre is not, however, the essence of the matter. The real question is whether the children should be out of the assembly at all during Sunday Eucharistic worship. A number of liturgists think not. Alexander Schmemann, the late and great Greek Orthodox liturgist, spoke out against preparing children for a lifetime of divine worship by removing them from liturgy. Gail Ramshaw Schmidt is in accord with Schmemann's position; she has documented impressively the impact that liturgical song, text, and gesture have on the very young child in ways that astonish the unsuspecting adult.[8]

Examples of the child's retention of liturgical impressions abound in the experience of family and friends: three-year-old Barbara repeating the refrain "Glory to God in the highest and peace to his people on earth!"; five-year-old Rachel dancing the song of Mary, "My soul glorifies the Lord . . ."; Mark, two and a half, holding a small missal on high and processing around his home chanting "Jesus! Glory!";

Stephen, two, opening a Bible and presenting to his family a "reading" about Jesus the Good Shepherd; Stefan, one and a half, chortling a Gregorian Easter "alleluia" at suppertime.

Can we, then, continue to remove small children from the Sunday liturgical experience without seriously reflecting on the concerns that numerous people, including some parents, have about this practice? I suggest that there are two major areas for consideration: first, the nature of the Sunday Eucharistic assembly as sign of the kingdom; and secondly, the nature of the liturgy as sacramental and thus sensorial, involving the whole person as participant.

The Sunday Eucharistic gathering shows forth the kingdom of God. On this day, God calls and assembles together those baptized into his Son and filled with the Spirit. They are all there, rich and poor, old and young, healthy and frail and handicapped, powerful and powerless, learned and unschooled, articulate and voiceless, women and men "from every nation, race, tribe and language," (Rev 7:9) collectively witnessing to the world and also to each other the freely given grace of God which knows no human boundaries. And yes, children, too, testify to the workings of God's grace among us! As Louis Weil writes, "The presence of children worshiping with their parents is important, [and] that presence is also important for single persons, for the elderly, and for all who make up the parish community. Children have an integral place in worship which bears significance for the corporate prayer of the whole church."[9] We are all living witnesses to one another as, for one hour a week, we become a visible embodiment of the Church, of the great multitude of God's people.

If members of the community draw life from the Sunday Eucharist, is it possible that not only the adult ·but also the child cannot live without the Sunday liturgical assembly? As Joseph Gelineau writes, "The child needs to be immersed in a cell of the ecclesiastical body where belief in the risen Christ lives . . . but parents, educators, or school friends provide only partial images. The total image of the ecclesiastical *koinonia* is provided only by the assembly of those who meet in the name of God to partake of the good tidings, their goods and services, prayer and eucharistic bread."[10] Children already baptized into the Body of Christ have the right to be included around the table of the Word and the table of Eucharist. They are not merely "Church of the future," as we like to say; they are Church here and now![11]

The second point to consider regarding children at worship is the nature of liturgy as tangible bearer of invisible sacred reality. Worship is where we touch and are touched by the Holy, whose presence is revealed to us in signs such as the assembly, ritual and human gesture and the earthborn gifts of water, oil, and bread and wine. We are appreciating anew in our time the importance of these aspects of the liturgy. We are reiterating that the beauty in the environment and in the music of worship can help lead us to the source of beauty. We are remembering that good liturgical celebrations build up and strengthen our faith. In a word, liturgy is where we can together be immersed in the Holy as complete human beings.

Although liturgy is formative of faith, it is not a gathering for the purpose of instruction. Liturgy shapes us in a much broader way. In our proclamation and silence and song, in our processing and dancing and bearing of gifts, in our gestures of forgiveness and healing and love, and in our blessing and sharing of bread and wine, we discover the face of our God and his mission for us as Church.

We have already noted the sensorial way in which little children interact with their environment. Seeing,

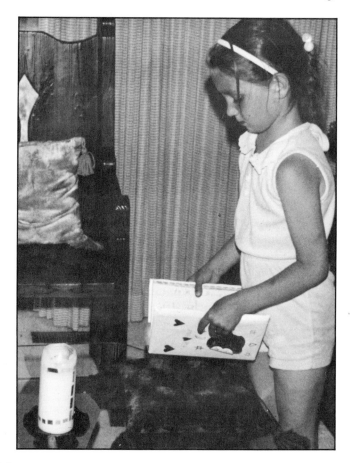

touching, tasting, smelling, feeling—these, rather than cerebral instruction, are their true teachers. Liturgical ritual wonderfully done is exactly that which engages the senses of the child and which offers in an irreplaceable way the first glimpse of how this community—these parents, these neighbors and friends and others—live by the Word and bread of God.

Yet, do we somehow feel that little children should learn something definite, something concrete which they can articulate or explain to an adult? Do we somehow feel that the child has to respond rationally to liturgy rather than affectively and intuitively?[12] We reveal this penchant over and over when we say that little children should be apart from the community for some or all of the Sunday liturgy, for, as it is said, they need to "understand on their own level," or "get the message." In one parish the tendency toward instruction during the so-called children's Liturgy of the Word is so strong that the children's leaders are actually called "liturgy teachers." There is a time for catechesis of the very young, but the hour of Eucharistic liturgy on Sunday is not it!

Some will come to the defense of children's Liturgy of the Word programs, saying that they are truly celebrations of the Word of God and not instructional in purpose. While in some places, such may be the case—and the *Directory for Masses with Children* affirms the validity of these programs—in general it is difficult to see how a splendid Liturgy of the Word celebrated in the sensorially rich environment of full Sunday assembly can be replaced. Even more difficult to defend is the practice of keeping children en masse out of the entire Sunday Eucharistic liturgy and relegating them to the church hall or basement.

Is it possible that our decision to send children into exile during Sunday worship emerges less from our passionate concern for the liturgical faith formation of the very young than from our failure to address some difficult underlying challenges? These challenges are: first, the thorough renewal of our Sunday Eucharistic worship, particularly the Liturgy of the Word; second, the welcoming and integration of children into the liturgical assembly; and third, the provision of assistance to parents in the earliest religious formation of their children or, alternately, some form of catechesis for little children outside times of liturgical celebration.

Regarding renewal of the liturgy, to be more specific, our parishes need to encourage the best liturgical practices for the sake of the children (and

everyone!). For instance, regarding the Liturgy of the Word, this means having a proclaimer who loves the Word of God and who can announce it with conviction, in a face-to-face manner, to an assembly which is visibly eager to hear. It means having a cantor who is genuinely a leader of prayer; it means that the cantor uses a psalm that has a good refrain melody and an easily remembered text so that all, including the children, have a prayer to carry home in their hearts. It means that the musicians and assembly are spirited participants in the Sunday's Easter song, the "Alleluia," while the movement of lights and incense surrounds the Book of the Gospel. It means having a gospel proclaimer who knows "by heart" the story of Jesus; a homilist who addresses us with scriptural insight, spiritual bread, memorable and nourishing; and a leader of intercessions who truly summons us over and over to call upon the Lord on behalf of all humankind.

We might highlight briefly the role of the homilist, who has a unique opportunity to make children welcome in the worshiping assembly. Ways in which the homilist can positively respond to the presence of little children include using concrete imagery and vivid language in the homily, telling a simple illustrative story when apppropriate to the scriptural readings, referring to familial experiences or other situations well known to the children of this particular assembly, and occasionally addressing a remark directly to the children. This is not to say that the homily should be addressed primarily to children nor that it should be construed as pedagogy for them, but rather that it should in some way recognize their presence within the community that is fed by God's Word.

The welcoming and integration of children into the Sunday assembly is another issue on which the parish as a whole needs to reflect and be challenged. When little children come to the community at worship, how are they received? Are they greeted personally and spoken to and welcomed warmly? Are they and their families given a place where they can see both the assembly and the sanctuary, or are they confined to the back, where they are almost certain to become bored and restless for the lack of visual connection with the liturgical happenings? (Of course, the architecture of most churches imposes distances on children, whose vision is already limited by their height; perhaps we ought to consider rearranging the church's seating—if not for ourselves, then for the sake of the children.) Are families with little children and all their attendant baggage and appendages in fact given enough space for comfort and some movement during the liturgical service? Are individual members of the assembly willing to give up a favorite place at the end of a bench so that a parent with a young child can move in and out with ease? Does anyone attempt to send an extra hymnbook over when necessary? Does anyone smile a greeting or offer a helping hand when, as is so often the case, families arrive out of breath after hurried breakfasts and hair-combing, the inevitable spills, and last minute diaper changes? In short, can it be said that thoughtful human kindness characterizes the welcome to and affirmation of parents with young children as they come to worship?

Liturgical ministries within the Sunday assembly are really an adult responsibility, but there are ways of encouraging active participation and initial sharing in ministries even by very young children. One of the first things that children can do is join in the liturgical responses, spoken and sung. Occasionally, the whole assembly—with special invitation to the children within it—could rehearse some of the dialogue or music of the liturgy, such as the "Amen," what it means, and how to really exclaim it; the singing of the "Holy, Holy, Holy" and its centrality in the Eucharistic Prayer (musicians might be more pastorally sensitive in their choice of the assembly's acclamatory song, using good music which is changed less often—young children love to sing music they know well!). Children can be taught to respect hymnals as prayer books of the parish community and to handle them with reverence and care. Little ones derive considerable pleasure from merely holding a book like everyone else; and as soon as they can recognize numbers and letters, they greatly enjoy helping to find the songs for the family.

Sharing in the presentation of the gifts is another way that little children can take an active part in Sunday liturgy. It is customary in many parishes to have the whole family process to the sanctuary with gifts of bread and wine. One hopes that single-parent families are not habitually excluded from this participation, but that they are sought out, invited, maybe paired with another family for the gift procession. The smallest children can be given something to carry, according to their capability. For instance, a two-year-old might be best at simply taking up the family's monetary contribution, while older family members carry the bread and wine. At our parish, special occasions such as the pre-Christmas collection of gifts/toys for charity or the Lenten "food bank" drive provide an opportunity even for toddlers to enter into the great tradition of the Church—bringing material gifts to Sunday Eucharist as part of active caring for others.

The welcome ministry of a parish could quite easily integrate into its ranks families with young children. A child of four or five could help with a specific task, such as handing out bulletins at the door after liturgy. Children of any age might be part of the actual welcoming team as suggested by Lucien Deiss; he proposes, perhaps more seriously than it first appears, that we turn our toddlers loose at the church door and let them melt hearts and bring cheer to the gathering (sometimes glum) assembly. In any case, parents with young children could be an asset to the church's hospitality ministry, doing in the *domus ecclesiae,* the "house of the Church," what they are probably already doing in their own homes—receiving others with love into their family.

Slightly older children (five- and six-year-olds and early school-age children) could be included in simple dance-like processions related to a major liturgical action such as the proclamation of the gospel. Gloria Weyman, well known as a leader in liturgical dance, has done extensive work with children in this field. She outlines various possibilities in a book coauthored with Lucien Deiss, *Liturgical Dance* (Phoenix: North American Liturgy Resources, 1984). A liturgical dance/movement project requires much careful planning and rehearsal to be a spiritually rewarding experience for children.

Probably the most important dimension of integrating young children into liturgy is to accept them for what they are: curious and questioning, occasionally noisy, periodically in need of hugs, rarely motionless for any length of time, and gifted with an amazing ability to overhear everything. As Ramshaw Schmidt notes, children can tune in and out; they seem to be distracted by something at liturgy, but can tell their parents afterward the entire story of the gospel.[13] The parish community's acceptance of young children as they are could even take on a more explicit dimension, so that parents at liturgy with infants or toddlers might be "twinned" with a retired couple or a teenager, someone who might provide that extra set of hands, that extra shoulder to rest on.

Lastly, parishes might consider putting less time and energy into alternate celebrations/catechesis for little children during Sunday Eucharist and instead redirect their efforts toward *parents* of small children. Could parishes not provide a short course for parents or a family-network group or resource people to contact or materials to borrow—even babysitters free of charge when young families are invited to meetings? Parents are often willing to do a great deal with their children but are stymied because of lack of resources and support. However, if parents are unable or unwilling to work with the religious formation of their young families, the parish might consider arranging for some form of catechesis outside Sunday Eucharist times. For example, the catechetical centers of Cavalletti and her associates hold sessions for children (ages two and a half and up) on Saturday afternoons, and some parishes offer pre-Eucharist classes for all age groups on Sundays.

One final thought on parish liturgy and the family of the young child. Would it be possible to have a liaison person, either a staff member at the parish or a volunteer, who could act as mutual information link between families and the parish's liturgical planners? When Advent is approaching, for example, the liaison could have a seasonal responsorial psalm as selected by the music leaders printed in the Sunday bulletin for people to learn at home. Or if a group baptism is to be celebrated on an upcoming Sunday, the liaison announces this in advance so that parents can prepare their children by speaking to them of baptism, looking at family baptismal photos, praying for those to be baptized. A long-term and consistent effort in such a linkage between families and parish liturgy is richly rewarding for everyone.

Sunday in the Home

Since in our tradition the Lord's Day is first and foremost for the Eucharist, it is fitting to make the Sunday Eucharist liturgy the focal point of the family's day. The following remarks are offered to families who wish to create a climate wherein children can experience the importance of Sunday Eucharist as well as the paschal character of Sunday.

In the same way that Jewish people welcome the Sabbath with a ritual at the Sabbath eve sundown, so the Church's longstanding manner of greeting the Sunday is with the prayer of the Liturgy of the Hours on Saturday evening. "First vespers of Sunday" (so-called to distinguish it from the vespers of Sunday proper) is the Church's common evening prayer, pointing forward to and already sharing in the Lord's Day. Immediately after supper on Saturday, the family could gather in a place somewhat apart (we use the more formal

environment of our living room) for a brief service whose primary links with Sunday and the Easter-ness of Sunday are: the lighting of the household paschal candle; the singing of Psalm 121 [122], "We shall go up with joy to the house of our God"; and the proclamation of all or a portion of the Sunday gospel. (For a complete outline of the service, see "Resources for Sunday" at the end of this chapter.)

Some Christian households use a slightly modified version of the Jewish Sabbath-welcoming meal to enhance their Saturday evening anticipation of Sunday. The Christian Church has been increasingly conscious of its roots in the Jewish tradition and recognizes that tradition as its matrix and birthplace. However, many Jewish people rightly have a sensitivity to the wholesale borrowing of their religious rituals. In fact, the doing of ritual proceeds from a faith experience shared within the community which is the source of the ritual. The Jewish Sabbath-welcoming rite proceeds from a unique faith perspective which sets apart the Sabbath day, honoring it as the completion of creation.

It is true that the early Church borrowed Jewish forms and ritual elements with great freedom, but the theological content of those forms and the understanding of symbolism was soon adapted in accord with belief in Jesus as Messiah and Lord. We have seen that the Christian Sunday is not the direct descendant of the Jewish Sabbath, and that the Sunday and Sabbath have quite different bases in faith experience.

It would be possible to use the Jewish Sabbath ritual as an inspiration for a Sunday-welcoming meal that recognizes the paschal character of Sunday. The lighting of the household paschal candle would be most fitting, as would be the sharing of bread and a cup of wine—the ties with Sunday Eucharist are very apparent (some East European Christians have such a bread-sharing ritual on Christmas Eve). The proclamation of the gospel or a selected part of it would complete the Sunday orientation of the meal. One Sunday-welcoming ritual is appended under "Resources for Sunday" later in this chapter.

The beautiful Jewish custom of lingering over the Sabbath evening, i.e., after the Sabbath-welcoming ritual on Friday, could well inspire Christian families to do the same. (This is certainly not always possible in a household with tiny children!) There might be leisurely conversation, interspersed with remarks on the gospel passage; a Sunday or paschal song from time to time; small children moving in and out of the group; and a conclusion of the evening with the sing-

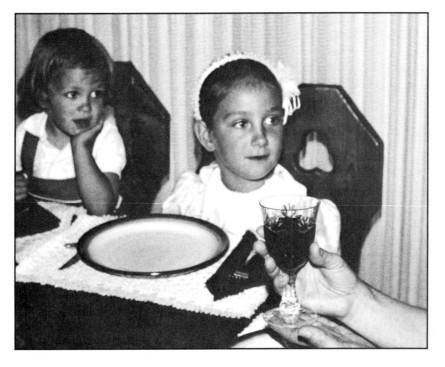

The Sunday-welcoming meal.

ing of an ''alleluia'' or a verse of Psalm 121 [122], ''We shall go up with joy. . . .'' Two or three families could gather occasionally on a Saturday evening for a common celebration of the Sunday-welcoming meal.

The family can prepare for Sunday Eucharistic liturgy in ways that direct young children's attention toward Eucharist as a special event. These ways include finding and filling the Sunday envelope for the monetary collection (occasionally older children who receive an allowance might add some money of their own), selecting and bagging food for the food bank barrel (contributing both money and food for the support of Church community and the poor are part of our venerable tradition—taking the gifts to the church and presenting them in the Eucharistic gathering are an important educational gesture for the child); even the bath-taking and setting out best clothes, however modest those clothes may be.

For our family, the best time to celebrate Eucharist with our parish is the mid-morning of Sunday. The children are fresh and rested. There is no sense of haste, as the whole morning is reserved and the day seems to arrange itself around the Eucharistic celebration. The Sunday mid-morning liturgy in our parish seems to attract a broad range of people, including the elderly

and handicapped who arrive on special buses, families with very young children, and many persons who have a high degree of commitment to parish life—altogether a wonderful cross section of the kingdom! Further, in our parish the mid-morning music leaders are a choir with strong traditional roots and a willingness to do contemporary music. This choir represents a ''catholic'' or universal approach to music for worship, and its repertoire extends beyond the songs of the last fifteen or twenty years. We want our children to share in the wealth of musical prayer forms and sounds that represent two thousand years of Christian prayer-in-song, from the ''Veni, Creator Spiritus'' to ''A Mighty Fortress Is Our God''; from Alexander Peloquin's ''Faith, Hope, and Love'' to Michael Joncas' ''On Eagle's Wings.'' Beautiful, powerful, and timeless music, like great art, forms us spiritually; and the many styles of music can reveal to us the many faces of our God. Can we offer our children less than the whole spectrum of the best?

It is commendable to arrive early (if that is ever possible with young children!) at the church building, to see and hear the flow of water at the baptismal font, to visit friends at the parish or to meet someone new, to deposit food or other contributions in the appropriate places, to take note together of the day's or season's decor, to be sure to hear the bells, to be able to share in any preliturgy instructions or brief music rehearsal. Just taking time to walk around in the church building fosters the child's familiarity with the "house of the Church," as it was called in ancient times. Eugene Walsh vigorously encourages a *purposeful* gathering of those assembling for Sunday Eucharist. He speaks of the "deliberate personal presence" of each one, and urges everyone to take time to become immersed in the community which is Church.[14] The parish and the household which habitually engage in purposeful gathering nurture the child's awareness of Church as family in which each one is responsible for the others, and in which each one contributes to "making eucharist."

It is valuable for parents to point out significant things to the child during the Eucharistic celebration. For example, the adult can draw the child's attention to the liturgical actions by quick comments, such as "See the procession coming in with the golden cross" or "Do you see how high they hold the Book of God's Word?" or "Notice how many ministers there are today to help share out Jesus' gift of himself." Children are always pleased to observe persons they know in ministerial roles. Our children at Sunday Eucharist love to see Jackie, Mom's piano student, now leading the ministry group; Colleen, our babysitter, at the keyboard; and Ed, our longtime friend, leading the psalm; Jim and Marion, our child's godparents, as Eucharistic ministers; Christopher, brother of a friend, one of the day's welcome ministers. We notice assembly, too, because assembly *is* the Church. We alert one another to the presence of people with whom we are acquainted, and we try to meet new people in the congregation whenever possible.

After Eucharistic liturgy one always hopes for a hospitality time at which coffee and juice are available. In any case, the family can make it a point to stay awhile, continuing conversations, expressing care for others, introducing people to one another, and welcoming newcomers or visitors.

On the way home we note aspects of the Eucharistic celebration which we have particularly appreciated. (When our child was two he offered the comment that he liked "all the walking around" best!) We sometimes discuss the meaning of decor/vestment color or sing again a song used in the celebration; usually we single out the gospel passage as the part of the Liturgy of the Word we want most to remember; often there

are spontaneous remarks on other parts of the liturgy, particularly the communion ritual (children seem to be fascinated by seeing God's people close at hand, walking by in procession).

It is important to note at this point that all the preceding suggestions constitute precatechetical activity with children. This activity imparts to them not doctrinal information but a basis for understanding the centrality of Sunday Eucharist for the family and the Church. For the child of two or three, formal catechetical instruction is a thing of the future; the family's enthusiastic attitude to and love of the Sunday Eucharistic gathering is the environment wherein the child's appreciation may begin to grow. Specific suggestions for catechetical instruction on the Eucharistic celebration for older preschool children are found in Cavalletti's book, *The Religious Potential of the Child*, cited previously.

On Sundays at home, one can make mealtimes special to underline the Easter-ness of the day. The family can light its paschal candle at all Sunday meals, and the table prayer can be a sung "alleluia" or resurrection-oriented prayer. One can try to serve something festal at each meal, even if it is only a warm raisin bread at breakfast or a pretty fruit dish for dessert at lunch. A household might want to establish its own customs of Sunday foods centering around family favorites or drawing from a collection like Vitz's *A Continual Feast*, which contains a sampling of Sunday recipes.

Sunday supper can be as elaborate as the family's day allows. In our household, Sunday supper means eating in the dining room with the best tablecloth and dishes and, from time to time, preparing a more elaborate meal together. Children can be invited to make placecards, a centerpiece decoration, or a dessert for the family on this day.

If the gospel of the day has been particularly striking in its imagery, if the child is not too weary, and a reflective quiet mood is upon the family, a parent might wish to spend some gospel-telling time with the child. In our home these occasions, although not frequent, have become a special time for our elder child and her father. They read the day's gospel and exchange comments and insights. Sometimes they conclude with an artistic expression of the good news they have shared together.

As we have seen, Sunday in its Christian origins was not primarily a day of rest but a day of Eucharistic worship. In our time, with so many societal factors eroding the family's leisure, prayer, recreational activity—even the family itself, it is most suitable that the Sunday be regarded as a day set apart for the kind of rejuventation that is a gift of the Lord. A family could spend time more generously and freely with one another, with neighbors and friends. Leaving aside as far as possible concerns of a pragmatic nature, the family might try to live the day in the festal spirit otherwise so foreign to a harried society. Enjoy music, the arts, sports, recreation and re-creation; visit the sick or aged, phone someone in need, spend time with a child, or invite someone lonely to share the day. Take off your watch and taste the freedom of timeless time, of which Sunday is a sign. Why not immerse your family in a kingdom day where love—not time—reigns supreme!

Those whom we remember at family prayers; age 5.

Resources for Sunday

1. Sunday "First Vespers"
A Sunday-welcoming prayer for Saturday evening
(Here, as in all "Resource" sections of the book, the prayers and songs are presented within a liturgical format of common prayer similar to the Church's Liturgy of the Hours, but they may be used in many other ways as the family finds suitable.)

Call to Prayer
Lighting of the paschal candle is accompanied by the acclamation:
(SONG 1)
Light and peace, in Jesus Christ our Lord.
Thanks be to God!

Psalm to Welcome the Sunday: Ps 121 [122]
(SONG 2)
Refrain: I rejoiced when I heard them say:
    let us go to the house of the Lord.

Verse: I rejoiced when I heard them say:
    'Let us go to God's house.'
    And now our feet are standing
    within your gates, O Jerusalem.

Scripture Reading: the Sunday gospel passage or selected verses
(see list in Appendix B)

Evening Canticle: Song of Mary *(Magnificat)*
(SONG 3)
My soul glorifies the Lord. Holy is his name.
My spirit rejoices. Holy is his name.
In God my Savior. Holy is his name.

See also SONG 34. Other settings such as those of Joseph Gelineau or of the Taizé community may be used.

Intercessions

Our Father

Blessing
Leader: May God, Father, Son, and Spirit, bless and keep us.
    All: Amen.

Celebrating the Weekly Pasch

2. A Sunday-Welcoming Ritual

A meal rite to be used in association with Saturday evening supper

All gather around the table, which has been made festive by best tableware and by the presence of a beautiful plate of bread, a goblet of wine, and the household paschal candle (see "Resources for the Three Days," p. 37).

A parent lights the candle and says or sings the following prayer:

(SONG 4) Prayers for a Sunday Welcoming Meal

Leader: (extending arms, if so desired)
    Blessed are you, O God, who give us this paschal light, light that shines in the darkness and brings us joy.
    All: Blessed be God forever! (Brief pause in silence.)
Leader: May the light of Christ fill our hearts on this day of resurrection,
    And may his peaceful light shine upon all peoples.
    All: Amen!

The parent takes the bread, holds it up and prays:
Leader: Blessed are you, O God, for your gift of bread, many grains made one, bread which nourishes our life and our unity.
    All: Blessed be God forever! (All consume a small piece of the bread.)

The parent holds up the cup of wine (the wine may be diluted with water for young children) and prays:
Leader: Blessed are you, O God, for your gift of wine, fruit of the vine, this cup which we share in thanksgiving and in gladness.
    All: Blessed be God forever! (All drink of the cup.)

After the meal there might be a psalm or other scriptural reading pointing forward to the Sunday Eucharistic gathering with the whole family of the Church. The psalm could be Psalm 121 [122] (see p. 23 above); and the reading, the gospel of the Sunday (see Appendix B).

---

3. Songs for Sunday

(SONG 5) This Is the Day

This is the day the Lord has made!
We are glad and rejoice in it.
This is the day the Lord has made!
We sing alleluia!

(SONG 6) The Lord's Day

The Lord's Day is our day to sing,
Praise the Lord forever.
Clap your hands for the Risen King!
Praise the Lord forever.
Earth and sky and sun so bright,
Dance in resurrection light.
Clap your hands for the Risen King!
Praise the Lord forever.

4. Reflections for Sunday

From time to time, a parent may want to verbalize with
and for the child what the family is already celebrating as the meaning of Sunday. Such conversations may
be more structured and formal, or they may take place
in a quite casual way when an opportune moment
presents itself.

1. Talk about the meaning of Sunday. The parent could share with the child some simple
reflections on the Lord's Day, using the following or similar words:

"Today, Sunday, is a very special day for
us and for everyone who belongs to Jesus' family. On this day we celebrate that Jesus, who
gave his life for us, arose, and lives forever. We
remember that Jesus is risen when we light our
paschal candle on this day.

"Today, Jesus our Good Shepherd calls his
people together as one family, the Church.
Through the ministers and the people of the
Church, he speaks to us and feeds us. We are
happy to be with our Shepherd, and with so
many others who belong to him.

"We are happy it is Sunday, the day the
Lord has made. On this day, we sing 'alleluia,'
a word which means 'praise God.' " (The child
could choose a favorite alleluia song to sing
from Appendix C, p. 139, or from those used
at the parish.)

2. Share the Sunday gospel. The child and parent choose a quiet place. A Bible or Sunday
Lectionary, and a candle can be nearby.

The day's gospel story could be told again
in a parent/child dialogue. It could also be
read. During the gospel reading, the parent
may light the candle to represent Jesus the light
of our life. The lighted candle helps the child
distinguish the actual scriptural passage from
the adult's paraphrased version of the same.

If the child is so inclined, he or she may
want to respond to the gospel by making a
drawing or a symbol (for instance, a brilliant
sun-mobile of construction paper expressing
the gospel, "I am the light of the world"). For
suggestions in finding symbols related to the
Sunday gospels, Gaynell Cronin's book *Sunday Throughout the Week* (Notre Dame, Ind.:
Ave Maria Press, 1981) is one which a family
might want to have on hand.

5. Activities for Sunday

There are some thirty Sundays of the year which are
outside the seasonal times on the liturgical calendar.
These "ordinary Sundays" are when we celebrate the
paschal mystery of Christ in all its fullness.

The following suggestions are based on the understanding of Sunday as day of resurrection and new life,
as day of recognizing the Spirit's movement in all creation, when we as families can be more aware of our
Christian calling within our own households and
beyond—to grow in love for one another and for all
God's people.

This list of ideas, it is hoped, might be a springboard
for others that the family will find appropriate for itself. It is also good to remind ourselves that there will
be many Sundays, especially when our children are
very young, when the family is happy enough to enjoy an unstructured, unplanned, uninterrupted time
as family . . . a day of at least some rest in the Lord!

1. Take a "season hike," looking for the mi-
raculous things of nature particular to summer,
spring, fall, winter. Little children like to take
along a basket or small bucket to hold their
collected treasures.

2. Make something together: a mural in paints
or crayons, a sculpture of snow, a giant sand-
castle, a mud-splashing pool for immediate use

(a chance for adults to enter into one of the venerable rituals of childhood). If your family enjoys making crafts together, consult some of the many excellent books available on this topic.

3. Visit someone who is alone, handicapped, or bedridden. Often there are persons in one's own parish who would appreciate the company of a family—this becomes for children a visible link with Eucharistic mission, caring for/sharing with those with whom one worships on Sunday. Bring a homemade gift (a card, some artwork, baking) from the family.

4. Go to a cultural event together: an art show, a craft fair, a symphony concert, or a choral presentation. Often young children cannot survive an entire musical performance. On occasion, our whole family has happily attended the first half of a music event and parted company in the second half, as one parent takes the smallest concertgoer into a lobby or park or garden for playtime.

5. Think of a lovely thing to do secretly for each other (names should be assigned or pulled out of a hat so that no one is left out). Share the results at the Sunday evening meal.

6. Cook a meal with an international flavor, planning either one special dish or, if your family is really ambitious, the whole meal! Use an international or ethnic cookbook for recipes which everyone can help prepare. One such book is Eve Tharlet's *The Little Cooks: Recipes from around the world for boys and girls* (New York: UNICEF, 1988). The older child(ren) can do some research on the country and culture the meal represents.

7. Have a story hour. Everyone brings a favorite book or story or poem to be read aloud. Finish with goodies (we inevitably have popcorn).

8. Make music together. Have a sing-along with simple songs that children can easily sing, or listen to recordings together (public libraries generally have fine resources for all ages), or have a dress-up-and-dance time for everyone. If your children study music, this could be the time they share their week's music-making with the family.

9. Assemble a "thanks-for-creation" collage. Each person brings a favorite photo or drawing or clipping or other small treasure which can be mounted onto a common poster.

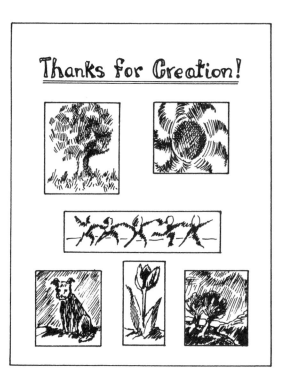

10. Bring out the family photo albums and share the stories of each child's growing-up and of memorable family events and occasions.

11. Play games: tag or ball outdoors, puzzles or board games indoors. There are many suggestions for cooperative games in books, such as *Games Manual* by Jim Deacove (Perth, Ont.: Family Pastimes, 1974).

12. Have a "Sunday festival." Decorate the party space with balloons or flowers, dress up in fantastic costumes, put on a play or variety show, end with a picnic (during winter or inclement weather, indoor picnics are a great hit too). Friends might be invited to share the festivities.

13. Have a treasure hunt, indoors or outdoors. Older children can help make clue-cards or maps, and the "treasures" can be anything from precious trinkets to colorful goodies to love notes!

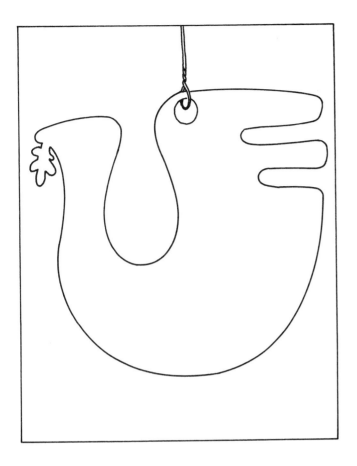

14. Host a peace party. Invite neighbors or friends and together make peace doves, sing peace songs, make small flags representing many nations (use a reference book for patterns), pray for peace. End with snacks.

15. Write/stage a puppet show or play (for a puppet show, make puppets out of old socks). Older children love writing scripts, and the little ones can be willing coworkers in designing puppet faces or assembling costumes.

16. Do some Easter-y activities. When I recently dropped a remark about Sunday being Easter, our three-and-a-half-year-old instantly responded that we should do an Easter thing. "How about we dye eggs?" he asked. And why not? On the occasional Sunday it would be possible to select an activity from "Resources for the Fifty Days" and so continue a linking of the weekly and yearly celebration of Pasch.

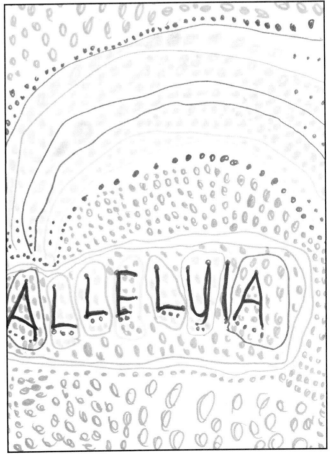

A Sunday decoration; age 4½.

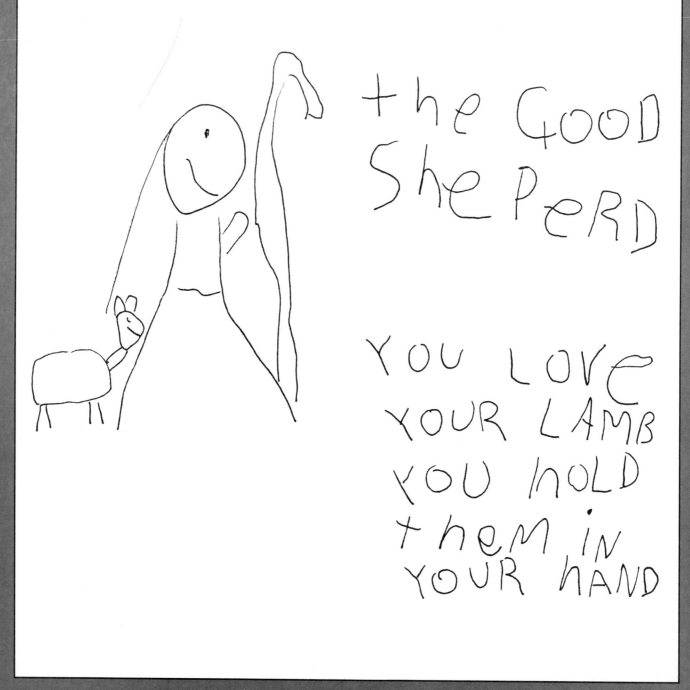

the GOOD
SHePeRD

YOU LOVE
YOUR LAMB
YOU HOLD
them IN
YOUR HAND

The Good Shepherd and the sheep; age 5.

s his life for his sheep!"

Chapter 2
THE PASCHAL THREE DAYS

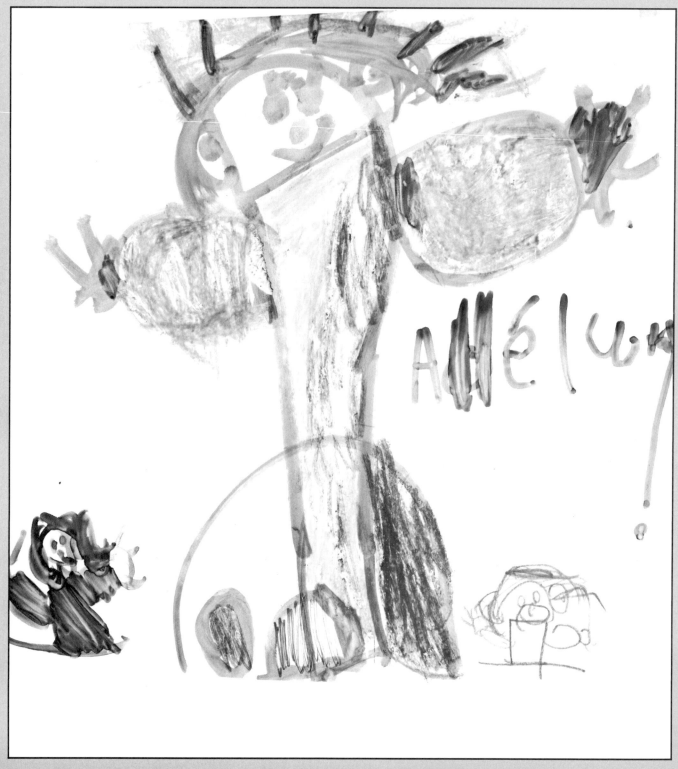

Jesus risen from the tomb, with figure at left showing great surprise; age 5.

Sketch of jeweled cross; age 4.

Origins and Spirit of the Three Days

Once a year the community of Christians assembles for a long night watch, a time of waiting for the Rising Sun of God. On that vigil night a new flame and an age-old song rise from the darkness. We hear it sung that "this is our passover feast, when Christ the true Lamb is slain . . . the night when Christians everywhere are restored to grace and grow together in holiness . . . the night when Jesus Christ broke the chains of death. Most blessed of all nights, when heaven is wedded to earth and man is reconciled to God!" (*Exsultet*, Paschal Vigil of the Roman Rite).[1] We hear the stories, both powerful and tender, of our Christian community's past and future. We baptize and anoint and welcome those who seek to live in the dying and rising of Christ, and we celebrate the festive Eucharistic meal of our wedding with the Lord. It is the most blessed of all nights, mother of all vigils, the great annual Paschal Vigil.

The community's ritual of the Easter Vigil embodies the entirety of our Christian life and faith: that Jesus Christ, who died for us, is alive with new life in the Father and that we too live in him by our baptism and

by the Spirit. Our whole life's journey, personal and communal, follows this pattern of dying and living again. It is our paschal way, shaped and in-spirited by the true Pasch who is Jesus Christ himself.

Our tradition of celebrating Easter Vigil has ancient roots that go back at least to the second century; it was then a one-night celebration, a unitive commemoration of the death and resurrection of Christ. The Vigil also became the privileged time of the year when new members were initiated into the community by baptism and Eucharist.

The fasting preceding the Vigil, originally one day in duration, later absorbed the preexistent Friday fast, so that the result was a paschal fast of Friday-Saturday, terminating with the early morning Easter Eucharist at the end of the Vigil. While this fast later took on the characteristic of accompanying the baptismal candidates in their fasting and praying before initiation, it also fulfilled the scriptural injunction of the Lord, who had said, "the time will come for the bridegroom to be taken away from them, and then they will fast" (Matt 9:15). Together, the two days of paschal fast on Friday and Saturday, plus the Sunday with its essential link to the resurrection—these became known very early as the triduum or three days of the Lord's passion, death and resurrection, the Christian Passover feast.

Church Fathers of the fourth and early fifth centuries considered the paschal triduum a single festal time, a comprehensive celebration of the mystery of redemption in Christ. Ambrose refers to it as "the three holy days . . . within which [Christ] suffered, lay in the tomb, and arose, the three days of which he said: 'Destroy this temple and in three days I will raise it up.'"[2] Leo the Great maintains that the triduum is the Pasch not only of Jesus but of his people: "If we unhesitatingly believe with the heart what we profess with the mouth, in Christ we are crucified, we are dead, we are buried; on the very third day, too, we are raised."[3]

Over the centuries, a complex series of changes and developments altered the shape and popular perception of the triduum and fractured its integrity. As if to witness to this process of shifting and fragmenting, each part of the triduum acquired its own specific name, "Holy Thursday, Good Friday, Holy Saturday, Easter Sunday," in turn reinforcing a tendency to historicize and isolate each day. Only with the *General Norms for the Liturgical Year and Calendar* of 1969 are we summoned to keep once again the

Three Days as a unitive celebration of Christ's paschal mystery:

"Christ redeemed mankind and gave perfect glory to God principally through his paschal mystery: by dying he destroyed our death and by rising he restored our life. The Easter Triduum *(triduum paschale)* of the passion and resurrection of Christ is thus the culmination of the entire liturgical year. The Easter Triduum begins with the evening Mass of the Lord's Supper, reaches its high point in the Easter Vigil and closes with evening prayer on Easter Sunday" (nos. 18, 19).[4]

What the General Norms invite us to is a renewed vision of the Paschal Three Days: above all, that they are collectively a single celebration of the whole paschal mystery, of both the death and resurrection of Jesus Christ. It is from the Passion According to John, always read at some part of the annual paschal celebration since ancient times and now proclaimed at the Good Friday service, that we discover the spirit of the Three Days.

John portrays Jesus as the Word of the Father, the Divine One who gives up his life of his own free will, as the one who embraces "this hour" as his hour of glory, as the one who is king enthroned upon the cross, there drawing all persons unto himself and giving birth to his Church in water and blood and the breathing forth of his spirit (John 17–19). For John and for the Church's paschal celebration, the cross and resurrection of Jesus are one event, a single moment as it were: dying-unto-rising, sorrow-unto-joy, cross-unto-glory. It was with this vision in mind that the Early Church jeweled its crosses. It was with this understanding that ecclesiastical poets could write that Christ reigned in triumph from the tree of the cross. "O Tree of Beauty! Tree of Light!"[5] cried Venantius Fortunatus; and again, "Faithful Cross! . . . O Tree of Glory!"[6]

Pasch, as Christ's passion, is further enriched by the concept of passage or passing over. Jesus, held in the chains of death for three days, has passed over to risen life. The community of God's people is also in passage. Of old, Israel was passed over by the angel of death and came through the waters of the Red Sea to freedom; now, Christians, marked by the blood of the Christ-Lamb, are led through the waters of baptism into life and light.

The Johannine Passion and the Passover imagery of Exodus shape and infuse the entire Three Days, from the triduum's opening liturgy on Thursday evening, to the solemn Liturgy of the Word on Friday afternoon, through the quiet aliturgical Saturday, which climaxes in the initiation rites and Eucharist of resurrection morning.

The Three Days in the Parish

The beginning of the Three Days is presently considered to be Thursday evening, somewhat in the manner of the Jewish tradition which begins the new day at sundown. Although originally the triduum encompassed no part of Thursday and at a later time had absorbed all of the day, it is important to remember that the major part of Thursday is really the last day of Lent, the final day of preparing for the triduum. Eucharist on Thursday evening orients the Church toward the whole of the Three Days. Even while it is called Evening Mass of the Lord's Supper, the liturgy begins with a focus on the image which dominates the entire triduum, "We should glory in the cross of our Lord Jesus Christ, for he is our salvation, our life and our resurrection; through him we are saved and made free" (Entrance, Holy Thursday, Eucharistic Liturgy of the Roman Rite).

Friday of the triduum in the Roman tradition originated as a service of the Word, that is, scriptural readings and prayers. A primary element in that Word service from ancient times to our own day is the proclamation of the Passion According to John, as we have noted above.

For so lengthy a reading as the Passion narrative, it is realistic to expect that children will simply tune in and out; the prime benefit of their presence will be less their comprehension of the Passion story than their witness of the solemn manner of its telling by the community. Children and perhaps the rest of the community, too, are probably better able to stay with the narrative when it is in fact done as a narrative, a storytelling by one person rather than by several readers. (Although this issue cannot be fully treated here, the use of multiple readers, mime, costuming, and other dramatic elements represents a progression toward dramatizing the Word within the liturgical context. The longstanding tension between drama's historicizing tendency and the transhistorical nature of liturgy would not be lost on children for whom the visual/dramatic has a powerful impact.) The Passion proclamation, if done by one narrator, can be interspersed with a short, specially selected acclamation in which even little children could share.

Following the scriptural readings and homily come the lengthy and broadly inclusive intercessions of Good Friday. These intercessions are one of the oldest fragments of our liturgical tradition and preserve the original Roman form of this prayer, that is, the deacon's announcement of the intention and a time for the assembly to kneel in silent prayer, followed by the presider's "collecting" prayer. In using this traditional form of the Friday intercessions, we join the prayers of the faithful as they have been done on this day across the ages. What is more, these intercessions give us a unique liturgical opportunity to use our whole bodies in prayer. There is a rhythmic beauty of posture, gesture, silence, and response in these prayers, which etch them on the memories not only of adults but also of children.

On Friday of the Three Days, the visual highpoint is without doubt the ceremony of the veneration of the cross. The cross presented to the community on this day should be of significant proportion, of beautiful wood, desirably carried into the midst of the community, and then set up in an otherwise barren sanctuary. Veneration by all can be a kind of free movement of genuflection, bowing, touching, or kissing the cross. The spontaneous choreography of faith can be a profound experience for a parish, including the spiritually receptive little ones who are learning through their whole bodies. Children, then, should be welcomed to draw near the cross, touch, stand a moment, and watch others do so, for it is their participation in this community's reverence for its Lord and for this sign of life over death. (Our daughter at four years appreciated the veneration of the cross more than any other part of the Friday service.)

The second day of the triduum, the day we call Holy Saturday, has no liturgy—this aliturgical character is one of its most primitive features. This day, which is in fact the Jewish Sabbath, has been thought of as the day of God's rest:

> The great Moses foretold this day when he said: "God blessed the seventh day." For this is the blessed Sabbath, the day of rest on which the only-begotten Son of God abstained from bodily work, as he had ordained that it would occur in death *(Text for Holy Saturday, Liturgy of the Orthodox Church).*

He who showed himself king upon the cross now sleeps in the tomb, and a great silence reigns over the earth, says an ancient homily (Office of Readings for Holy Saturday, Liturgy of the Hours of the Roman Rite).

We the Church remain with the Lord during this day, empty of food but full of prayer, a great awe encompassing our lives as individuals, as families, as community, as universal Church. We wait and watch, that is, literally, we keep vigil.

A parish could arrange prayer hours for the community throughout Friday and Saturday of the Three Days. The cross of Good Friday might remain in the sanctuary, where parishioners could take their turns at silent prayer, beginning after the Friday major service and continuing until late Saturday. On the hour throughout this time, there could be a short common prayer consisting of scriptural reading and intercessions (prominent among those remembered should be the catechumens, those preparing for baptism at the Vigil). For families with young children, even a brief sharing in keeping vigil in this manner is a good way to experience the meaning of triduum; for everyone, a supportive parish witness of prayer helps to keep the days immersed in paschal mystery.

It is self-evident that in a parish where the Friday-Saturday is considered a time of prayer and fasting, the church building should be fully available at this time to the people who are the Church! Rehearsals of ministers, extensive cleaning, music practices—all these will have been done far ahead to free both the space and the people for the main work of the Three Days, to keep the Pasch. And certainly the celebration of the sacrament of reconciliation, which in the recent past has occurred routinely during the Three Days, is not to be scheduled during this time.[7] Returning to the Lord and to the community is one of the urgent spiritual tasks of Lent in preparation for Pasch, and to seek that reconciliation now is to have missed the invitation of the past forty days!

As Holy Saturday draws to a close, the private vigils of Christians are gathered into one community watch, the Paschal Vigil. We come together in the darkness of night. We light the fire necessary for seeing, and we greet the brilliance of that new light, sign of the Risen Christ, leaping flame of the Spirit already hovering over us in this night of new creation! The rite of the Easter candle reaches a high point in the chanting of the *Exsultet* or Easter proclamation, a lyrical prayer text calling God's people and all creation to rejoice, for "Christ has conquered!" The chanting of the *Exsultet* should be solemn and excellent. The paschal candle itself should be of impressive size, noble (and of fragrant beeswax, as custom dictates). Everyone, even children, should be able to hold a

A child depicts her own baptism in the midst of a singing parish community; age 6½.

small baptismal candle with Easter fire, even if it means an adult must help.

In any vigil service, scriptural readings, each followed by a psalm and prayers, are the most important element. On this night of Paschal Vigil, the Roman Rite uses nine readings of the Word of God. The panorama of salvation appears before us: from the Genesis account of creation, through the powerful prophetic literature which speaks of the call, the mercy and love, the wisdom, the judgment and the redemption of God, through to the gospel announcement of the resurrection of the Lord. The scriptural proclamation can be rich and exciting if the parish's best readers are selected for this liturgy and prayerfully prepare their readings until the Word shines brightly through their narration. Cantors, choir, instrumentalists, and assembly can share in the responsorial psalms in an appropriate variety of ways.

We have already noted that, quite early in the Church's history, the Paschal Vigil was the setting for baptism. In our own day, after a lapse of some centuries, this night is again the primary occasion for the adult rites of Christian initiation. The baptism, confirming, and first Eucharist of new Christians is most suit-

able to this vigil night, for as Paul writes: "When we were baptized we went into the tomb with [Christ] and joined him in death, so that as Christ was raised from the dead by the Father's glory, we too might live a new life" (Rom 6:4). In addition, those who are reborn in baptism are themselves a sign of resurrection to the community of the Church, a sign that Christ is still conquering death and rising to new life! Part of the present baptismal rite at the Easter Vigil is the renewal of baptismal promises by the community, a fitting conclusion to the long Lenten journey which has led to this night and these life-giving waters.

Initiation, then, should always be part of the Vigil and not postponed to another time for the sake of shortening the service. Water in abundance, flowing oil, lighted candles, graceful white garments—all these speak of the wonder of rebirth in the Lord. Children, even those three or four years old, are spellbound by the baptismal rite. Liturgy planners might try to ensure that as much as possible of the rite be visible to the very young members of the assembly. When the baptism and confirmation are over, there could be a procession of ministers and the newly initiated throughout the church building, with opportunity for

34

parishioners to greet, welcome, and congratulate the new members.

Eucharist, celebrated at a time now well into the early hours of Sunday, proceeds simply, with Eucharistic Prayer acclamations in which everyone can share, with Communion under both kinds (while this should be regular practice at all Eucharistic liturgies it is, in fact, not). The newly baptized are welcomed to the table of the altar for the first time. First communions of children might possibly take place at this time, if parents consider it appropriate.

The Eucharist could conclude with the blessing of Easter food, where customary. A parish party is a wonderful way to continue the festivity, with wine, cheese, Easter eggs, blessed bread, and glad fellowship unto the "Morning Star which never sets" (*Exsultet,* Easter Vigil of the Roman Rite).

Having the Vigil at a late hour is most important if we take seriously the meaning of vigil, that is, watching and waiting for the new day. Tasting the passing of time which bridges one day to the next, night to the morning; experiencing the length of night as we wait for the Rising Sun—these are an intrinsic part of the experience of keeping vigil. To shy away from a complete and late-night Vigil serves only to destroy the Vigil itself as it comes to resemble more and more any other Saturday evening liturgy. Such a niggardly attitude toward giving time for vigil also deprives the parish, the family, and its little ones of what can be the most profound liturgical experience of the Church year. . . . And yes, one *can* take the little ones, provided one is flexible as to their state of waking or sleeping at any given time. The older preschooler is usually too engrossed in this dramatic liturgy to sleep through much of it.

Originally, the Eucharist ending the Vigil service was celebrated very early in the morning, around 3:00 or 4:00 A.M., and no other Eucharist was celebrated on Sunday. With the decrease in adult baptisms and decline in popular understanding of the Vigil, a separate Eucharist came to be celebrated on Easter Sunday morning.

In a parish which celebrates an authentic and powerful Easter Vigil, the later Sunday morning liturgy is often felt to be exactly what it is, a *partial* sharing in the culmination of the Three Days, a culmination which took place during the vigil celebration. Although many people are conditioned to come to a service only on Easter Sunday morning, the parish could begin a long-term catechesis emphasizing the importance of participation in the Paschal Vigil. Gathering the whole parish for the Vigil may yet be a distant ideal, but someone must embark upon the journey of formation that will see us all gathered to celebrate annually the "most blessed of all nights" (*Exsultet,* Easter Vigil of the Roman Rite).

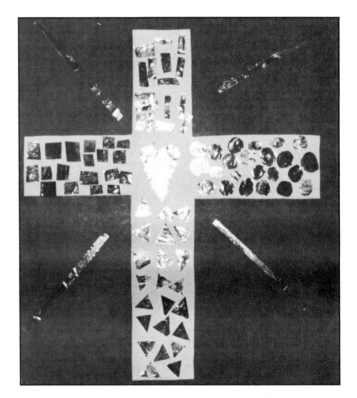

Jeweled cross in collage, with foil heart in center; age 6½.

The Three Days in the Home

When a parish community has prepared thoughtfully and prayerfully and energetically for the Three Days, all will be in readiness for a rich experience at the liturgical level. For families, the schedule of parish celebrations will determine much of the shape of the Three Days, but each family will want to make its own domestic commitment to keeping this time in a special way. The following checklist prepared by this author has been printed in our parish bulletin a month before the Three Days:

What are your family's plans for the Paschal Three Days? The parish liturgy and parish prayer of the Three Days is nearly prepared. Is your household ready? Here's a partial checklist, based on liturgical tradition and spirituality:

- Plan to be free for entering fully into the prayer and liturgies of the Three Days. Can those who work outside the home arrange for days off on Good Friday, Holy Saturday, and Easter Sunday?
- If you are a homemaker, get all spring cleaning done before Holy Thursday evening (a Christian custom linked with the Jewish tradition of thorough cleaning and throwing out the old leaven before sundown of the Passover).
- If you are a university student with exams around the corner, finish as many papers and projects as you can ahead of time to be able to share in the spirit of the Three Days.
- Sign up your family's name for prayer hours (see large sheet on parish bulletin board).
- Study and reflect on the liturgies to discuss as a family during the Paschal Three Days; adults could explore in advance the meaning of the cross, of the waters of baptism, of the paschal candle, and so on.
- Plan ahead a simple fast-day menu for Good Friday/Holy Saturday; prepare ahead some special once-a-year foods for Easter Sunday.
- Try to meet one or more catechumens soon, and pray especially for these persons now and during the Three Days.
- Think of one new thing, even a token article, like a new necklace or a new hair band or a new tie, which every family member can wear for the Easter Vigil or Easter Sunday service—a sign of our putting on the newness of Christ as we did in baptism.
- Discuss as a family the mood your household hopes to achieve for the Paschal Days, a sense of prayerful quiet revolving around the parish liturgy.
- Let friends and relatives know your Easter season visiting begins after the completion of the household/parish Paschal Three Days. The approaching Fifty Days of Easter are *the* time of year for rejoicing, festivity, hospitality!
- Remember to keep Holy Saturday free to be a truly restful day when we prepare for the long, strenuous, but the richest and most splendid liturgy of the Church's year!

At home, the Three Days take on the spirit of a family retreat. This is a time of quiet, of prayer, of reflection. To make room for all of those, a family can eliminate frenzied last-minute shopping and housecleaning. The family's participation in parish liturgy and prayer times will take up considerable time; and at home, common prayer of some part of the Liturgy of the Hours could further punctuate the days (see "Resources for the Three Days"). It is good to have plenty of opportunity for rest, especially on the Saturday, when enough daytime sleep for everyone means that all can share fully in the night Vigil.

A family can decide together how the Three Days may be kept in their home. Both the simple meals of fast and abstinence on Friday-Saturday and the festival fare of Sunday may include once-a-year recipes that make this time distinct (see "Resources for the Three Days"). Listening to the radio and viewing television are really inappropriate at this time, unless there are feature programs related to the Three Days. At our home, even the children's bedtime stories are chosen in a unique way at this time; we look at icon books together or at classic religious art volumes or at miniature paintings of the Passion, reprinted from a medieval Book of Hours.

In speaking to little children about the meaning of the Three Days, one helpful approach is to use the Good Shepherd parable, particularly the aspect of the Shepherd giving his life for his sheep (John 10:11). Liturgical texts on these days keep the Shepherd image before us: "Our Shepherd, the source of the water of life, has died . . . but now man's captor is made captive" (Responsory, Roman Rite Morning Prayer,

Saturday of the Three Days). The family's prayer and song and discussion can support this understanding. In our home, we find that this emphasis for the Three Days—the Shepherd laying down his life in love for his sheep—is more suited to the mental and emotional capacity of the very young than an overly historical explanation might be.

We have found that the household's triduum is more focused and unified when family activities echo or prepare for the liturgical services or reflect their meaning. On Good Friday, for instance, family members can make and ''jewel'' a large cross. On Saturday, it is appropriate to decorate a household paschal candle for use during the Easter season and on Sundays of the year. The family could also decorate eggs on the Saturday; these eggs, along with Easter breads and other Easter foods could be arranged in a basket and taken along to the Vigil for the traditional blessing of Easter foods, where customary.

Children can help to find a sparkling glass jar (with lid) to take to the Vigil so that the family can bring home Easter/baptismal water for the Easter season. Friends of our family, who live very near their parish church, take along a covered lantern to carry home the paschal fire which they use to kindle anew their furnace pilot light—a whole year of household warmth from the Easter flame! (Taking home the paschal fire is actually an ancient Christian custom.)

In our experience, Sunday of the Three Days seems to be a considerably shorter day than the preceding two. In a household where the young children have kept Paschal Vigil along with family and parish, a sleep-in fills much of the morning. Brunch or a dinner shared with extended family or among a group of families could continue the festivity begun at the liturgy. A sing-along of Easter music or a short prayer service could conclude the gathering (see ''Resources for the Three Days'').

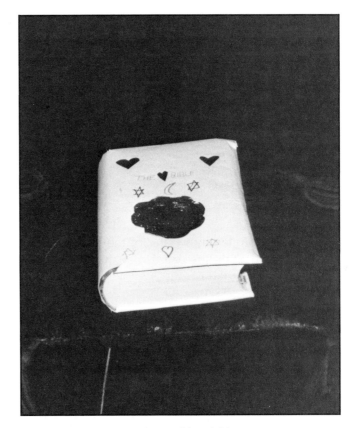

Enthroned Bible, cover designed by child, age 6.

Resources for the Three Days

1. Morning and Evening Prayer for the Three Days

During the Three Days in our home, as no one goes to school or work, we celebrate Morning Prayer together (or join the parish Morning Prayer) to capture the tone of these days and to help set them apart as a unique time in the Church year. We omit the Evening Prayer on the Friday and Saturday because of the late-day parish liturgical celebrations on those days. An Easter Sunday evening prayer might be celebrated with relatives or friends.

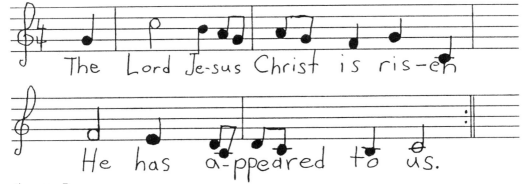

The Lord Je-sus Christ is ris-en

He has a-ppeared to us.

Song of resurrection; age 7.

Call to Prayer

(SONG 7)

(Leader says or sings each line first, all repeat):

O Jesus Christ,

Shepherd Lord,

You showed your love by death on a cross. (Friday, stop here)

Raise us up to new life with you. (Saturday, stop here)

Alleluia! (Sunday)

Psalm for the Three Days: Ps 15[16]

(SONG 8)

Refrain: Keep me safe, O God; you are my hope.

Verse: My heart rejoices, my soul is glad;

Even my body shall rest in safety.

For you will not leave my soul among the dead,

Nor let your beloved know decay.

Scripture Reading: John 10:14-15

Canticle

(SONG 9) Song of the Cross

Leader: Salvation comes to us

All: In the cross of our Lord, Jesus Christ;

Leader: And life and resurrection,

All: In the cross of our Lord, Jesus Christ.

Leader: The Good Shepherd saves us.

All: We glory in his cross!

Leader: The Good Shepherd loves us.

All: We glory in his love!

Intercessions

Our Father

Blessing

2. Songs for the Three Days

(SONG 10) We Adore You, Christ

Leader: We adore you, Christ, and we bless you.

All: By your cross you have saved the world.

(SONG 11) We Worship You, O Lord

Leader: We worship you, O Lord.

We venerate your cross.

We praise your resurrection.

All: Through your cross you brought joy to the world.

3. Activities for the Three Days

A REFLECTION TIME

The parent and child find a quiet place to be together, taking with them a Bible and a candle. The parent may explain the meaning of the Paschal Three Days in the following or similar words:

"Jesus, the Good Shepherd, loves his sheep. He is light for the sheep. He says that he loves the sheep so much that he even gives his life for them. So, for a little while, when Jesus gave his life, darkness covered the light. Jesus told us this could happen when he said, 'The Good Shepherd gives his life for his sheep.'

"The darkness stayed only a very short time. When Jesus rose, the light of Jesus returned and it will never go out again. The light of the Risen Jesus is so strong that it will shine always.

"During these three special days, we stay close to Jesus, our Good Shepherd, and we listen to his words to us" (the adult lights the candle and reads from the Scriptures, John 10:14-15).

BOOKS TO SHARE

Many attractive books of icons, church mosaics, and classical paintings are available at libraries or for purchase at better bookstores. Even young children find these fascinating. The adult might select a few suitable pages and point out to the child some salient gospel-related aspects of the artistic representation.

For our younger preschooler, we have come to favor icons and mosaics rather than paintings, which tend to be somewhat more graphic about the physical suffering of Jesus. Nevertheless, a book such as *Easter* (New York: Harper and Row, 1984), a collection of paintings of the passion, death, and resurrection of the Lord, can be used selectively with young preschoolers and with older children; this volume also has the advantage of providing a scriptural text with each pictorial representation.

MUSIC

Great musical classics of the past, such as the *St. Matthew* or *St. John Passion* settings by Bach, or the paschal section of Handel's *Messiah,* as well as contemporary works can provide the aural environment of these days. Scripturally/liturgically based texts are the best ones for children to hear on the subject of Jesus' Pasch. Recent collections such as John Foley's

Wood Hath Hope are suitable, as are selections from the Taizé community.

OUTDOOR ACTIVITIES

Warmer weather beckons the family outdoors for long, quiet walks in the park or in the country, somewhere that can offer reflective moments and a close look at nature.

On the Friday of the Three Days, the day when we honor the wood of the cross, the family might want to pay particular attention to trees and all the ways in which trees and wood are important in our lives. Very young children are happy even to find and touch/hug interesting trees (or to find all the ways in which wood is used inside the house).

On the Saturday of the Three Days, when we "rest with the King who sleeps in the tomb," the nature walk might concentrate on how nature is still restful (and not yet in blossom?), still awaiting the return of life.

On the Sunday, when we celebrate new life, the family might search out any signs of rebirth in nature, any harbinger of spring—the first crocus, a bud on the tree, the sound of a bird returning from the South. (In some parts of Germany, the family's Easter afternoon walk is enhanced by the children's discovery of chocolate eggs which mysteriously fall from a parent's pocket onto the path.)

4. Special Activities for Friday of the Three Days, "Good Friday"

JEWELING A CROSS

Materials: one sheet of bristol board in ruby or red (the liturgical color this day); another sheet of similar or lighter-weight paper in white; an X-Acto knife and steel-edged ruler, or scissors; glue; gummed foil paper of various colors.

Activity: *either* draw a large cross on the white sheet, and about half an inch away from your drawing repeat the lines to create a double-line drawing of the cross; using the steel-edged ruler and X-Acto knife cut away the outline of the cross; mount on red bristol board to obtain a negative image of the cross. (If desired, the white paper can be cut down on all sides before being attached to the red, to create a "frame" of red when the two sheets of paper are joined together.)

Or, more simply, draw a large cross on the white sheet, cut out with scissors, and glue onto red bristol

Jeweled Cross

(22 in. × 28 in. / 56 cm × 71 cm)

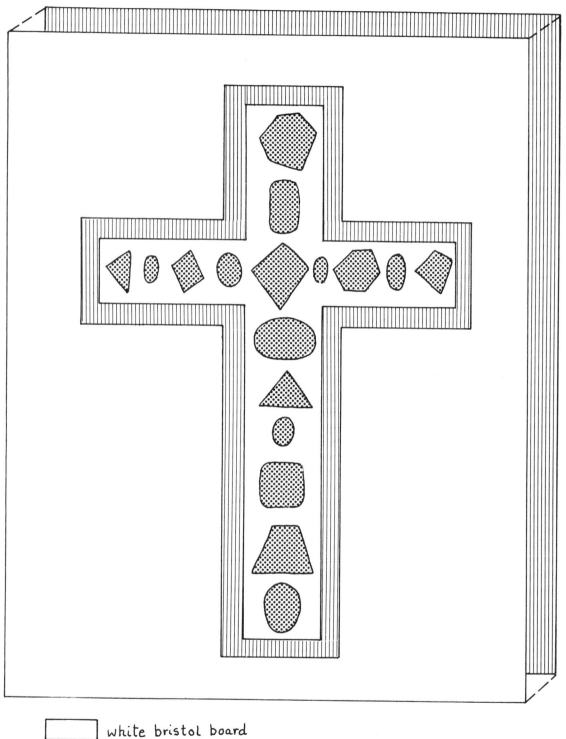

▢ white bristol board

▥ red bristol board

▦ multi-coloured foil paper

board (the older preschooler is usually capable of doing the whole process of drawing, cutting, and pasting).

Even a very young child can cut out or tear out shapes of ''jewels'' from foil paper and stick them onto the white cross shape. The adult can use this opportunity to explain that Jesus, the Good Shepherd, loved us so much that he gave his life for us on the cross, and that is why the cross is so beautiful for us. The cross reminds us of his love!

When completed, the jeweled cross can hang in a prominent place—a feature wall near the family table or on the refrigerator door, or wherever it can be seen constantly by all for the duration of the Three Days.

PLACECARDS

A very easy activity for a child is making placecards for the family to use at mealtimes during the entire Three Days. Using any kind of medium-weight paper, the child can draw or be helped to draw and cut out for each family member a cross (about 3 x 5 inches or 7 x 12 cm works well). Names may be printed on the crosses and/or the crosses may be ''jeweled'' with bright-colored foil or gummed paper shapes.

MAKING HOT CROSS BUNS
See recipe, page 42

5. Special Activities for Saturday of the Three Days, ''Holy Saturday''

The character of the Saturday as a restful aliturgical day leaves ample spaces of time for quiet family activity. Nevertheless, in our household, we try to complete all our activities by mid-afternoon to have enough time for bathing, a quick supper, and long early-evening naps in preparation for the Vigil.

DECORATING A PASCHAL CANDLE

A large, colorfully decorated candle can serve the family throughout the Easter season and on all Sundays of the year. Before making decorations, the family might try to remember together what is on the paschal candle at the parish (some of the symbols traditionally used are the cross and five grains of incense representing the five wounds of Christ). Decorations for the home candle might include a cross or symbols of the new life which comes to us through the cross— water, flowers, or other visual reminders of Jesus' love (our daughter included red hearts one year).

Materials: large white candle, lightweight paper of bright colors; if available, a hot-wax glue gun.

Activity: decorative symbols can be drawn and cut, then pasted on with wax-glue (used sparingly so decorations are not lumpy) *or* affixed on the edges by an adult using a heated knife to fuse the wax and the decoration. The symbols are better placed lower down on the candle where they will stay intact for a longer time as the candle gradually diminishes.

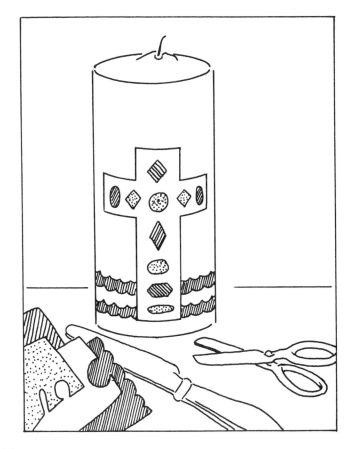

HOT CROSS BUNS—A Good Friday Tradition

The famed English hot cross bun, already well known in medieval times, was originally eaten only on Good Friday. This recipe is adapted from Norma Jost Voth's *The Festive Breads of Easter* (Scottdale, Pa. and Kitchener, Ont.: Herald Press, 1980).

3½–4 cups	Flour	875–1000 ml
¾ cup	Lukewarm milk	175 ml
½ cup	Lukewarm water	125 ml
1 pkg	Active dry yeast	1 pkg
1 Tbsp	Sugar	15 ml
¼ cup	Sugar	60 ml
1 tsp	Salt	5 ml
¼ cup	Melted butter	60 ml
¼ tsp	Allspice	1 ml
½ tsp	Cinnamon	2 ml
¼ tsp	Nutmeg	1 ml
2	Eggs	2
½ cup	Currants	125 ml
⅓ cup	Diced fruit peel	75 ml
	Egg glaze	

In a large mixer bowl, combine 1 cup (250 ml) flour, milk, water, yeast, and 1 Tbsp (15 ml) sugar. Beat well. Set in warm place until frothy. Melt butter and cool. To the yeast mixture, add remaining sugar, salt, melted butter, and spices; beat in eggs, one at a time. Add 1 cup (250 ml) flour, and beat 5 minutes with electric mixer. Gradually add remaining flour, currants, and peel. Turn out onto floured board, and knead until smooth and elastic (8–10 minutes). Place in greased bowl, turning in order to grease top of dough. Cover with towel, and set in warm place until doubled in volume. Punch down. Turn out onto lightly floured board, and knead lightly for 2 minutes. Divide dough into 24 equal parts, and shape into buns. Place well apart on greased baking sheet. Cover and let rise until almost doubled in size (about 30 minutes).

Egg glaze: After making a cross on each bun with a sharp knife, brush with egg white beaten with 1 Tbsp (15 ml) water. Bake at 375 degrees F (190 C) for 15–20 minutes or until golden in color. Let cool on wire racks.

Although icing is often used on hot cross buns, purists consider it an unsuitable modernity and prefer the original knife-mark cross. Others add strips of pastry dough over the crosses before baking.

DECORATING EGGS

Various decorating techniques yield lovely results even with young children. Older children who can draw more skillfully can be helped to choose some Christian symbols to put on eggs. Decorating time offers a good opportunity to discuss the meaning of Easter eggs. In medieval times they became a symbol of the rock tomb out of which Jesus emerged to new life. It is appropriate, therefore, that in the Christian home, eggs be decorated with religious and liturgical designs, such as the cross, the rising sun (Son!), water, candle, and so on.

A family might want to have among its household paschal treasures a *pysanka*, the decorated Easter egg of the Ukrainian tradition. At egg-coloring time, the *pysanka* can be both a starting point for conversation on religious symbolism and an inspiration to young egg-dyers to do some unique designs of their own. Actually, children of early elementary ages can make a simple *pysanka* if they have developed some patience, and if they are well supervised during the hot-waxing stages. Information on the technique is available through libraries, some handicraft stores, and best of all, through people of Eastern Rite churches, who are themselves experts in the significance and the making of *pysanka* designs.

The suggestions below are largely intended for younger children for whom some immediacy of result is important.

Materials:

- White hard-boiled eggs: to prepare without cracking, cover room-temperature eggs with water and bring to a full boil; remove from heat, replace lid, and let stand for 25 minutes; and finally, rinse in cold water.

- Dyes, made most easily from commercial preparations, can also be made, though in a more time-consuming way, from natural materials such as onionskins for yellow, beets for red, blueberries for blue, broccoli or spinach for green, coffee or tea for brown (in each case, boil the material for at least five minutes, or longer to obtain darker colors, then strain).

- For different techniques, the required items are indicated below.

Activity:

- Crayon or candle-wax designs
  With ordinary wax crayons of any color, or candle stubs, the child can make symbolic designs of new life in Christ.
  A very young child unable to draw specific symbols may simply make what we like to call "joy" designs, freely coloring on the egg before dipping it in dye.

- Masking tape designs
  This technique works especially well for designs such as the cross, the sun, or the candle. Narrow strips of masking tape (best cut by the parent) can be affixed on the egg to make the desired pattern; dip into dye, and afterwards allow to dry thoroughly before removing tapes. For additional color surprises, the egg may then be dipped in another color.

- Yarn design
  Young children may succeed quite well in making some symbolic or free designs with yarn. After the egg has been dyed, a child or parent can draw on it a design with liquid glue; let it dry partially, then add yarn.

- "Joy" eggs
  This is the simplest and quickest way for a small child to fill an egg with delightful color. Add 1 Tbsp (5 ml) of vegetable oil to each cup of dye, and dip eggs in one color after another—we find that two to three colors work best. The delicate mottled effect of rainbow colors is a joy-sign of Easter!

6. Special Activities for Sunday of the Three Days, "Easter Sunday"

The Easter Sunday menu traditionally includes a high-rising bread, often studded with colorful "royal jewels," in honor of the resurrection of Jesus. (In East European traditions, Easter bread itself is called *paska*.) This bread would be made in advance of the Three Days.

EASTER BREAD

2 pkg	Active dry yeast	2 pkg
1 cup	Sugar	250 ml
½ cup	Warm water	125 ml
1 cup	Unsalted butter	250 ml
1½ Tbsp	Salt	20 ml
1 cup	Warm milk	250 ml
3	Eggs	3
2	Egg yolks	2
6-7 cups	Flour	1500–1750 ml
½ cup	Brown sugar	125 ml
½ tsp	Cinnamon	2 ml
½ cup	Currants	125 ml
½ cup	Fruit peel	125 ml
Small bottle	Maraschino cherries	small bottle

In a large mixing bowl, combine yeast, sugar, and water. Set aside until frothy. Stir ½ cup (125 ml) butter and the salt into warm milk (the butter does not have to melt completely). Add to yeast mixture. Beat in the whole eggs and egg yolks. Blend thoroughly. Add flour, one cup at a time, stirring well after each addition. After the first five cups of flour, turn out onto a floured counter (dough will be very sticky); continue adding remaining flour until the dough can be kneaded with hands. Knead a *full 10 minutes* until dough is elastic and pliable. Put dough into a greased bowl, turning in order to grease top of dough. Cover lightly and let rise in a warm place until doubled in volume.

Punch the dough down on a lightly floured board. Cover while preparing the baking tins and the coating mixture. Generously grease two 2 lb. coffee cans or some other suitable tins with equivalent capacity; line bottoms of tins with wax paper. Melt remaining butter and cool slightly; mix brown sugar and cinnamon on a plate. Pinch off dough by pieces to make one-inch balls. Dip the balls in the butter, roll in brown sugar mixture, and layer loosely in the tins, sprinkling currants and fruits in between (cherries display their color best when placed on the outside) and on the top. Fill tins only two-thirds full. Pour remaining butter over top. Let rise till dough reaches to tops of tins. Bake in a preheated oven at 325 degrees F (160 C) approximately 50-60 minutes or until bread sounds hollow when tapped. If bread browns too quickly, place foil lightly over the top. Let breads cool for a few minutes before removing gently from tins.

AN EASTER DAY GATHERING

The family might like to continue the festivity with a brunch or dinner. If guests are invited, these might include an elderly person who would otherwise celebrate alone or a single-parent family or someone who has lost a spouse. A potluck works well for the occasion and relieves the host of having to cook a great deal during the Three Days.

The children might make a giant Easter banner together, using bright felt letters and/or shapes glued onto cloth. For such a banner, children could be invited/helped individually to choose a symbol or color that they found important at the Vigil celebration (or at any liturgy of the Three Days).

If the weather is fine, everyone can fly kites or identify spring birds or find butterflies. All these activities have a resurrectional dimension—rising, new life, the gift of freedom—which might be drawn to the children's attention.

The gathering might conclude with a prayer service (using "Resources for the Three Days," p. 38 above) or with an Easter sing-along or an Easter evening walk, during which the Emmaus story (Luke 24:13-35) is told.

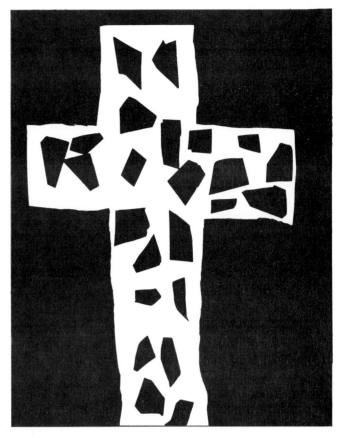

Jeweled cross in collage; age 3½.

Easter processional; age 6½.

Chapter 3
EASTER'S FIFTY DAYS

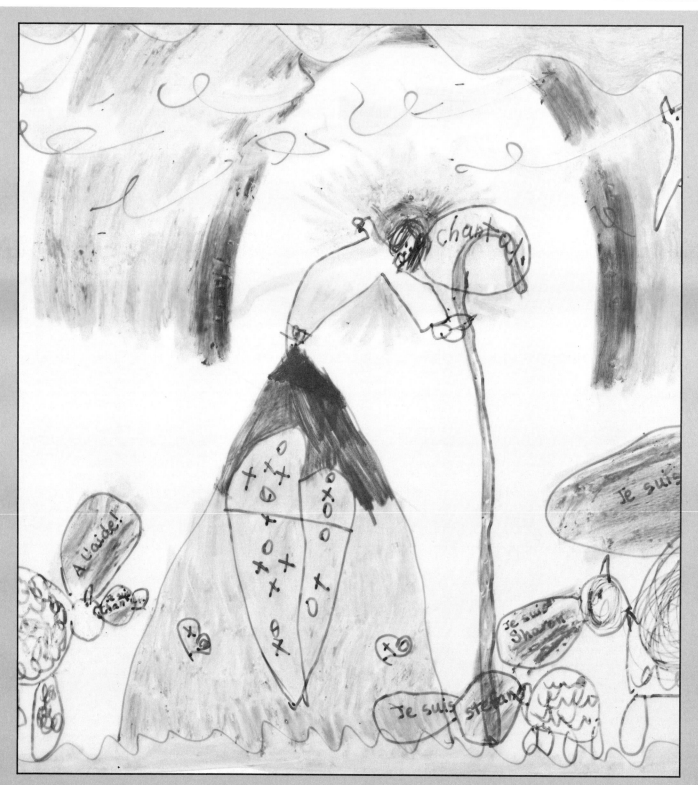

The Good Shepherd summons the flock by name; age 6½.

Paschal candle; age 6.

Origins and Spirit of Easter's Fifty Days

With the alleluias of the Paschal Vigil and Easter Sunday, the season of joy has only begun. Celebrating the Fifty Days of Easter gives the Church sufficient time for the riches of the Three Days to unfold. Fifty Days of Easter give new members of the Church—those reborn in the baptism of the Vigil—the opportunity to reflect on, and rejoice in the marvelous things God has done for them. Easter Day itself stands at the head of this time, and is both the end of the Three Days and the beginning of the Fifty.

Eastertime is the oldest season of the Church's liturgical year. In the early Church the season as a whole was known as Pentecost (from *pentekostē,* the Greek word for fifty). It was celebrated as a comprehensive feast of the paschal victory of the Lord Jesus Christ: resurrection, ascension, gift of the Spirit, and birth of the Church, all understood together as different aspects of the same mystery.

It is from the Gospel of John and the Letters of Paul that one can glean a unitive understanding of Christ's paschal mystery as it was celebrated during Pentecost in the first centuries. We have already taken note of

John's vision of Christ on the cross: Jesus as king upon his royal throne, lifted up and drawing all to himself, now Lord of glory (these are resurrection/ascension themes; see John 17–19); Jesus as the one totally empty and open to his Father's transforming gift of Spirit, and then as the one through whom the Spirit flows to give birth to Church, to a whole new eschatological creation (Spirit, Church, New Creation themes; see John 17–20 and Pauline writings such as Rom 8). There is really no separation possible between the paschal mystery of Christ and the outpouring of the Spirit. It is by the Spirit's hovering presence that Christ is anointed as servant for us in his baptism until he is consecrated for us in his self-gift on the cross; it is by the Spirit's presence that we receive Christ's continuing self-gift for us in the Eucharist; it is by the Spirit's work in us that we are able to share in the paschal mystery and to live our daily lives for the upbuilding of the new creation and the praise of God. As Christians, we live the risen life of Christ by the power of the Spirit poured out within us!

From the writings of the early Fathers of the Church, the most complete witness to the Easter season comes from the theologian Tertullian. Referring to the Easter Fifty Days as a whole, as "the Pentecost,"[1] Tertullian describes this span of time as a "space" in which one can experience the expansiveness, freedom, and boundlessness of resurrection life. The Fifty Days are a space filled with the presence of Christ Risen, who shows himself over and over to us, his Church, just as he manifested himself to his apostles. Everywhere we turn, there is the Risen Lord—with us at table, at a campfire on the lakeshore, on the road as we journey. Everywhere we turn, there is his Spirit outpoured, shaping the new creation. Indeed, the New Creation is actualized—made visible—by our very celebration of the Fifty Days. The whole Pentecost is thus a gathering-in of God's people by God himself, a fashioning of the members into the very Body of the Risen Christ by the power of the Spirit.

The Fifty Days are the Lord's gift, his invitation and his grace—ours is the privilege of keeping "this most joyous space,"[2] as Tertullian calls it. Truly, the feast of the fifty is the day the Lord has made. We are glad and rejoice in it (Ps 117 [118]).

We have already noted that the Sunday of each week has been regarded in our tradition as a sign of the end time, the *eschaton* or eternity. Likewise, the annual Fifty Days were seen as a symbol of the world to come, and because of their strong affinity to the weekly resurrection day, were called collectively "the great Sunday."

Basil the Great sees in the number fifty an eschatological meaning. Seven, the scripturally perfect number, is multiplied by itself, taking us from the Sunday of the Pasch to the final Sunday of Easter. Each of the Fifty Days of the Pentecost is equal to the others, and when the fiftieth arrives, it is as the first, ranking with it in honor and celebrating the same comprehensive mystery of our redemption in Christ. Thus, the Pentecost—the Fifty—is "a likeness of eternity, beginning as it does and ending, as in a circling course, at the same point."[3]

Writing about the season of Easter, Augustine takes up the eschatological theme, saying that the Fifty "joyful days point to a future life when we are destined to reign with the Lord."[4] He declares that the Fifty Days are a taste of eternal blessedness, for the Risen Lord is present, and we the Church are already in possession of that which is promised.

To appropriately show our resurrected life, we are neither to kneel in prayer nor fast during the Fifty Days, according to the Church fathers and early liturgical tradition. Kneeling for prayer is suitable in times of trouble; but in these Easter days when we experience the gift of risen life in such abundance, we pray standing to show that we gladly and gratefully possess whatever good we could hope for in Christ. Fasting is enjoined upon us when the bridegroom is taken away (Mark 2:19-20); but now as we rejoice in his radiant presence, as we celebrate the marriage of the Lamb, fasting has no place in our spiritual expression.

Above all, in the acknowledgment par excellence of our risen existence, we sing "alleluia!" In this one word, which means "praise God" (*Hallelu Yahweh* in Hebrew), we are in touch with the Exodus, the decisive act of God for his people Israel. In this one word, says Augustine, we sing of our new passing over in Christ, joyful *now,* and joyful in eternity for the full delight of the eternal Easter. For Augustine, Christians are an Easter people, and alleluia is their food, their drink, and their joy, even unto eternity.[5]

After several centuries of such abundant theological reflection on the Fifty Days of Easter, it is surprising that until recent years many of us had not even heard that there was a Fifty Days! The disintegration of the unitive Easter season actually began quite early, and for a variety of reasons, one of which may have been the tendency toward historical commemoration in the liturgy. There is evidence that at least in fourth-

century Jerusalem, the fiftieth day of Easter was celebrated as the feast of both Christ's ascension and the coming of the Spirit. After the fiftieth day became entirely a Holy Spirit feast, the term Pentecost came more and more to designate this single day.

Influences from Jewish tradition came to bear on the fiftieth day as a celebration of the coming of the Holy Spirit. The Jewish Feast of Weeks, a grain-harvest festival, was celebrated seven weeks after the Passover and later became a commemoration of the giving of the law to the people of Israel. Since the Feast of Weeks coincided with the fiftieth day of Easter, some Christian writers drew a parallel between the giving of the law on Sinai and the giving of the new law written on our hearts by the Holy Spirit.

The Lord's ascension, originally celebrated as part of the paschal mystery, was later commemorated separately at some time during the Fifty Days. Finally, based on the time-frame of the Acts of the Apostles, which assigns Christ's ascension to the fortieth day after his resurrection and the Spirit's coming to the fiftieth day (Acts 1:3 and 2:1, respectively), Ascension Thursday came into being as a distinct feast during Easter's Fifty Days.

The Ascension feast isolates an aspect of the paschal triumph of Christ, one we have already heard about in the texts of the Paschal Three Days. Jesus, having emptied himself, even unto death on a cross, is now at the right hand of God. "God raised him high and gave him the name which is above all other names . . . Jesus Christ as Lord," writes Paul. In the ascension, we celebrate Jesus as king and Lord "to the glory of God the Father (Phil 2:9, 11).

While it may have been spiritually profitable to accent distinct aspects of paschal mystery by giving each an individual day of celebration, the effect of such a development on the oneness of the Fifty Days was ultimately devastating. The unified Easter season eventually fell into two parts, the first forty and the last ten days. The new feasts with their strong doctrinal thrust soon came to overshadow the unitive paschal mystery celebrated in the original Fifty Days.

The Second Vatican Council, without seeking to dilute the feasts of Ascension and Pentecost, *does* emphatically call attention anew to the Easter Fifty Days as a totality, saying that "the fifty days between Easter Sunday and Pentecost are celebrated as one feast day, sometimes called 'the great Sunday' " (*General Norms for the Liturgical Year and the Calendar,* no. 22). We now speak of the Sundays *of* Easter, no longer the Sun-

The Risen Jesus; age 3½.

days *after* Easter; and the paschal candle remains lit throughout the season to the fiftieth day, inclusive.

A significant step toward reintegrating the Fifty Days theologically is the manner in which the scriptural readings for the Sundays of Easter have been selected. On the first day of the Fifty, Easter Sunday, we hear the post-Pentecost sermon of Peter, and we witness in him the fiery zeal given by the Holy Spirit (Acts 10:34, 37-43). On the last day of the season, the fiftieth day of Easter, we hear the gospel of a resurrection appearance, when on ''the first day of the week'' the Lord appears to his own (John 20:19-23). Another unifying factor in the Easter season is that the new Lectionary supplies readings for the whole of the Fifty Days.

The Rite of the Christian Initiation of Adults offers a very strong impetus toward the cohesion and importance of the Fifty Days. First, the new practice sets initiation squarely into the context of the paschal mystery; and second, it underlines the fact that the normal context of the latter stages of initiation is the paschal cycle, Lent/Three Days/Easter season. The final stage of initiation, the so-called *mystagogia* or post-baptismal teaching, is the one which corresponds to

the Fifty Days. For both the newly initiated and their communities, the object of this time is to ''move forward together, meditating on the gospel, sharing in the Eucharist, and performing works of charity. In this way they understand the paschal mystery more fully and bring it into their lives more and more'' (Rite of Christian Initiation of Adults [RCIA], 37).

The Fifty Days of Easter in the Parish

It has recently been written that the Church of our day may not be able to celebrate a lengthy season like Easter's Fifty Days because our cultural context and our life cycles have changed so since the early centuries. True, much is different in our lifestyles today. However, if we look theologically at the Fifty Days, we cannot deny the validity—even the necessity—of keeping a season that unfolds, explores, and celebrates the central mystery of our Christian life.

To better understand what can happen during the Fifty Days, we might take our cue from the *mystagogia*. The ''neophytes,'' newly baptized at the Paschal Vigil, continue to meet throughout the Easter season for spiritual sharing, prayer, celebration, and mutual support in good works. What the neophytes experienced in their paschal initiation becomes the source of fifty days of reflection, thanksgiving, and mission. The pattern of spiritual growth follows that expressed in Psalm 33[34]: taste, and then come to see, to contemplate the goodness of the Lord. After such an experience as Pasch, we the Church need the Fifty Days to allow the paschal blessings to unfold in our lives.

The neophytes' visible presence to the community is part of the richness of the Fifty Days, particularly for all who witnessed their initiation at the Paschal Vigil. Whatever gatherings the parish might have for its newly initiated, the family could try to attend one or more of these in order to come to know the neophytes, support them, pray with them. Another possibility for parishioners to meet the neophytes might be at a Sunday Eucharistic gathering, at which the newly baptized might wear their white garments and be specially honored at the hospitality time after the liturgy. The presence of the neophytes in the parish community during the Fifty Days underscores the ongoing nature of Christian initiation. In them we see that by continuing in prayer and in following the gospel, we live out our baptismal commitment and become ever more what we are called to be! The new members of the Church become witness for the whole parish community, bringing them "renewed vision and new impetus" (RCIA, 39).

Helping the community deepen its baptismal spirituality, then, is a major Easter responsibility of the parish. Keeping neophytes present to the community is one aspect of this pastoral task. Ensuring that the initiation of infants and children be celebrated at this season is another challenge. Why baptize, for instance, just before Lent, or confirm at the end of June, when the Church's prime season for initiation sacraments is the time of paschal mystery? What better gift to children, or to anyone, than to have their entry into the dying and rising of Jesus, the sealing of the Spirit, the Eucharistic table, at the season of Pasch? There is pedagogical wisdom in the Church's previous longstanding practice of initiating only at paschal time; for then, every annual paschal initiation becomes a reliving, a renewal of one's own. In our family, both children were baptized on the fiftieth day of Easter; our six-year-old daughter is already excited and overjoyed to be present at the baptismal liturgy, which is usually celebrated in our parish on the anniversary of her baptism.

Besides the presence of the newly initiated, what is there in our parish that we can point out to our families as signs of the high festal season of Easter?

Throughout the Easter season, the majestic paschal candle stands before us. Jesus Christ, resplendent Risen One and source of light, is with us through his Spirit, shining forth as does the waxen pillar of light which now, in the Fifty Days, replaces the cross as central liturgical symbol. While we generally tend to identify the light of the paschal candle with Christ, it is worth noting that the Holy Spirit's presence is also frequently represented by a flame. The Easter candle becomes another reminder that resurrection and the Spirit-gift are inseparable—that the mystery we celebrate in these Fifty Days is indeed one.

The parish's decor committee will have to plan for a constant and generous supply of flowers and greens for the Fifty Days, a supply more lavish than at any other time of year. If the artists have not managed to prepare a splendid banner for this year, this could be the moment to plan ahead for next Easter . . . perhaps a single large-scale hanging, dramatic in color, symbolic of the one comprehensive paschal mystery of Christ and of the Church. Our parish has a striking tripartite banner grouping featuring the tree of life/cross, water, light, and tongues of fire; it remains hanging for—and only for—the Fifty Days of Easter.

There is a beloved image of Christ which the Church has long associated with the paschal season, that of Christ the Good Shepherd. In the early Christian period, representations of the Good Shepherd antedate and outnumber other depictions of the Lord. From the first four centuries, catacomb art includes several hundred Good Shepherd drawings; after the fifth century the Good Shepherd continues to be represented in mosaic art, statues, and paintings.

For Christians of ancient times, the image of Christ the Shepherd succinctly expressed their whole paschal faith. Jesus gives his life for his sheep (John 10:11); he leads them by the waters, anoints them with oil, and feeds them with a rich banquet (these are baptism, Spirit, and Eucharist symbols); and he takes his own to green pastures forever (Ps 22 [23]). Christ's Pasch, his dying, rising, glorification; its continuation in us by the sacramental life of the Church; the taste of and longing for eternal Easter—this nucleus of faith is contained in the Good Shepherd representation. Throughout the Fifty Days of Easter, the preaching, songs, decor, and catechesis could be much enriched by this loved but often overlooked image.

In particular, the Good Shepherd figure and par-

The child depicts her baptism, with Christ-light emanating from herself; age 6.

able is a cornerstone in the spirituality of the very young child, according to Cavalletti.[6] If, as this book will propose in the following pages, the shepherd image is to be presented to the child as an important aspect of Easter prayer and celebration, the parish's conscious pointing to Christ the Shepherd is highly desirable and supportive for the child.

The musicians' energies, sometimes dissipated by frequent change of repertoire, should be better focused than ever in this longest of liturgical seasons: one good set of acclamations for the liturgies of Word and Eucharist, plus paschal hymns and songs, something new and enough that is old (i.e., classic or beloved traditional)—these can unify and sustain the season very well. Constant change is not the same as creativity! All of us, including our little children with their need for repetition, should be able to identify an Easter liturgy in our parish when we hear one. We should be able to take home in our hearts Easter music that we have done several times and not only once during the Fifty Days!

In fairness to musicians, however, and to preachers and even to ourselves as community, all of us have had very little help in understanding the unity of the Fifty Days. Most of our hymns, our prayer texts, and our spiritual formation regarding the paschal season tend to be divided into the separate thematic categories of resurrection, ascension, and coming of the Spirit. What can we do in our parishes to recognize these different aspects of the paschal mystery and still preserve the oneness of the Easter season, the fifty-day "great Sunday"? And how can a parish ensure that its celebration of Ascension and Pentecost are kept in the larger paschal context of the Fifty Days?

First, whatever liturgical rituals are being used to unify the Easter season, i.e., baptismal-water sprinkling rite, entrance procession with paschal banners, seasonal refrains and acclamations repeated every Sunday, and so on, should continue on the days marking the Lord's ascension and on Pentecost Sunday (The United States has retained Ascension Thursday, the fortieth day of the Easter season, while Canada celebrates the ascension on the seventh Sunday of Easter; Pentecost, of course, is always the eighth Sunday of Easter.) Second, it is probably the tone of the preaching and the selection of music which will help the community most immediately to develop an understanding of the unity of the paschal mystery. Let us hope that what we hear and what we sing at the liturgies of the seventh and eighth Sundays of Easter will keep us squarely in the Fifty Days, "the great Sunday" of the Lord.

The Fifty Days in the parish are usually filled with sacramental celebrations, not only the sacraments of initiation, as we have already noted, but also weddings and ordinations. How fitting it would be to have many of these take place at the Sunday Eucharistic liturgy, when a parish assembly is present! Such celebrations need not overshadow the paschal season but rather, by careful planning and catechesis, can be experienced as an integral part of the Fifty Days. Such celebrations can then reveal even more clearly how the Spirit of God is among us, fashioning the New Creation ushered in by the Risen Lord.

The Fifty Days of Easter in the Home

Given that our parishes themselves seem to experience a difficulty sustaining the celebration of the Fifty Days, the home has to overcome even greater hurdles. What to do? Above all, one has to believe in the greatness of the Easter season and appreciate the implications of this time; and then, realizing how great a challenge it may be to invest in this new enterprise, commit oneself to the Fifty Days!

In our hemisphere, the Easter season happily coincides with spring and a rush of new life everywhere. Nature, too, can be a teacher, especially for the young child, whose affinity with and wonder at the natural world have been well documented. The Fifty Days can be a time to discover birth and rebirth, to delight in colors and sounds of the earth and sky, to experience the pulsing of the Spirit in all of creation!

Easter decoration in the home need not be expensive to be tasteful and pleasing. A friend of mine plants pots of daffodil bulbs over several weeks of the winter and assures her household of glorious sunlit flowers throughout the Fifty Days. If a home has no green-thumb gardener, streamers and little rosettes of bright crepe paper are easy to make, and children eagerly help with them.

The household paschal candle decorated on Saturday of the Three Days can be a table centerpiece all through the Easter season. A vividly colored tablecloth will keep the family's dinner table appropriately festive (two tablecloths can be sewn from one of those cheerfully patterned bedsheets available inexpensively at department store sales). Since the whole season is "the great Sunday," the home's Sunday-best dining

pieces can be used as regularly as one may dare with small children!

Books of Easter art and recordings of Easter music, if you do not have them on your own shelves, can be found at a public library or sometimes at a diocesan center or a larger church or at a university or college nearby.

A family can build up its supply of Easter decorations and other paschal season items, much as is done for Christmas. Often, lovely fabrics and books and the like are available for a reduced cost at unpredictable times of the year. Become a year-round Easter season collector. Our house is in the process of assembling paschal music on videos, records, and tapes; we also have an unintentional accumulation of Easter baskets for our decorated eggs, baskets ranging from our daughter's first efforts in paper when she was four years old to some imported woven baskets and an elegant silver basket given us by another family.

Environment is only the setting for the family's activity; it is what you *do* that is Easter! Privileged among the daily rhythms of the Fifty Days is our common prayer. In this season of newness in Christ, family members may themselves find a special Easter aspect of their prayer at this season. For instance, our daughter, at five years of age, wanted to dance the Song of Mary (*Magnificat*) at evening prayer during the Easter season. The family might wish to sing its prayer in entirety during the Fifty Days (see "Resources for the Fifty Days").

In celebrating the paschal mystery of the Lord, we discover that we have been joyfully and eagerly welcomed into the Shepherd's fold; we have become royal sons and daughters, heirs of the kingdom; we have been lovingly received at the marriage feast of the Lamb. The Fifty Days of Easter is a preeminent time to extend hospitality as it has been extended to us. It is a time to let the hospitality and care of the Lord flow through us—to those around us, to those in need of concern and support, to those who are already beloved to us. Host a potluck, a picnic, a quiet evening meal, an Easter festival, a fiftieth-day party. Visit someone who needs you.

Because of the duration of the Easter season, it is almost imperative for a family with young children to use an engaging visual symbol to maintain its focus for fifty days. For four years, since our elder child was three, we have centered our children's Easter activities around a large poster-board "tree of life"—it is painted with the image of the cross entwined with fifty flowers which open to reveal a daily activity for the child/family (much in the manner of Advent calendars, which we do not use in our home since the appearance of our Easter tree). The idea for a flowering tree came to us in connection with the imagery of the tree as found in Scripture, liturgy, and the Fathers of the Church. The tree of Eden became the tree of death, but the tree of the cross becomes the tree of life and joy, bringing us the fruits of salvation. In writings such as those of Andrew of Crete, we hear; "Rightly could

I call [the cross of Christ] the fairest of all fair things and the costliest, in fact as well as in name, for on it and through it and for its sake the riches of salvation that had been lost were restored to us."[7]

The cross which we jeweled during the Three Days has sprung to life and burst into full living beauty. This cross has become the paschal tree of life. In its branches, both the great and the least significant find a home and receive nourishment and grace.

Resources for the Fifty Days of Easter

1. Morning and Evening Prayer for the Fifty Days

Call to Prayer

(SONG 12)
(Leader says or sings each line first, all repeat):
Jesus is our light,
Light of the world,
Alleluia.

Psalm for the Fifty Days: Ps 22[23]

(SONG 13)
Refrain: The Lord is my shepherd; there is nothing I
shall want.
Verse: The Lord is my shepherd;
There is nothing I shall want.
Fresh and green are the pastures
Where he gives me repose.
Near restful waters he leads me,
To revive my drooping spirit.

Scripture Reading: the Sunday gospel passage or selected verses (See Appendix B)

Canticle: for morning, Song of Zechariah *(Benedictus)*, see p. 153
for evening, Song of Mary *(Magnificat)*, see p. 140

Intercessions

Our Father

Blessing

2. Songs for the Fifty Days

(Additional songs and refrains are suggested in connection with the activities of each of the weeks of Easter.)

> (SONG 14) Our Shepherd Lord Is Ris'n
> Our Shepherd Lord is ris'n! Allelu, alleluia.
> O let our voices ring! Allelu, alleluia.
> His light shines in our hearts, Allelu, alleluia.
> For fifty days we sing Allelu, alleluia.
>
> (SONG 15) Alleluia Clapping Song
> Alleluia, alleluia, alleluia
> Alleluia, alleluia, alleluia
> Alleluia, alleluia, alleluia

3. Activities for the Fifty Days of Easter

The following pages include enough activities for the entire Fifty Days. The activities can be modified, shortened, lengthened, or repeated as the children involved find profitable—and fun! It has been our family's experience that the length of an activity has little to do with its significance in the child's mind. The quality of the experience and the sharing with a loved one are what seem most important.

Seven themes derived from scriptural/liturgical sources are suggested, one for each of the seven Easter weeks. For each thematic area, I include some background notes; these are intended primarily for parents, to enrich the understanding of the vast spiritual wealth of the Easter season. The more extensive comments on specific paschal themes/images are included for the Fifty Days because there is little material available for this season as compared to Lent or Advent-Christmas. There are, of course, numerous Easter themes other than those I have suggested, and families are encouraged to substitute or rearrange as suitable.

I also sketch a brief introductory reflection[8] which parents might wish to share with their children early in the week, for the whole week of activities grows out of that theme or image. Although this reflective sharing can be done quite formally, it is possible that it be part of rather more casual conversation between parent and child.

A visual focal point and unifying center for all these activities is desirable. Our family has used the flowering tree-of-life poster (see p. 55). A tree that has its fifty flowers from the beginning rather than from having accumulated them as the season progresses is more truly expressive of the theology of the Easter Fifty

Days; that is, all the richness of the paschal mystery is present from the outset, and it is ours to discover.

The flowering paschal tree may be made as follows:

Materials: medium to heavyweight bristol board, 22 x 28 in. (56 x 71 cm), in brilliant yellow or another festive color; a lightweight white paper of the same size as the bristol board; X-Acto knife; acrylic paints; glue.

Activity: Sketch and then paint on the bristol board a large cross entwined by seven vines of flowers (seven flowers per vine and eight on the last vine, for a total of fifty). When paint is thoroughly dry, cut approximately four-fifths of the way around each flower to create a hinged door which will open with some ease. Glue the white paper onto the back of the bristol board; gently lift the flowers open, write the Fifty Days' activities on the white paper, and close the flowers carefully afterward.(One year I wrote all the activities in advance, but found I had to adjust things often as our season moved along; now, I write activities for a day or two, or up to a week at a time. Also, until the child is able to read, consider sketching on the back of the flower a tiny drawing relating to the day's activity; then, even the non-reader has something to discover inside the flower.)

Tree of Life

(22 in x 28 in / 56 cm x 71 cm)

actual size:

cut

lift to write message

▨▨▨ brown

⸬⸬⸬ yellow

▭ white

55

First Week of Easter—Land of Milk and Honey

Scriptural/liturgical orientation—a note for parents

The image of the people of God journeying toward the Promised Land is fresh in our minds from the Lenten season and paschal celebration. Of old, God gave his word that he would lead his own into a land flowing with milk and honey, a land of choicest blessings: "I will give to you and to your descendants after you the land you are living in . . . I will be your God" (Gen 17:8).

"Promised Land" in the Hebrew Scriptures came to have both historical and symbolic dimensions. In the Christian experience, the Promised Land has been thought of as the *eschaton*, eternity, the fullness of the kingdom. It is the home to which our Good Shepherd leads us.

As the image of Promised Land is so deeply rooted in the Hebrew Scripture and is so richly complex, its multiple facets will unfold over many years for each of us. For the very young child, it is sufficient to speak of Promised Land in the context of the Good Shepherd.

1. REFLECTION OF PARENT AND CHILD ON "THE LAND OF MILK AND HONEY"

At a quiet time, the parent and child could come together in the prayer corner or outdoors or wherever appropriate. The parent introduces the reflection in the following or similar words:

"The Good Shepherd brings his sheep into beautiful places where he stays with them and cares for them. The place where the Good Shepherd is with his sheep is so full of good things that we sometimes call it the 'land of milk and honey.' We are happy the Good Shepherd has brought us here. Sometimes we sing and dance for joy!"

Conversation on the above topic, silence, spontaneous prayer, or a song could follow.

2. AN EASTER MORNING DANCE

As Eastertime is fifty days long, this dance may be done on any of the sunlit mornings of the season, but at our house we like to begin the first Sunday of the Fifty in this way.

Materials: a recording of triumphant Easter music, for instance, a hymn tune such as "Jesus Christ is Ris'n Today" or a classic such as the "Hallelujah Chorus" from Handel's *Messiah*; tambourines, bells, drums, rhythm sticks—all these can be homemade, improvised from anything which rings, clangs, rattles, or resounds.

Activity: the whole family might do a free dance together or a processional dance through the home, a sheer joy response to the Pasch of the Lord (for a scriptural description of such a moment after God delivered his people from Egypt, see Exod 15:20-21).

It might be noted here that dance for the Lord, at home as well as at the Church's common worship, should not only be pretty and calm and slow under the guise of being reverent. Our God moves abruptly at times "to disrupt the temple, to lay low the mighty, to shake the foundations. Dance may very well witness to the God who speaks in the stillness; but if it is to be faithful to the biblical record, it must also witness to the God who speaks through mighty acts."[9]

With very young children, free dance is accomplishment enough on an Easter morning! The older preschooler would be ready to join in a simple line-dance with the family (or with friends invited for Easter dancing later in the season). The following step fits duple and quadruple rhythms ("one-two," and "one-two-three-four" respectively) in which many festive hymns and songs are written: three steps forward and one step back, three steps forward and one step back, and so on, indefinitely.

3. A SONG FOR THE LAND OF MILK AND HONEY

> This song may be used not only during this week but during the entire Easter season:
>
> (SONG 16) Milk and Honey Song
>
> We've come to the land of milk and honey, Halleluia!
> We've come to the land where it's always sunny, Halleluia!
> And now we see the tree of life,
> and the Shepherd Lord who is our light.
> We've come to the land of milk and honey, Halleluia!

4. AN EASTER DISPLAY

All family members could help in setting up a display of Jesus the Shepherd leading his people to beautiful places (this is really a festal elaboration of what the child has already done in connection with the initial

Good Shepherd presentation—see "Resources for Lent," p. 79). The display might be in the prayer area, or if possible, near the family table, where it can be seen and referred to often at mealtimes.

Materials: Good Shepherd and sheep figurines or paper models (see "Resources for Lent," p. 81); three sheets of paper, one brown, one blue, one green—these could be construction or tissue paper, tissues, pages from wallpaper sample books, or simply crayon-colored paper; spring flowers of any kind, a green plant or two.

Activity: on the display area, arrange the colored paper—brown, cut to an appropriate size for the desert, blue for a river of water, green for the verdant place where everything is full of life. The children can help arrange greens and flowers in "the Promised Land." Finally, they can set up the shepherd and the sheep as leaving the desert behind and coming together to the place of beauty and life.

5. MILK AND HONEY COOKIES

The following recipe makes a quite nutritious cookie, and in a large enough quantity to freeze and use often during the Fifty Days.

1 cup	Butter	250 ml
1 cup	Honey	250 ml
2	Eggs	2
1 cup	Milk	250 ml
2 tsp	Vanilla	10 ml
1 tsp	Baking soda	5 ml
2½ cups	Whole wheat flour	625 ml
1 Tbsp	Baking powder	15 ml
¾ tsp	Salt	3 ml
1 tsp	Cinnamon	5 ml
2½ cups	Rolled oats	625 ml
1¼ cup	Raisins	300 ml

Preheat oven to 350 degrees F (180 C). Cream together butter and honey. Beat eggs, milk, vanilla, and baking soda, and add to butter-honey mixture. Sift flour, baking powder, salt, and cinnamon into mixture. Add rolled oats and raisins. Drop by teaspoons onto a greased cookie sheet, about two inches apart. Bake for about 12 minutes until cookies are spread out and slightly browned.

6. DECORATIONS IN THE HOME

Whatever decorations are already up in our home by the beginning of Easter season, more keep appearing as part of our Fifty Days celebration! This week, as we think of how the Good Shepherd brings us to a place of life and gladness, we make colorful floral decorations for our home and some extras to share with others.

<u>Materials</u>: crepe paper in vibrant colors, including green; or bright construction paper or tissue paper or any scraps of medium-weight paper, available inexpensively at commercial print shops; fine wire or green twisters from shopping.

<u>Activity</u>: if using crepe paper or tissue paper, cut strips about 2″ x 18″ (5 x 45 cm), roll up, bind tightly at bottom with wire or twisters, and let the child pull at the paper gently to ''fluff up'' the flowers. Leaf shapes made of green paper may be added.

If using construction paper or other flat paper, everyone can draw or trace floral shapes to cut out.

The flowers may be used to decorate windows, doorjambs or doors, children's room, etc. (be sure to use masking tape, and to be gentle in removing it when the season is over, to avoid damaging wall or furniture surfaces). One year, we made additional flowers for our grandparents' home and decorated their kitchen for the Fifty Days.

7. DYEING EASTER EGGS

We do a repeat of the Easter-egg dyeing at some time during this week, partly because we give away eggs to friends and relatives (an old Christian custom of gift-giving at Easter), and partly because it is such a delightful activity for the child and a good pedagogical moment besides.

For suggestions on dyeing/decorating eggs see ''Resources for the Three Days,'' p. 43.

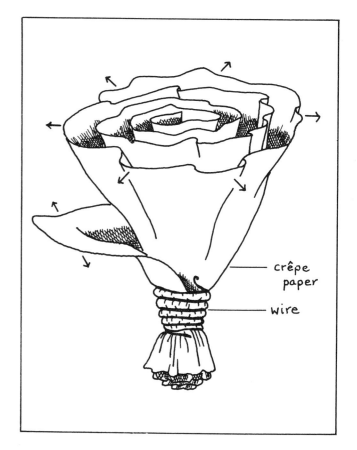

crêpe paper

wire

8. OTHER ACTIVITIES

■ Find an interesting rock, and paint it with poster paints or thick tempera paint (to preserve, apply a coat of varnish when paint is dry). If the child is old enough to grasp this, the parent might explain that Jesus is sometimes called ''our rock'' because he is so strong in loving and protecting us.

■ Find green, wear green (an easy activity that very young children enjoy!).

■ Make an Easter-egg gift: using a small box to which you can add a cardboard handle or, using a plastic berry-basket, insert ''straw'' made of shredded crepe paper or tissue paper or paper napkins; put a decorated Easter egg inside and give this as a gift to someone.

Second Week of Easter: Light

<u>Scriptural/liturgical orientation—a note for parents</u>
The light image has had a dramatic liturgical expression at the Easter Vigil. The paschal "light of Christ" continues to be present, represented by the paschal candle used at home and in the parish; that light is celebrated again and again in the baptismal services and spirituality which are part of this season.

Light is closely associated with baptism into Christ. Everyone is familiar with the part of the ceremony in which the newly baptized person, after emerging from the water, receives the light taken from the paschal candle which symbolizes Christ. Both scriptural and patristic writings refer to baptism as illumination, being filled with light. In the words of Justin, "this washing [baptism] is called illumination, since those who learn these things are illumined within."[10]

Cavalletti believes that for the child coming to understand baptism, light is the "linking point" or nucleus image which contains the whole meaning of baptism. She emphasizes that, for the child, this nucleus may not necessarily be the most important liturgical sign, which in baptism is water and not light. It is Cavalletti's experience that the child easily associates the image of Christ the light with the Good Shepherd.[11]

1. REFLECTION OF PARENT AND CHILD ON "LIGHT"

Parent and child choose a quiet place to be together, preferably in a room that is somewhat darkened. Set up the household paschal candle there, and have on hand the child's baptismal candle (or other small candle) as well as the child's baptismal gown if possible. The parent presents the week's theme in these or similar words:

"When Jesus rose, his light shone on the whole world (the adult lights the paschal candle). The light of the Risen Jesus is so strong that it will shine always and always. And now Jesus gives his light to all who come close to him. Many people receive it in their hearts!

"On the day I was baptized I received this light. You received this light from Jesus, too, at your baptism (with the small candle, the child takes light from the paschal candle).

"At our baptism, we put on a beautiful white gown (the adult shows the white garment). This wonderful gown we wore showed on the outside the light that

Jesus put inside our hearts. Our baptismal gown showed everyone that we became completely different, all new, full of light."

Conversation on the above topic, silence, spontaneous prayer, or a song could follow.

2. DRAWING OF BAPTISMAL LIGHT

Children may be invited to draw themselves at baptism. When did they receive the light of Christ? How did they look when full of light?

3. A SONG OF LIGHT

The family might learn this song for the week. It could be used at the family Evening Prayer when the paschal candle is lit to begin the service (see p. 53 above).

> (SONG 17) O Light of Christ
> Leader: O light of Christ,
>   All: Shine in our hearts.
> Leader: Wonderful light,
>   All: Shine in our hearts.
> Leader: Be with us always,
>   All: Shine, shine in our hearts.

4. BAPTISMAL DISPLAY AREA

The parent could encourage the child to examine its white baptismal garment, perhaps referring again to its symbolism as in Item 1 above. Choose a special place to hang it, or set it where the child and the family can see it often (it could remain there for the whole Fifty Days).

The child's baptismal candle can also be displayed, either near the white garment or in the prayer area or another suitable place. It is good to allow the child to touch, hold, and carefully help with the candle in this project.

5. CARD FOR GODPARENTS

At some time when speaking to children about their baptismal day, the question of godparents and their role may arise. Possibly the godparents were the ones who actually received the lighted candle on behalf of the child in the liturgical ceremony of baptism. In any case, children can be told that the godparents are to help them always live in the light of Christ.

Children could make a drawing or a special card, or write a message to their godparents as a thank-you gesture.

6. WATCHING A SUNRISE

In spring with its earlier sunrises, this may be more difficult to do, but the family (or several households together) could make a project of it on a weekend.

An early rising, a gathering in a park or on a hillside, some silent time to watch the changing hues of dawn, an Easter song or prayer, and a simple breakfast of buns and Easter eggs and fruit—all these would make for a memorable morning honoring Jesus the Risen Light, the Risen Sun of God.

7. A "CANDLE" DESSERT

<u>Materials</u>: banana, pineapple rings, and/or assorted fruit chunks, maraschino cherries, or large fresh red berries.

<u>Activity</u>: cut bananas in half and stand one half vertically on each dessert plate, using pineapple ring as a base if desired; top with a cherry or berry secured with a toothpick; add fruit chunks around base.

8. OTHER ACTIVITIES

- At the parish church, find the paschal candle, touch it reverently, examine it carefully, and talk about its meaning.
- Draw a picture of the Paschal Vigil service of light.
- Find white, wear white.
- Make candleholders to use at home or share with others.

<u>Materials</u>: small jars or glasses, white glue, small paint brushes, salt (coarse or fine grain).

<u>Activity</u>: using glue, paint designs on the glass or jar, and roll immediately in a plate of salt; when the glue has dried thoroughly, insert a votive candle or other small candle which will stand securely.

Third Week of Easter: Water

<u>Scriptural/liturgical orientation—a note for parents</u>

Water, one of the most ancient and universal religious symbols, has profound significance in the Judeo-Christian tradition. In the beginning, there were the dark primeval waters over which God's creative Spirit hovered (Gen 1:1-2); the flood of Noah's day purged and judged, but also preceded a universal covenant, a new world order (Gen 6–9); the waters of the Red Sea, through which God's people passed from slavery into freedom, became a central symbol in the salvation story of Israel (Exod 14). When Jesus was baptized in the Jordan, once again the Spirit of God hovered over the waters, and the Father proclaimed his delight in his Son. In his baptism we recognize not only Jesus' nature and mission, but also the mission of each Christian baptized into him (Matt 3:13-17, Mark 1:9-11, Luke 3:21-22). From the side of Jesus on the cross there flows water (John 19:34), water which becomes a river of life, flowing crystal clear and filling the city of God with life (Rev 22:1-2).

1. REFLECTION OF PARENT AND CHILD ON "WATER"

There should be on hand a large, preferably clear, bowl filled with water, and a lighted paschal candle. The adult may speak of water to the child in these or similar words:

"At our baptism, the light of Jesus came to us so that we could become sheep of the Good Shepherd with his light in our hearts. The light came to us in many ways. One way the light of the Shepherd came into our hearts is through water.

"Water is good to drink, and it is also used for washing. We know that water makes things grow, like the little seed that grows into a big plant. Water is so important that without it we could not live; nothing on the earth could live!

"When we are baptized, we are put into the water so that we become filled with light, filled with new life. The water is given us in the name of the Father and of the Son and of the Holy Spirit. Here is how we were baptized (the adult places his or her hands into the water, scoops some upward, and using the child's name, says the words of baptism): 'N., I baptize you in the name of the Father and of the Son and of the Holy Spirit.' (The child is invited to do the water gesture and repeat the baptismal words.)"

Conversation on the above topic, silence, spontaneous prayer, or a song could follow.

2. A GOOD SHEPHERD SONG

The refrain below could be used by young children during this and following weeks. A slightly older child can learn a full stanza of the Twenty-second (-third) Psalm from one of the settings in a parish hymnal.

(SONG 18) The Lord Is My Shepherd

The Lord is my Shepherd,
By restful waters he leads me.

3. WINDOW TRANSPARENCY

Materials: tissue paper in blue, or blue and white, or several shades of blue; transparent glue such as mucilage, one large piece of construction or poster paper.

Activity: fold the construction paper in half to make a "book," and cut out the inside of each half to create two frames; paste one sheet of white or light-colored tissue paper onto one of the frames—this will be the backdrop for the remaining work; cut or gently tear strips or other shapes from the blue paper; paste lightly onto tissue backdrop, overlapping as desired; when the water-design is complete, fold down the second frame over the working side of the transparency and glue securely; trim any excess tissue; hang it in a window where there is plenty of light.

4. VIEWING THE LIGHT IN WATER

Find a beautiful clear-glass jar or pitcher or other container, preferably with little or no decor on it. Fill with fresh water. Let the child view it against the sunlight to see how "full of light" the water is. Together thank God for the gift of water.

---

5. POPPY SEED CAKE

Remembering that it is water which makes seeds grow into new life, make this simple cake (poppy seeds are significant in many East European food traditions, as they are taken to represent the seed which fell into the ground and in dying, gave new life):

3	Eggs	3
1½ cups	Sugar	375 ml
1½ cups	Dairy sour cream	375 ml
1½ tsp	Vanilla	7 ml
2¼ cups	Flour	550 ml
3 tsp	Baking powder	15 ml
½ tsp	Baking soda	2 ml
¼ tsp	Salt	1 ml
½ cup	Poppy seed	125 ml

Beat eggs well, add sugar, and beat again until light and fluffy. Mix in sour cream and vanilla. Sift flour with baking powder, soda, and salt. Add flour mixture to cream mixture along with poppy seeds, and mix gently with a folding motion. Bake at 350 degrees F (180 C) for 35-40 min.

---

6. A WALK BY THE WATERS

If you have a river, lake, stream, or pond nearby, take a family walk there. Look for the movement of water, how it catches light; enjoy its soft or powerful sounds. Linger awhile and sing a Good Shepherd song.

7. BAPTISMAL PHOTOS

Children love to see the pictures of themselves and hear stories of their baptism. Take time to show baptismal pictures to the child, explaining the place, the actions, the people present.

If the photos are not already mounted in an album, the child could help do this; or possibly older children might like to make a poster display of their baptismal photos to be hung near the area previously arranged with white garment and candle.

8. OTHER ACTIVITIES

- Have the children make drawings of themselves touched by/immersed in the waters of baptism.
- Find blue, wear blue.
- If you have an aquarium, or can locate one at a school or some public building, spend time watching the fish move through the waters (to an older child, you can explain that sometimes people have spoken of Christians as little fishes, swimming in the baptismal waters. An image of a fish and the Greek letters for ''fish'' were early Christian identity codes).

Fourth Week of Easter: the Good Shepherd Calls by Name

Scriptural/liturgical orientation—a note for parents

In numerous passages of Hebrew Scripture, God is described as a shepherd. This shepherd gathers his scattered flock to lead them home (Jer 23:3-4); and he feeds them, rescues the stray, and cares for the weak and the wounded (Ezek 34:11-31). Many human leaders appointed as shepherds of God's people ultimately fail in their task of caring for the flock, and it seems that God himself must tend his sheep.

In the Christian Scriptures Jesus describes himself as the Good Shepherd (John 10:11), the one who loves the sheep to the point of giving his life for them. The Church at prayer has, from the beginning, used Psalm 22[23], the shepherd psalm, as referring to Jesus.

The paschal character of the Good Shepherd image has already been noted (see p. 50 above). On the Fourth Sunday of Easter, the liturgical texts are related to the Good Shepherd and the gospel of the day is always from John 10.

Quite often the parish emphasis on priestly and religious vocations on Good Shepherd Sunday blurs the paschal image of Jesus the Shepherd. Consequently, the community tends not to grasp fully the liturgical/scriptural richness of this image of the Lord. Parents can try at home to offset the imbalance experienced on the parish level.

1. REFLECTION OF PARENT AND CHILD ON ''THE GOOD SHEPHERD CALLS ME BY NAME''

The figures of Good Shepherd and sheep may be used for this conversation, just as during the Lenten-time presentation (see ''Resources for Lent,'' p. 79). The adult's comments to the child could be something like the following:

''Jesus says to us, 'I am the Good Shepherd . . . the sheep that belong to me listen to my voice; I know them and they follow me.' So Jesus is the *good* shepherd for us all, not just any shepherd. And why do we call him Good Shepherd, do you think? What does he do for his sheep? He knows each one of them. He feeds them and looks after them. The sheep hear his voice because he calls each one of them by name. Every sheep has a name, and every one is special to the Good Shepherd. The name the Good Shepherd calls you is the one you were given in baptism. You are N., and you belong to the Good Shepherd.''

Conversation on the above topic, silence, spontaneous prayer, or a song could follow.

2. THE PSALM OF THE GOOD SHEPHERD

Any of the Good Shepherd songs (settings of Psalm 22 [23]) used commonly in the parish may be sung by the family. If used, the psalm refrain setting below should be done smoothly, at an easy pace; a boisterous approach contradicts the comforting mood of the text.

(SONG 19) Jesus
Jesus is my shepherd and he calls me by my name;
He walks with me ev'rywhere.

3. A NAME DECORATION

Remembering that the Good Shepherd calls each of us by name, the children can be helped to make a paper decoration of their own name.

Materials: one sheet of construction paper or other medium-weight paper, and scissors.

Activity: fold paper in half lengthwise; draw child's name in bold, wide lettering, ensuring that all letters touch each other in at least one place and also touch the top of the fold; cut carefully through the folded paper to get a two-sided name design.

Children may further decorate their names with markers or stickers and may hang them as window decorations or mobiles or mount them flat on white paper to use as nameplates on their bedroom doors.

4. A SHEEP DESSERT

Materials: pear halves, shredded coconut, chocolate chips or firm raisins, a few lettuce leaves.

Activity: for each dessert needed, place a pear half flat-side down on a lettuce leaf; make "eyes" on the pear-shape with chocolate chips or raisins, and sprinkle with coconut.

5. MEETING THE PARISH'S NEWLY BAPTIZED

Especially if children have witnessed the Easter Vigil baptisms or others taking place during this season, they should be given the chance to meet the parish's newly initiated members—even one person. Introduce the newly baptized person(s) to the child by name, the name given at baptism; perhaps exchange a few comments about the baptismal ceremony. Ask for the neophytes' remembrance in prayer, and remember them by name at family prayer. Look for them at parish liturgies in the future.

6. A "FRESH GREEN PASTURES" WALK

If it is possible to arrange, this is an opportune time for a visit to the parish cemetery. Unusual as this may initially seem in our death-denying society, cemetery visiting has long been customary for many religious traditions, and certainly for Christians.

Today, as in the past, it is important that young children grow up feeling comfortable with the presence of death in the midst of life. Cemetery visits provide one context in which parent and child can discuss the topic of dying with naturalness and ease.

An Eastertime cemetery walk can include viewing headstones and searching for names inscribed there. The parent and child can speak of how the Good Shepherd calls us by name in baptism and throughout our lives; and how, at our death, the Good Shepherd calls us by name to be with him always in "fresh green pastures."

Or, if for some reason the cemetery walk is not feasible, find a place with abundant green grass in a quiet park, a meadow, or your own yard. Enjoy the new spring grass. Talk about how Jesus the Good Shepherd leads his sheep into the best pastures.

7. WELCOMING GUESTS

During the season of hospitality, think of some person(s) who would appreciate a meal or evening with your household—a single-parent family, an elderly neighbor, a widow or widower, someone new to the block or to your parish.

Make cards (or placecards for mealtime) featuring each person's name; give them to your guests to take home.

8. OTHER ACTIVITIES

- An older child who can print some of the alphabet could decorate cookies or muffins with first initials of family members; it is easiest to use a "cake-mate" squeeze-tube of icing for the initialing.

- Name bookmarks: using pieces of stiff paper cut to about 2" x 5" (5 x 12 cm), print with markers the names of bookmark recipients (or if the children can print, let them do so); the children decorate around the name with free designs or Easter symbols.

- The child could identify its own favorite color, then find it everywhere, and wear something in that color.

Fifth Week of Easter: The Victorious Cross, Baptismal Sign

Scriptural/liturgical orientation—a note for parents
Throughout Christian history, the victorious cross of Christ has been a central image in Christian symbolism. The cross is traced upon the forehead of each candidate for baptism, and the sign of the cross is used as a prayer gesture throughout the life of a Christian. The cross is raised aloft in processions, venerated in worship, hymned by poets and musicians; it adorns churches, schools and homes, surrounds life on every side, and marks the last resting place of those who die in Christ.

The Scriptures and the Fathers of the Church deeply enrich our understanding of the cross. In the Gospel of John, particularly, we are presented with the vision of the cross as royal throne, place of Christ's ascent to the Father and of Christ's kingship, and source of the life of the Church. In patristic writings, we hear that the cross is a tree of life standing in happy contrast to the tree in paradise which brought death. The tree of the cross brings light, not darkness; joy, not sadness; the fruits of salvation and not the fruits of destruction and death. The patristic image of the cross as victory of light over darkness would be a suitable manner of speaking of the cross to the young child.

1. REFLECTION OF PARENT AND CHILD ON "THE VICTORIOUS CROSS"

The parent and child could come together at the place where the jeweled cross of the Paschal Three Days

is displayed (see "Resources for the Three Days," p. 39) or where the family has its representation of the cross. The adult may introduce the reflection in the following or similar words:

"Do you remember how we celebrated the cross of Jesus not long ago? (The child might be able to contribute some memories of the Three Days, their ceremonies, songs, or gestures at worship, or home activities.)

"We know that the cross is the sign of Jesus' victory over darkness. At baptism, our parents and godparents and the Church's minister made that sign on our foreheads to show that we belong to Jesus, the Good Shepherd and to his light—it shows that we are full of his light and that we live always in his light. The sign of the cross we received in baptism was traced on our foreheads in this way (adult traces ✚ on child's head). That sign is also in our hearts to stay with us always."

Conversation on the above topic, silence, spontaneous prayer, or a song could follow.

2. LOOKING FOR CROSSES

While walking or driving, or when at the parish liturgy on Sunday, look for all the crosses you can find on the outside and inside of the church building(s).

Intricately crafted crosses of our two-thousand-year-old tradition are sometimes depicted in art books or displayed in art gallery showings. Better still, they can often be found in various churches, especially those of the Eastern Christian rites, incorporated in icons or other decorative arts. Exploring one of these ways of celebrating the cross might be an afternoon project for the family.

If your family is using the tree-of-life Easter poster, look at it with more care today. Invite the little children to trace their hands over the "wood" of the cross and over the flowers emerging from it (see p. 55 above).

3. MAKING THE SIGN OF THE CROSS

Even if the child already knows the gesture of the sign of the cross, it could be used at a very special time today and with extra attention to its meaning (see introductory comments in Item 1 above). It might be the first gesture of the morning or the very last before bedtime.

If the household has baptismal water which was brought home from the Easter Vigil, that water may be used in making the sign of the cross gesture.

If this activity is done on Sunday, the child may be shown how to use the parish's baptismal water from pool or font for the sign of the cross.

4. A SONG HONORING THE CROSS

(SONG 20) Lift High the Cross

Leader: Lift high the cross,
　　All: Lift high the cross of Christ!
　　　　All people, come, adore and praise his holy name.

Or, if desired, the Song of the Cross given for the Three Days could be used (see p. 144).

5. A NATURE PROJECT IN HONOR OF TREES

Take an outdoors walk together, and find many varieties of trees. Look for trees with different leaf shapes, trees with blossoms, trees in which birds make their nests.

Or, if your family intends to plant a tree this year, make a family project of it as today's activity.

---

6. A JEWELED CROSS DESSERT

Using a home-baked or commercial cake or a loaf or muffins or plain cookies, decorate in a festive way for a special dessert. Ice with a simple butter or cream cheese icing (recipe follows), making the shape of a cross in icing of contrasting color; or with glazed cherry halves or halved colorful gumdrops or raisins and pieces of dried apricot or other dried fruits.

Cream Cheese Icing

1 pkg (4 oz)	Cream cheese, softened	125 g
1 Tbsp	Milk	15 ml
1 tsp	Vanilla	5 ml
	Pinch of salt	
2½ cups	Icing sugar	625 ml

Blend cheese, milk, vanilla, and salt. Gradually add sugar, beating until icing is smooth and of spreading consistency. If necessary, stir in additional milk, 1 tsp (5 ml) at a time. Fills and frosts two 8- or 9-inch (20 or 23 cm) layers or a 9 x 13-inch (23 x 33 cm) cake.)

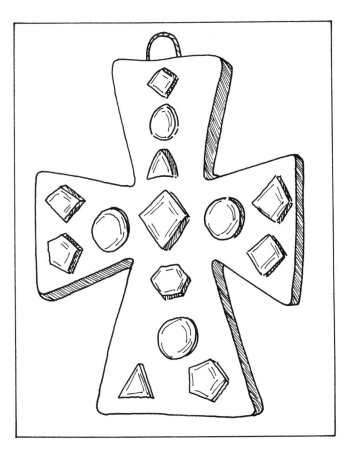

8. OTHER ACTIVITIES

- If the child has a cross necklace or pin (with secure holding devices for safety's sake!), it can be worn with special attention one day; a cross could also be made from stiff cardboard decorated with gummed foil or plain tinfoil and strung on an attractive cord or ribbon (use a paper punch or thick needle to make a hole).

- At a mealtime or prayertime, let all family members recall their baptismal signing with the cross: each person traces the cross on the forehead of the others (help young children by gently guiding their hands).

- Find purple or another rich jewel-tone color everywhere, and wear something in that color.

7. BAKER'S ART TO KEEP

A cross for the home or to give away to others may be made quite easily with a doughlike material which can then be baked for permanence.

Materials: one part salt, two parts flour, one part water; rolling pin; cross-shaped cookie cutter, or stiff paper made into a cross pattern, and a knife; a fork; paper clips or a strong drinking straw; water color or poster paints.

Activity: mix salt, flour, and water, and knead for about two minutes; roll out and cut shape of cross with cookie cutter or knife; designs or patterns may be made by adding small flat pieces for "jewels" or by creating free block-like patterns on the cross; if the crosses are to be hung, use the drinking straw to make a hole in the top of each cross or unfold the arms of a paper clip to make a long U-shape and insert deep into dough for a hanger; before baking, prick each piece here and there to allow air to escape; bake at 275 degrees F (140 C) for an hour, or until the pieces are golden yellow and hard-sounding when tapped with a fork; when cool, paint as desired (to preserve the pieces, later apply several coats of varnish or polyurethane on both the back and the front).

Sixth Week of Easter: the Father of Jesus

N.B.: For the very young child, the image of Jesus is sufficient without the introduction of God, Father of Jesus. For the sixth week, a suitable alternate theme is creation/new life, for which some of the following activities could be modified and others added.

Scriptural/liturgical orientation—a note for parents
Jesus speaks of his relationship to God as one of son to a father. It is often said today that Jesus' references to the fatherhood of God were culturally and historically conditioned; nevertheless, we acknowledge the enduring truth contained in those references.

From the Hebrew Scriptures we already know that God is like a parent, like a mother lovingly holding her child in her arms (Ps 130[131]), like a father leading and training his child (Deut 8:5-6). The Father whom Jesus describes is a loving and caring God (Matt 6:26-34), and always a forgiving God (Mark 11:25) who becomes the model for human forgiveness.

Jesus uses the Aramaic word *abba* (akin to "dad" in our language) to address God the Father. This manner of speaking reveals Jesus' own intimate relationship with God: Jesus is Son of the Father. The privilege of that close relationship becomes ours, for as Jesus' sisters and brothers by baptism, we can also say *abba* to God (Rom 8:15).

1. REFLECTION OF PARENT AND CHILD ON "THE FATHER OF JESUS"

The parent may introduce the reflection in the following or similar words:

"When Jesus talked to God he used a special name, just as we do when we speak to our parents. We call our parents our mother and our father, but usually we have a special name for them: mommy or daddy. The special name shows how much we belong to our parents and how much we love them.

"When Jesus calls God by a special name, *abba*, he is calling God 'daddy.' What do you think this shows? Just as you belong to your parents, Jesus belongs to God.

"And Jesus has something wonderful to tell us! It is that God loves each of us very much, too, and that by our baptism, we also belong to God. Now we can call him our parent as Jesus does."

Conversation on the above topic, silence, spontaneous prayer, or a song could follow.

N.B.: If using the father terminology is considered inappropriate for some reason, another of the child's close relationships may provide a better image upon which to draw (e.g., parent, mother, grandparent). The adult may say, "Jesus calls God 'daddy,' just as you use the word 'mommy.'"

2. LEARNING THE OUR FATHER

For the young child, a short phrase of the Our Father is sufficient to learn: "Our Father, who art in heaven, hallowed be thy name."

Repeat, slowly, several times with the child until the prayer is committed to memory. For the older child, of course, a greater part or all of the Our Father may be prayed together.

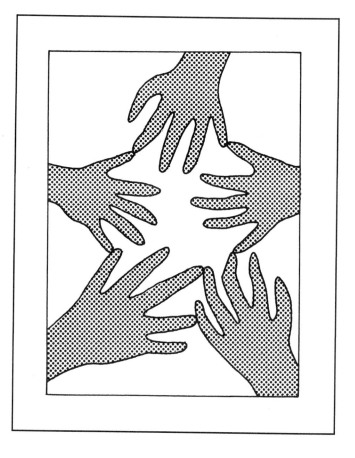

3. A "HANDS-IN-TOUCH" DRAWING

The child traces its hand onto a sheet of paper, then that of its father (mother, grandparent, aunt or uncle, or whomever). The hands should touch at some point. Coloring, decorating, or labeling may proceed as the child is able.

If desired, the adult may wish to show the child a reproduction of Michelangelo's creation painting from the ceiling of the Sistine Chapel, in which God reaches out to a person with the touch of life.

4. NATURE HIKE

Go on a long walk to find all the beauty that God puts around us for our enjoyment. Take along a basket or other container to hold prize finds like rocks, shells, twigs, and wild flowers. At home, these treasures may be arranged into a display or mounted on cardboard with a thick flour/water paste.

5. SINGING A SONG

(SONG 21) A Trinity Song
May the love of God our Father be in all our homes today.

68

6. A SPECIAL NAME FOR GOD OUR FATHER

Explore further the name Jesus called his Father, *abba;* this is also the name we may call him since he is our Father too. If the child knows or is learning the alphabet, this is an easy name to spell by arranging either commercial plastic letters or homemade cut-out letters into A-B-B-A.

7. SOMETHING SPECIAL FOR SOMEONE SPECIAL

To celebrate the love of our family's daddy, make something for him: a cut-and-paste art piece or a drawing; or his favorite dessert for supper. (If the father-figure for your child is someone else, mail that person a card, or arrange a visit or phone call for this day.)

8. OTHER ACTIVITIES

- When praying the Our Father phrase (see Item 2 above) use the simple and ancient *orans* gesture of prayer—arms extended.
- Paint a giant mural (two or three children, or even the whole family might participate, with each having a particular section to do) showing all the good and beautiful people and things with which God surrounds us.
- Find yellow or gold everywhere; wear yellow or gold.
- "Creation/new life" activities, such as searching for signs of spring.

Seventh Week of Easter: The Holy Spirit is with us

N.B.: For the very young child, the image of Jesus as Shepherd is sufficient without the introduction of the Holy Spirit. For the seventh week, a suitable alternate theme is celebration of family/community, for which some of the following activities may be modified and others added.

Scriptural/liturgical orientation—a note for parents
From the first words of the Scriptures, the Spirit of God, like a mighty wind, is present in power, creating a new order (Gen 1:2). Sometimes this Spirit acts with overwhelming strength in individuals (Judg 3:10); and at other times the Spirit is described as a more interior presence, bringing forth new life for the good of many (Isa 11:1-2; 42:1).

Jesus promises his followers that the Spirit will be with them, leading them "to the complete truth" (John 16:13). The Risen Jesus at God's right hand becomes the source of the Spirit (John 16:7) for the New Creation.

Liturgically, during Easter's Fifty Days, the Church celebrates the Risen Lord and his life in us, the new life made possible in us by the Holy Spirit. It is by the Spirit of God poured out within us that we live in Christ (Rom 8:9); it is by the Spirit of God poured out within us that we can say *abba,* Father (Rom 8:15); it is by the Spirit of God poured out within us that we become one family in Christ, one community in faith, one Body (1 Cor 12:13). Resurrection and new life, both individually and ecclesially, are thus inseparable from the presence of the Spirit.

The approaching fiftieth day of Easter—Pentecost—is therefore not a new element of the season but a kind of celebrative summary of the whole Fifty Days. The life of the Risen Lord goes on through the work of the Spirit in each of us, in the Church, in the world.

1. REFLECTION OF PARENT AND CHILD ON "THE HOLY SPIRIT"

This time of reflective sharing is best taken in a peaceful place and at a relaxed time. The adult can use the following or similar words.

"Jesus loves us so much that he wants us to always be happy and peaceful, never to be afraid. He tells us that the Holy Spirit will be inside us to help us in whatever way we need. He says to us, 'the Holy Spirit will be with you always . . . he will teach you everything.'

"When we are very still, when we are thinking or praying, the Holy Spirit speaks to us in our hearts. We want to listen very quietly to the voice of the Spirit in us. The Spirit helps us to be kind and helps us do good things. We are happy that the Holy Spirit is always with us.

"Sometimes we show that the Holy Spirit is with us through the sign of hands" (the adult demonstrates the gesture of "laying on of hands," i.e., both hands, palms down, placed on the head of the child; the gesture should be done slowly and reverently and retained for a few silent moments).

Conversation on the above topic, silence, spontaneous prayer, or a song could follow.

2. LISTENING TO THE SPIRIT IN SILENCE

Choose a peaceful time in the household, or go outdoors where you and the child can experience undisturbed stillness. Explain briefly that when we are quiet and listening well, the Holy Spirit helps us think good and happy things. (With a very young child, simply experiencing silence for a little while is sufficient.)

3. AN ART PIECE

Other people that we know also have the Holy Spirit speaking inside their hearts. The child can help to enumerate some of those people—relatives, friends, or parishioners well known to the family. Depict them by making a cut-out:

Materials: construction paper or other medium-weight paper, scissors, crayons, or markers.

Activity: using a strip of paper approximately 5″ x 18″ (12 x 48 cm), fold accordion-style so that each surface is about 3″ (8 cm) wide; draw people-figures on it; cut out, ensuring that you do not cut the figures apart from one another completely (the hands and feet should be joined); decorate, color, and label with names of persons the child knows.

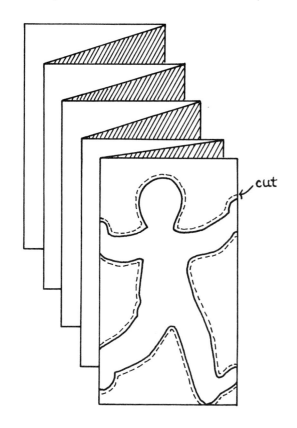

4. A HOLY SPIRIT SONG

(SONG 21) A Trinity Song
May the gift of God the Spirit keep us as one family.

5. A PARISH-AND-CHILD PORTRAIT

Have the child choose one of its baptismal photos (a close-up of the child is best), or another photo taken around the time of its baptism. Glue or otherwise mount the photo on a medium-weight sheet of paper, either 8½″ x 11″ (21.5 x 28 cm) or somewhat larger.

Explain that at baptism, the community welcomed the child into the Church. All the people of the parish pledged to help the child live as part of this family of the Church.

Draw several people around the child's photo, blessing, touching, reaching out in welcome.

6. SPRINGTIME PICNIC

Think of someone who would enjoy getting outdoors and having a meal with your family, for instance, a handicapped person or an elderly couple. Prepare a simple lunch and plan some songs, or take time to enjoy nature. Discover the Spirit of God in other persons, in all creation!

7. SPRING-FRESH FRUIT DESSERT

Chop an assortment of fresh fruits (apples, bananas, melons, berries), and have the child toss with honey-sweetened yogurt or any fruit-flavored yogurt.

You might point out, while working, how the many fruit pieces, though all different sizes and colors and shapes, come together to make one wonderful dessert.

8. OTHER ACTIVITIES

- Make a collage with magazine pictures of people helping one another, caring and sharing.
- Make an Easter bread for the fiftieth day of Easter, this coming Sunday.
- Do some planning and preparation for a fiftieth-day party.
- Find red everywhere; wear something red.

The child gives her family's names to the sheep and includes someone crying to the Good Shepherd for help; age 6½.

The Fiftieth Day of Easter

Although this day is usually called Pentecost, originally the entire Easter season was called "the Pentecost," the fifty, and kept as a unitive celebration of the Risen Lord sharing his new life with us by the Spirit. It is most enriching to celebrate this day as a completion of Easter rather than as only a separate feast.

A suitable conclusion of Eastertime might consist of an informal afternoon gathering of families for playtime and snacks and prayer, or a meal together—a casual brunch after Eucharist or a potluck supper in the park. Sometimes parishes plan an event for this day which includes those baptized at the Vigil; having families participate in such an event is ideal.

For decor at any gathering, children might bring bold Easter flags or banners they have made of brightly colored paper or felt. These flags can be stapled to slender sticks for planting in the ground at an outdoor gathering, or they can be hung (perhaps mounted on lengths of colorful wide ribbon or paper) as indoor decor.

The day could conclude with a short prayer service (using "Resources for the Fifty Days," p. 53 above); or with an evening walk like that on the first day of the Fifty—this time the conversation could touch on how each one experienced the presence of the Spirit of the Risen Lord during the days of Eastertime.

71

Chapter 4

LENT

Jesus in the desert amid the grains of sand (Gospel of the First Sunday of Lent); age 5.

Jesus is transfigured, surrounded by colorful rainbow "lights;" age 5 (Gospel of the Second Sunday of Lent).

Origins and Spirit of Lent

The origins of Lent are closely linked with the final preparation of candidates for baptism at the Paschal Vigil. For many centuries, this important aspect of Lent eluded us due to changes in baptismal practices. In our day, thanks to the restored Rite of Christian Initiation of Adults, we once again have the opportunity of Lenten journeying toward the Vigil with baptismal candidates (also called catechumens).

During the first centuries of Christianity, becoming a Christian was a lengthy process that took several years, and it was only after one gave evidence of an authentic Christian life that one could enter into the final prebaptismal period we eventually came to call Lent. For those chosen for Easter baptism, there was an enrollment ceremony at the beginning of Lent. A fine account of such a rite comes to us from a Spanish woman visiting Jerusalem at the end of the fourth century: "Then one by one those seeking baptism are brought up. . . . The bishop asks their neighbors questions about them: 'Is this person leading a good life? Does he respect his parents? Is he a drunkard or a boaster?'. . . . And if his inquiries show him that someone has not committed any of these misdeeds, he himself puts down his name."[1]

For those catechumens accepted for baptism, Lent was the time for the scrutinies—prayerful discernment of the person's life—and for the presentations of essential traditions of faith, such as the Creed and the Our Father. It was, of course, a time of intense prayer for freedom from sin, a time of fasting and of complete immersion in Christian living.

The length of Lent has varied in its long history and in different locales. Early in the Church's life, the prepaschal preparation was a week long (this is the time-frame for what is often still called "Holy Week"). Later, there is evidence in Rome of a Lent of three weeks' duration. The Johannine gospels of the third, fourth, and fifth Sundays of Lent in Cycle A of the Lectionary are a vestige of the three-week Lent and its orientation toward paschal baptism. In the gospels of these three Sundays respectively, the Samaritan woman seeks living water (John 4:5-42), the blind man yearns for light (John 9:1-41), and Lazarus is raised to life (John 11:1-44).

It is important to remember that the baptismal preparation was not simply an individual effort on the part of the catechumens. The community at large was also engaged in fasting, prayer, and good works, spiritually accompanying those on their way to the baptismal font.

By the early fifth century, Lent had also become the time for reconciliation of penitents. Christians who had seriously sinned presented themselves before the bishop at the beginning of Lent, declaring their willingness to do rigorous penance, to fast, and to make restitution for their wrongs. These penitents, attired in sackcloth and sprinkled with ashes, were separated in some way from the community until the end of Lent, when they would be reconciled with the Church in time for the celebration of the Pasch. Other members of the community could join with the penitents not only in the supportive gesture of fasting and praying, but also in the wearing of sackcloth and ashes. The latter would be both a witness of solidarity and a way of concealing before the non-Christian populace the identity of the "public sinners." The liturgical descendant of the Early Church's Lenten penitential practice is the Ash Wednesday ceremony, in which all members of the Church are marked with ashes and summoned to change their hearts and lives.

The penitential and conversion aspects of Lent became increasingly important, particularly when the practice of adult baptism declined and the prebaptismal orientation of Lent diminished accordingly. From early medieval times to our own day, the pentitential dimension of Lent is the one familiar to most Christians.

The classic Lent of forty days is the length of season typified in the Scriptures and known to the Church Fathers. There are many significant "forty's" in biblical literature. Forty days or forty years symbolize a time of preparation, usually by prayer, fasting, and journey, which precede a theophany of immense importance. At the end of a long spiritual road, God shows himself. For forty days and forty nights, Elijah journeyed to his meeting with God (1 Kgs 19:8); Moses fasted forty days before receiving the law on Mount Sinai (Exod 24:18); the children of Israel trekked for forty years in the desert before reaching the Promised Land (Deut 8:2); and Jesus, following in the steps of those ancestors of faith, prayed and fasted in the wilderness for forty days and forty nights (Matt 4:2; Mark 1:13; Luke 4:2).

Leo the Great and Augustine, Church Fathers who have given us many writings on the season of Lent, draw on this scriptural imagery of the number forty. Leo, inspired by the gospel account of Jesus in the desert, writes: "As we approach . . . the beginning of Lent . . . let us prepare our souls for fighting with temptations."[2] Similarly, Augustine sees the Church's task on the Lenten journey as one of intense spiritual struggle, discipline, and good works,[3] he sees the number forty as representing our earthly life with all its sufferings.[4]

For the whole church—for catechumens, penitents, all the community of faith—the forty-day journey may be rigorous and demanding. Despite the hardship of this preparation time, a destination beckons and leads us forward. That destination is a theophany, a manifestation of the glory of God, which for us will be none other than the Pasch, the death and resurrection of Jesus Christ.

For complex reasons, related to the computation of days of fasting and to a shift in understanding the unitive nature of the Three Days, Lent extended itself backward to begin on what we now call Ash Wednesday, and eventually extended itself forward to absorb the Friday and Saturday of the Three Days. The latter development had such far-reaching implications in the Church's understanding and customs that we in our day have not escaped its consequences, namely, that the triduum often seems split into two parts: Friday-Saturday, which tend to attach themselves to Lent, and Easter Sunday, which seems to belong exclusively to the resurrection season. Eventually, Lent as-

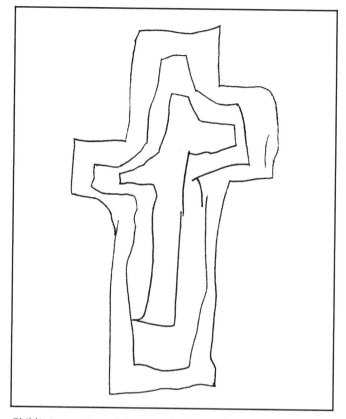

Child's impression of the cross in his parish church; age 4.

sumed such importance that it came to overshadow, up to our own times, the older and theologically more important Fifty Days of Easter.

Today, the Church is challenged to reevaluate and reorient its Lenten understanding. The Second Vatican Council has proposed quite clearly how one may put the whole paschal cycle into perspective. The order of priority is triduum, the Fifty Days of Easter, and then Lent (see, for example, the *General Norms on the Liturgical Year and Calendar*). Lent is no more and no less than a serious preparation for, a journey toward, the great yearly Pasch.

What then should Lent be in our lives? Patristic and scriptural writings summon us above all to an integrity in our Christian living. They summon us to a wholeness that can be fostered by the three great traditional Lenten practices of prayer, fasting, and almsgiving.

Writing about the spirit of Lent, Augustine emphasizes the primacy of prayer, but always in the context of the quality of our Christian living: "By humility and charity, by fasting and almsgiving, by temperance and forgiveness, by sharing blessings and by not retaliating for evils, by declining from wickedness and by doing good, our prayer seeks and attains peace."[5] Fasting and Lent became synonymous in later times and places, but for Leo the Great in the fifth century, physical fasting alone is incomplete and indeed futile. "Let us engage in this solemn fast with alert faith," he writes, "and celebrate it not as a sterile abstinence from food . . . but as a form of great-hearted generosity."[6] And explicitly linking almsgiving to fasting, he adds: "Let a man give to the weak and poor what he refuses to spend on his own pleasures."[7] In yet another Lenten sermon, Leo becomes bolder still: "Our fasting does not consist merely in abstinence from food; in fact, there is no profit in depriving the body of nourishment unless the spirit turns from injustice and the tongue abstains from quarreling."[8] These very sentiments are closely akin to the prophetic cry addressed to the people of Israel: "I hate and despise your feasts, I take no pleasure in your solemn festivals. I reject your oblations, and refuse to look at your sacrifices. . . . But let justice flow like water, and integrity like an unfailing stream (Amos 5:21, 22, 24).

In our time-honored tradition of preparing ourselves for the annual paschal celebration, we are challenged to adopt not a series of practices but a renewed way of living. To keep Lent one does not merely do certain things, but one does everything a Christian should always do.

Lent in the Parish

Lent points foward. Its whole significance derives from the time for which it prepares, the Vigil and the Three Days in their entirety, and the Fifty Days of Easter. Happy the parish which has in its midst catechumens preparing for Easter initiation, for they embody this forward orientation of Lent. By their presence, the catechumens remind us of the call to turn our lives to the Lord and of the promise that our dying unto self will be transformed into glorious life. The catechumens, in their journey toward the Pasch, are an icon of what Lent is for the whole Church.[9]

Parishes who have catechumens would do well to ensure that these icon-persons are present to the community during Lent. It is desirable that the rite of election be done at one of the parish's Eucharistic liturgies on the First Sunday of Lent, so that the parishioners can hear the testimony of people recommending the catechumens for baptism and can also come to realize the thrust of the Lenten season toward the celebration of Pasch. On other Sundays of Lent, the scrutinies will be done at the Eucharistic liturgies, possibly at different times from Sunday to Sunday so that more of the parishioners can come to share in the catechumenal journey.

In all instances, whatever ceremony is taking place with the baptismal candidates, visibility is important. The parish community, young and old alike, needs to see the people whom we will welcome as brothers and sisters at the Vigil. Likewise, the gestures and words surrounding the ceremonies need to be strong, engaging, compelling. There should be no perfunctory movement, no inaudible testimony, no impersonal touch, for people and their actions are sacramental and grace-bearing for the community.

As we have seen, conversion and reconciliation are an important element in our Lenten spiritutality, but one in which very young children can share less easily due to their age and level of spiritual development. One vital dimension of conversion includes social awareness, and this is a point at which a parish's Lenten endeavor could involve children in some way. In our parish, for instance, on the First Sunday of Lent, each family receives a sharing box to be used in collecting money for Third World development. On the Fifth Sunday of Lent, families bring their boxes of money to the Eucharistic celebration. Perhaps after Eucharist on one of the Lenten Sundays, a short film on the developing countries might be shown, a film which is somewhat comprehensible also to the children present in the assembly.

If the spiritual environment of Lent is the desert, the decor of a parish assembly space should reflect that by sparseness and utter simplicity. Even as we fast, emptiness characterizes the place in which we gather for Lenten prayers and worship. The mandate of Lent's decor committee should, perhaps, be to purge the liturgical environment of all unnecessary items, to de-decorate rather than to decorate for Lent.

As in other seasons, the music of Lent is best unified within itself. One suitable set of acclamations can be used throughout the Forty Days, and could even be used at all Eucharistic liturgies, if all music leaders can come to such a consensus. Then, not only do the Lenten liturgies "sound like Lent" at any Sunday liturgy a parishioner happens to attend, but some of the acclamations like the "Praise to you" surrounding the gospel could be used at the Thursday evening Mass beginning the Three Days—at last, an acclamation common to all members of the parish. Further, from the point of view of the family, it is hard to exaggerate the usefulness of doing one set of acclamations at liturgy throughout Lent, or throughout any season for that matter. One year, some friends with young children tried to link their home experience of Lent with the parish liturgy by singing the acclamation "Lord, by your cross and resurrection . . ." as a meal prayer throughout the season; midway into Lent, their parish music leaders found a new, more elaborate one to do!

For children, one of the most memorable liturgies of Lent is the Passion (Palm) Sunday service. For the Sixth Sunday of Lent, parish planners might invite all children to bring a branch of their own for the palm procession—an evergreen branch or a pussy willow. Regardless of whoever comprises the day's liturgical procession, children will want to be and should be included, walking in the footsteps of those Hebrew children who long ago welcomed the Lord into Jerusalem.

To support its people in their celebration of the whole paschal cycle, a parish could give out on the First Sunday of Lent a one-page calendar incorporating Lent, the Three Days, and the Fifty Days of Easter. On it might be a notation of the dates and times of Lenten events such as those connected with the baptismal candidates, a reminder of Lenten fast days (the parish may want to declare all Fridays as communal fast days), the schedule of triduum services, and occasions of the Fifty Days, such as baptisms, first Communion, and confirmation, along with events planned for the newly baptized during the Easter season.

Lent in the Home

As Lent begins, it is fitting that the family sort out the relationship of Lent to the rest of the paschal cycle. The triduum is the central celebration of the paschal time, and from it flow the Fifty Days; Lent as the preparatory season should not overshadow either of these times. Keeping the entire paschal cycle in perspective will free us from severely overloading our Lent, from feeling that we must annually invent entirely new projects to make this season outstanding and memorable for ourselves and our families. Committing ourselves to the whole paschal cycle should not lead to a lazy Lent but to allotting a proper proportion to it.

Considering the possibilities of Lent for very young children, one must bear in mind their spiritual and psychological growth patterns. The insights of religious

educators involved in such initiatives as *The Canadian Catechism* series[10] and Cavalletti's Good Shepherd catechetical centers remind us that the early years of childhood are a time for growing in awareness of gifts given, a time of delight in the possession of love, a time of happiness in secure relationships. It is a time to know the Lord and rejoice in his presence. Aspects of morality (and also doctrinal learning) will be essential to full Christian development, but the preschool years of the child are not the time for these topics. In fact, as Cavalletti emphatically points out, to introduce ethical and dogmatic considerations too early is to intrude on the child's true development and to disrupt the basis on which later spiritual and moral formation should rest.[11]

We have seen that the goal of Lent is holistic, that is, each member of the Church is to live more intensely as a Christian in whatever way is appropriate to his or her state of life. For the very young child, Cavalletti's proposal that Lent be a time of coming to know Jesus as the Good Shepherd seems entirely fitting. Lent can be the period in which the first presentation of the parable of the Good Shepherd is made and the child given the time and space in which to prayerfully contemplate this image.

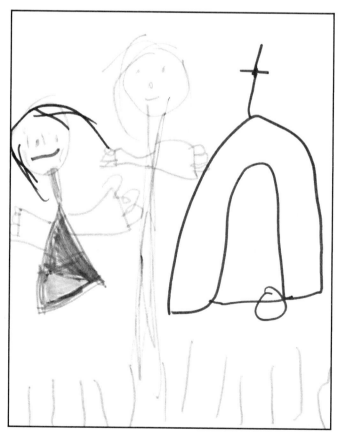

In this manner, Lent can lay a foundation not only for the child's later spiritual and moral development but also for its ability to grasp the meaning of the paschal celebration. The child can gradually come to understand the Three Days as the time of the Good Shepherd's giving his life for his sheep, and the Easter Fifty Days as a celebration of that gift to his flock.

For the slightly older child, let us say four and a half or older, one who has worked with the Good Shepherd image during previous paschal cycles, the Lenten season might include a weekly activity centered around the Sunday gospel. In our home, our elder child does drawings of the Sunday gospels to hang on the "Lenten tree" poster (see "Resources," p. 84–85). In another family, the child does her Lenten gospel pictures with felt markers on heavy transparent plastic; mounted on windows, they make wonderful "stained glass" meditations for the family.

In our household, although the little children are not able to participate in the ascetic practices associated with this time, we try to maintain the flavor of the traditional Lent. In our daily dining area, we have a small display table where an enthroned Bible, an empty wooden bowl, and a small sharing bank for money keep before us important aspects of our Lenten living—prayer, fasting, and almsgiving.

Besides regular Lenten family prayer, there is time for reflective prayer in connection with the children's Good Shepherd and/or gospel activities. The family could also pray in Lenten song at various moments throughout the day; for instance, at mealtime, we sing the Lenten gospel acclamation, "Praise to you Lord," which is used in our parish, or a seasonal song (see "Resources," p. 79).

Simple food is a Lenten norm in our household, with adults sharing in the parish's call to communal fast and abstinence on the Fridays of Lent. We contribute as a family to the alms-sharing box the money saved on our fast days, and we pray for those with whom we will share it.

With the older preschooler, five to six years, it would be possible to have during Lent a "sharing meal" modeled in part on the more adult-oriented austerity meal. The menu for a sharing meal could be jointly researched by parent and child. What foods would someone in Central America or Africa eat? How is that food obtained, and at what cost? What is a normal meal for our family and what does it cost? The difference in cost between the two meals can be donated to a development project or the parish's share-

Left: Jesus arrives at the tomb of Lazarus with Mary (Gospel of the Fifth Sunday of Lent); the "stone" is at lower right of tomb door; age 5.

Below: Jesus and the Samaritan woman converse at the well (Gospel of the Third Sunday of Lent); she brings her stool, a bucket, and a kite; age 5.

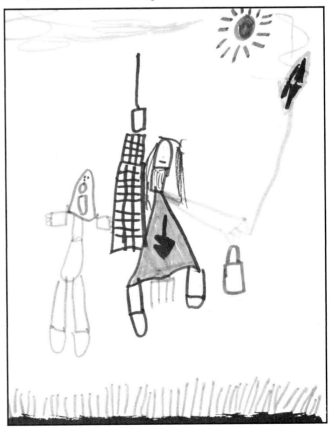

Lent fund. Older children like to do research on how food is produced elsewhere and enjoy examining globes and maps; they can present some of their insights to the family when the sharing meal is held.

Lent in the home needs to have a desert stillness, a peaceful atmosphere to invite reflection on the part of the whole family and specifically of the child. If the family is using the Good Shepherd parable materials with the child(ren), there should be plenty of time for the spontaneous use of those materials. Lent should have for the child and the family the same sort of quietness which Church regulations used to impose by prohibiting dances, parties, and movies.

Now the entire community has the opportunity to voluntarily embrace its desert. Together, the catechumens, the parish, and the children set out on their forty-day journey into the wilderness to which the Lord calls. The invitation is to travel light, leaving behind extra activities, some social engagements, some professional overtime—or, boldly now, all of them.

The mighty heroes of our faith—Moses, Elijah, the whole people of Israel, John the Baptist, Jesus himself, ranks of Christian saints—have walked this way before us. In the words of the fine Lenten hymn entitled ''The Glory of These Forty Days,'' we pray:

> Then grant us, Lord, like them to be,
> Full oft in prayer and fast with thee.
> Our spirits strengthen with thy grace,
> And give us joy to see thy face!

We sense that Lent looks forward to the fulfillment of our hope. We know that the journey will end with a vision of the paschal Lamb on a cross of glory, the Lord reigning from a tree. We welcome the Forty Days as gift and walk forward to see the face of our God.

Resources for Lent

1. Morning and Evening Prayer for Lent

Call to Prayer

> (SONG 22)
> Leader: O blessed light, pillar of fire,
> All: Lead us through the desert, Lord.

Psalm for Lent: Ps 129[130]

> (SONG 23)
> Refrain: With the Lord there is mercy,
> and fullness of redemption.
> Verse: My soul is waiting for the Lord,
> I count on his Word.
> My soul is longing for the Lord.
> More than watchmen for daybreak.

Scripture Reading: the Sunday gospel passage or selected verses (see Appendix B)

Canticle: for morning, Song of Zechariah (*Benedictus*), see p. 153
for evening, Song of Mary (*Magnificat*), see p. 140

Intercessions

Our Father

Blessing

2. Songs for Lent

(SONG 24) Song of the Forty Days

Leader: Lent is a time to share and pray,
   All: Lord, for this we thank you;

Leader: A time to walk in Jesus' way,
   All: Lord, for this we thank you.

Leader: Forty days, a gift, a grace;
      Lord, we long to see your face!
      Soon will dawn our Easter days,
   All: Lord, for this we thank you.

(SONG 25) Lenten Journey Song

Leader: Jesus, Lord, we walk with you
   All: On our Lenten journey.

Leader: Your word shows us what to do
   All: On our Lenten journey.

Leader: Shepherd, Lord, you give us light,
      Living waters and new life.
      Jesus, Lord, we walk with you
   All: On our Lenten journey.

(SONG 26) Prayers from the Gospel

Leader: Jesus, I am thirsty.
   All: Give me living water.

Leader: Jesus, I am blind.
   All: Let me see again.

Leader: Raise me up to live with you.
   All: Raise me up to live with you.

3. A Pre-Lenten Carnival

Before Lent, the Christian community has for centuries kept carnival, literally ''good-bye-to-meat'' time. Carnival is a time of revelry and excess before the dying of Lent, a time of feasting before the fasting. One of the culinary customs of carnival includes pancakes because, in the Church's older tradition, this was the time to use up eggs and dairy products which would be forbidden, along with meat, during the strict Lenten fast.

On the day, or sometimes several days, before Lent, our home is declared a carnival scene. The relative order of the household gives way to uncalculated exuberance, playfulness, topsy-turvy rules on every side, and all manner of surprise as the irrational within is freed to show itself! One day we indulge in fantastic dress-up and face-painting, adults alongside the children. Another day, we stage humorous skits or play rough-and-tumble games. And the days are never complete without a time when we reverse roles, parent and child, old and young, for in the world of carnival those in authority become as children, and the weak rule the world! Finally, the pancakes eaten and the mad costumes folded away, we settle into the silence of Lent.

4. Two Six-Week Projects for Lent

<u>Presenting the Good Shepherd Parable; or Making a Lenten Tree</u>

For the very young child, the object of Lent is simply to come nearer to the Lord Jesus. The parable of the Good Shepherd provides a beautiful entry point to a child's relationship with the Lord, and a weekly activity based on this parable could constitute the entire Lent for the child.

For an older child, let us say four and a half to six, who has already in a previous Lent explored the Good Shepherd parable, making a Lenten tree with drawings of the Sunday gospels offers another avenue of drawing closer to Jesus through his Word.

Whatever age your preschooler, if the child has not kept Lent under the guidance of the Good Shepherd parable, that would be a good place to begin.

COMING TO KNOW THE GOOD SHEPHERD

For those who have read Cavalletti's *The Religious Potential of the Child,* it is clear that the Good Shepherd parable can provide a foundation for the little child's relationship with the Lord.[12] Allowing the child to discover the meaning of the parable through its own reflection, prayer, song, art—this is the ideal proposed by Cavalletti. The adult merely presents the scriptural message and steps back to permit the work of the Lord to take place within the child. A flexible attitude is important on the part of the adult, so that the child is able to take whatever time desired or needed to explore the parable. Activities suggested for each week should be repeated or modified or reduced—whatever the adult and child find spiritually fruitful.

<u>First Week of Lent: Materials for the Parable</u>

Following Montessori's sensorial approach to educating children, Cavalletti and her co-catechists introduce the Good Shepherd parable to the very young child (two and a half years and up) not only with the Word of Scripture but also with tangible materials—small im-

Gospel of the Fourth Sunday of Lent: the man born born blind is going to wash the mud from his eyes, while Jesus (upper left) and the girl in braids (the child's self-depiction) watch; man at lower right is the one who questioned whether this was truly the man born blind; age 5.

ages of the Good Shepherd, the sheep, and the sheepfold. The child is then able, over a period of time, to return repeatedly to this set of images and reenact the parable of the Good Shepherd. The experience of Cavalletti is that, by use of such materials, the child can absorb, literally take unto itself, the message of Jesus.[13]

(In our family, both our children used the tangible materials in connection with the Good Shepherd parable. Our daughter, at five, had the shepherd figure put each of his sheep to rest with a kiss each night for many months. Our son, at three, daily lets the shepherd lead his flock to water for a leisurely drink, then lines up the sheep in readiness to follow the shepherd to pasture. These repeated actions are more than mere play; they seem to have become rituals of considerable significance which both children have explained in terms of Jesus the Good Shepherd.)

If a family wishes to use figures in the presentation of the Good Shepherd parable, these could be purchased from a store which deals in woodcarvings or directly from a woodcarver. (Friends of ours ordered a set from a craftsman who responded with a shepherd figure approximately 11″ [28 cm] high, and with six wooden sheep.) Cavalletti suggests that the Good Shepherd figure be of the kind best known to the Early Church, that is, the youthful shepherd gently carrying a sheep on his shoulders.

As an alternative, the family could make its own Good Shepherd set. A set made of heavy construction paper can be very lovely, although it will be less durable for frequent handling by children and may have to be remade eventually. Plans for a shepherd set are given below.

Making these figures well, especially if little children are helping, can be quite time consuming. Families opting to make Good Shepherd sets may need to take more than one session to do so and can adjust other Lenten activities accordingly.

If the family chooses not to use the tangible materials in the presentation of the parable of the Good Shepherd, it may wish to move forward with the introduction of the parable to the child during this first week of Lent.

Good Shepherd, Sheep, and Corral

Materials needed:

Bristol board
Pencil
Scissors
Crayons
Glue
Pipe cleaner
Shoe box

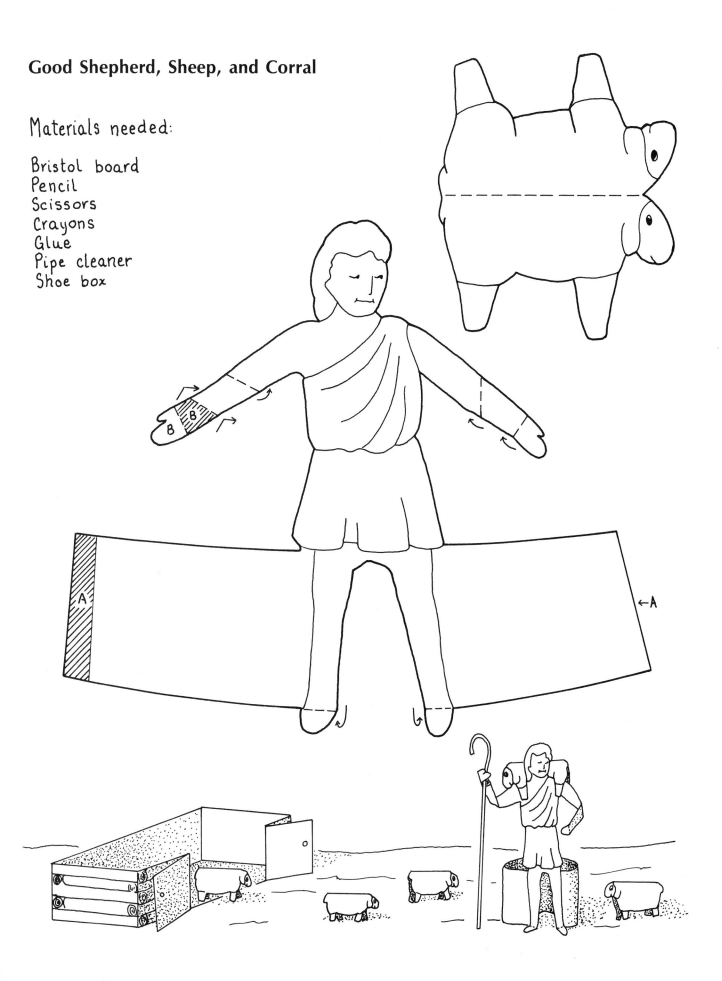

Second Week of Lent: Presentation of the Good Shepherd Parable

If materials are being used in the presentation of the parable, they should be ready and at hand (see First Week of Lent above) to be shown after the parable is told. It is best to do the presentation in a place where the materials can remain undisturbed and accessible to the child, perhaps in the family prayer area or in a prayer corner in the child(ren)'s room.

The adult does the presentation in the following or similar words:[14]

"Jesus has something special to tell us about himself. He says, 'I am the Good Shepherd.' There are many shepherds, but only Jesus is the Good Shepherd. The Good Shepherd knows his sheep and calls each one by name; he loves the sheep and cares for them.

"The sheep are happy to be with the Good Shepherd. When they hear his voice they follow him. The Good Shepherd loves his sheep so much that he will do anything for them. He will even give his life for his sheep.

"What kind of sheep do you think these could be? Are they sheep like those we see in the fields? Jesus the Good Shepherd says that his sheep are very special. We belong to the Good Shepherd, and he knows our name. How wonderful it is to be sheep of the Good Shepherd! We can listen to what Jesus tells us about himself." (The adult may light a candle and read from the Scriptures, John 10:3-5, 11, 14-16.)

If materials are being used, this is the time to bring out and set up the sheepfold and figures of the Good Shepherd and sheep. Show the child, slowly and with care, how the shepherd leads the flock into the sheepfold; then how they follow him out because they know his voice; how he will do everything out of love for his sheep, even die for them—lay down the image of the shepherd—but also he rises and lives again and will never abandon his sheep—place the image in erect position. Afterward, leave the materials accessible to the child.

After presenting the parable, invite the child to retell the story. Ask the child to think about the question "Who are the sheep?"

N.B.: Cavalletti suggests that the wolf image be left out of the Good Shepherd parable for children of very young age. Nevertheless, there will be a chance while presenting this parable to assure children in various ways that Jesus the Shepherd is stronger than the wolves and monsters that populate their imaginations and their nighttime closets.

Third Week of Lent: A Song

Any part of the presentation of the parable may be repeated if the parent feels it would be useful, and/or the following song may be learned during this week:

> (SONG 18) The Lord Is My Shepherd
> The Lord is my Shepherd,
> By restful waters he leads me.

Fourth Week of Lent: Another Aspect of the Parable

The adult and child can explore a further dimension of the parable, that of the Good Shepherd seeking out the lost sheep. If the child is using parable materials, they can be part of this presentation as well.

The parable may be introduced in the following or similar words:

"Jesus is the Good Shepherd and he loves his sheep. He knows each sheep by name, and the sheep know and love him.

"One day, when it is already dark and time to go to sleep, the Good Shepherd finds one sheep missing. Do you think he cares about that sheep? Will he leave the lost sheep alone in the darkness, away from its home? He loves the lost sheep very much. He will go to find it. All the other sheep are safe together inside their sheepfold. The Good Shepherd closes the gate so they can stay there safely, and goes looking for the lost sheep that he loves so much.

"He calls the name of the sheep; he looks everywhere. When he finds his sheep, he is very happy; he picks it up in his arms, then sets it on his shoulders and carries it home.

"Let us listen to what Jesus tells us about the sheep that was lost and found." (The adult may light a candle and read from the Scriptures, Luke 15:4-6.)

After presenting the parable, invite the child to reflect on some aspects of it by a few simple questions, allowing the child to discover for itself as much as possible the meaning of the parable.

Fifth Week of Lent: A Good Shepherd Picture

Invite the child to make some representation of the Good Shepherd parable, either by a cut-and-paste method or, for the very youngest child, by drawing. The slightly older child may wish to make a small booklet of drawings about the parable.

The child may want instead to work with the figures or to repeat some part of the activities of the previous weeks.

The Good Shepherd leads his sheep to the waters; age 3½.

Sixth Week of Lent: Common Reflection and Prayer

The sixth week of Lent tends to feel short. It commences with the dramatic and long liturgy of Passion (Palm) Sunday and includes the last few days of Lenten preparation for the Pasch. By Thursday evening, we are already beginning the Paschal Three Days. There is little time, consequently, for additional projects with the family.

Any activity one does with the child could begin to link the image of Jesus the Good Shepherd with the liturgical celebrations which will form so large a part of the Paschal Three Days. The adult and child could together speak of the Good Shepherd's love for the sheep, and how he would even give his life for the love of the sheep. Nothing is too much for the Good Shepherd! We praise and thank him for his great love for us.

It is possible that the child's prayer of response will be a silent one; if it is verbalized, the adult (or the child, if older) might wish to print it to keep.

A LENTEN TREE

This is better done only if your household is planning to do the other two "trees" of the paschal cycle, i.e., the jeweled cross for the Three Days (see p. 39–40) and the flowering Easter tree for the Fifty Days (see p. 55). The latter two may be done without the Lenten tree, as they represent the major parts of the paschal cycle; it seems better, however, *not* to do the Lenten tree project without the others, as it sets Lent into an isolated prominence which is ever in danger of surpassing the Three Days and Eastertime.

Materials: a bristol board poster sheet, 22 x 28 in. (56 x 71 cm), in purple (the liturgical color of Lent) or possibly in a shade of brown (to symbolize the desert journey of Lent); a thin, bare branch with at least six smaller arms or twigs extending from it—the branch should be roughly the same size as the paper; a needle threaded with sturdy brown cord; six lightweight, white sheets of paper, 8½ x 11″ (21.5 x 28 cm) or so.

Activity: stitch the branch onto the tree, taking care not to pull too tightly, or the bristol board may tear or pucker; at the beginning of Lent, mount it in a prominent place.

Lenten Tree (gospel drawings of Cycle A) (22 in. x 28 in./56 cm x 71 cm)

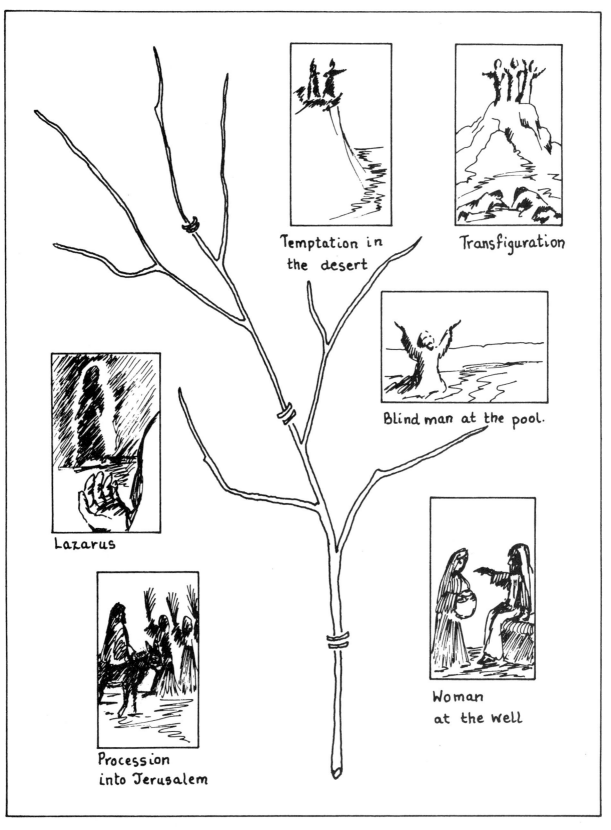

Temptation in the desert

Transfiguration

Blind man at the pool.

Lazarus

Procession into Jerusalem

Woman at the well

During each week of Lent, read the Sunday gospel with your child. On each of these occasions, a candle is lit for the time of the actual gospel reading, to set apart the words of Jesus. After reflecting/praying together, invite the child to draw the gospel story on a sheet of white paper. Song 26 (see p. 151) may be used at some time during this activity.

The reading/reflection/drawing may take place during the day or two following the Sunday; or a family may prefer to do this activity on the Saturday before the particular gospel is to be proclaimed at the liturgy.

A strong preference for the Lenten Cycle A readings exists among people involved in the Rite of Christian Initiation of Adults. It is my experience that Cycle A is also preferable for children, particularly as regards the gospels of the third, fourth, and fifth Sundays. The latter gospels are vivid and dramatic expressions of Jesus' care for others, and descriptive of Lent as preparation for baptism/baptismal renewal. The readings of Cycle A for Lent are given in Appendix B.

5. Other Activities for Lent

Children can help in all aspects of arranging the home environment for this important time of year. Even very young children are able to carry out with success and enjoyment segments of larger tasks in which older family members are engaged; for instance, a little child can carry certain items, or hold a roll of tape, or put things in boxes for storage, or run errands from room to room. Parents could use the opportunity to explain briefly what the project at hand is and why it is being done.

SIMPLIFYING THE HOUSEHOLD ENVIRONMENT

On one of the days at the beginning of Lent, the family might join together for a general de-decorating of the house and a simplifying of the environment:

- Put away some of the exuberantly decorative items of the home (you may welcome them back all the more during the Eastertime, or you may find you can live very well without them).

- Reuse and recycle toys, either by exchanging with another child or by giving away to charity toys no longer needed.

- Remove dated children's art from bulletin boards, refrigerator, and so on, to make room for the art of the new seasons.

- Wherever possible, pare down, eliminate; your family may even find it enjoys a less encumbered environment throughout the year.

SETTING UP A DISPLAY CORNER

During the paschal cycle—Lent, Three Days, Eastertime—a display area will be of importance to mark the movement of the days and seasons. Such an area would best be in a place where the household regularly gathers, for instance, at the family table or in the prayer corner. The area chosen should have enough wall space for three large posters (of the standard bristol board size), which will be made during the paschal cycle, and also a flat surface for setting up objects pertinent to the seasons.

For Lent itself, the display corner might include the following items:

- a Bible, "enthroned" on a stand or dignified cushion, open to the Lenten Sunday gospel particular to each week.

- A "sharing box" for collecting alms (see p. 86).

- An empty bowl, wooden or pottery or other, to symbolize fasting.

- A cactus, to remind us that Lent is a desert journey.

All these objects are more oriented to the adults and older children of the family than to very little ones; nevertheless, they can help set a household tone for Lent which children come to understand and appropriate over the years as they are ready.

MAKING A PASCHAL CYCLE CALENDAR

If your parish does not provide a complete home calendar of Lent/Three Days/Eastertime, make your own. A one-page format is desirable, as it shows the unity of the entire cycle. The suggested pattern at the end of this section (see p. 89) may be copied and filled in with parish/community activities for this time. Make extra calendars for friends too!

SHARING, OR "ALMSGIVING"

Sharing can take a variety of forms and includes the giving of many kinds of goods, not merely material ones. Time, attention, care, forgiveness, love—all these are "alms" for the giving.

Some projects which the household could plan and preschoolers participate in, as appropriate to their age, are listed below. It is not necessary to explain to the very young child every aspect of why we ought to do such and such, for concepts of moral responsibility can come later. It is sufficient that the household commit itself to the Lenten journey so that the family and child can actually engage in rather than only talk theoretically about it.

Adopting a Grandparent

Often grandparents live geographically far away from their families, while lonely elderly people live nearby and can be seen every week in one's own parish or neighborhood. Lent could be a time to begin a closer bond with an elderly person by visiting regularly, even briefly (for often older people prefer shorter visits) and phoning, taking over a meal or some special food on occasion, and remembering that person in prayer. This is an activity in which even the youngest children can participate.

Caring for One Another

Each week, everyone could choose another member of the family for whom they can do something good (the choosing can be done by mutual agreement or by drawing names). Explain to young children that the "good thing" to be done can be a hug shared, a helpful gesture, a kind word, a cooperative action, or time spent with the other person.

An Alms Box

Make a sharing box for Lent, using a small slotted box which the children could cover with pictures of people in need (or if your diocesan social justice center provides home-collection boxes, use one of these). Our household contributed money to the box regularly on Fridays and randomly, as family members wished.

An older child can begin to understand the connection between the household's Lenten austerity in food and the resultant savings set aside for the poor. The first simple explanation we offer is something like: "The money we saved by having just a soup supper, we are giving to people who don't have enough to eat."

Family Sharing Projects

One night a week could be family time, with a specific theme or activity selected for each of these evenings:

- Cooperative games; if you don't know any, use a handbook such as *Games Manual* by James Deacove (Perth, Ont.: Family Pastimes, 1974).

- Mend-and-repair tasks, each person bringing books or toys or household items to be fixed.

- Family memories, with each member sharing "I-remember-when" stories of family activities or special events; bring out the photo albums.

- Greeting cards for the paschal time: have available various kinds of paper, scissors and glue, and crayons and marker—let everyone create cards to be used for Eastertime.

■ Planting spring seeds: if you plan to have a garden, the family can prepare the pots and soil and plant seeds for the "bedding plants."

■ Recycling household items.

If recycling goods is not already part of your family's lifestyle, Lent is a good time to take some first steps; for further ideas see Kathleen and James McGinnis' *Parenting for Peace and Justice* (Maryknoll, N.Y.: Orbis Books, 1981) and Milo Shannon-Thornberry's *Alternative Celebrations Catalogue* (New York: The Pilgrim Press, 1982).

The whole family could participate in projects such as:

—going through closets and setting aside for charity those clothes or household items which are still good, but which are no longer necessary to keep.

—collecting old newspapers and magazines from your house (and perhaps from the neighbors also) to take to a paper recycling center. In our city, the recycling center is operated by handicapped adults, and our family visits the plant periodically to see a friend at work there, shredding "our papers!"

—making a spring-shopping outing to a second-hand clothing store, a good way to both save money and learn values of sharing and stewardship.

FOOD FOR LENT

The family's Lenten menu could be marked by some degree of austerity, both as a reflection of gospel values and of solidarity/sharing with those less privileged. Neither of these values has to be explained in detail or depth to young children; as part of the family's lifestyle, more visibly in Lent but also year round, it is hoped, simplicity in food is part of a long-term education in nutrition, stewardship, and responsible purchasing for socio-economic change. For the preschooler, merely growing up in a home where such concerns are woven into the fabric of life is sufficient; merely being part of a Lent where such concerns are accentuated is formation enough.

LENTIL STEW

6 cups	Water	1500 ml
2 cups	Lentils, preboiled and soaked	500 ml
1	Medium onion, chopped	1
1 tsp	Dried basil	5 ml
½ tsp	Salt	2 ml
1 cup	Celery, stalks and tops, chopped	250 ml
¾ cup	Carrots, sliced	175 ml
1-28 oz can	Stewed tomatoes	1-796 ml can
⅓ cup	Salad oil	75 ml
1½-2 Tbsp	Vinegar	25-30 ml

N.B. Lentils should be preboiled for about three minutes, then left to soak in the boiled water for four hours. Drain off soaking water and use fresh water when beginning stew recipe.

Boil 6 cups water and slowly add the soaked lentils. Reduce heat and simmer for one hour. Sauté onion and basil in oil. Combine all ingredients except vinegar and seasonings, and cook for 1½ hours or until lentils are tender. Add vinegar before serving. Season to taste with salt and pepper. Serve with rice.

In our home during Lent, we try to spend less time on elaborate meal preparation and use the time saved for family projects, reading or praying together. Slow-cooker meals, one-dish dinners, and so on, meet our needs admirably.

In various countries, certain foods, such as specific breads or soups, are served only in Lent. The family could choose one type of dish to serve weekly throughout the season as its culinary reminder of the Lenten journey. The recipe above is one possibility, a rather plain lentil stew. Lentil dishes were popular in the time of Jesus.

Pretzels, now used widely at social gatherings, actually have their beginning as Christian Lenten bread, going as far back as the fifth century. Since the ancient Lenten fast allowed for no dairy products, small breads were made of flour, water, and salt. As a reminder of the call to prayer during Lent, the breads were shaped in the form of arms crossed in prayer (a prayer gesture of the earlier centuries was to cross one's arms over one's breast).

Children are capable of assisting in pretzel-making. The family may want to make enough pretzels each week to serve everyone at supper every evening. At the meal prayer, each person might hold a pretzel as the blessing is sung or spoken.

LENTEN PRETZELS

1 cup	Whole wheat flour	250 ml
1 cup	White flour	250 ml
1 tsp	Salt	5 ml
½ tsp	Baking soda	2 ml
¼ cup	Butter	60 ml
½ cup	Buttermilk	125 ml
1	Large egg	1
	Sesame seeds or coarse salt (optional)	

Mix flour, salt, and baking soda; add butter and combine thoroughly. Add buttermilk and egg, and mix well. Turn out on floured board, and knead until smooth and elastic. Roll dough between hands to form long, pencil-thin ropes about 8 inches (20 cm) in length. Place these on greased cookie sheet, folding each into "little prayer arms." Sprinkle with sesame seeds or sparingly with coarse salt, if desired. Bake at 400 degrees F (200 C) for approximately 10 minutes.

A Calendar for Lent—Paschal Three Days—Eastertime

FEBRUARY 21	22	23	ASH WEDNESDAY 24	25	26	27
28 LENT I	MARCH 1	2	3	4	5	6
7 LENT II	8	9	10	11	12	13
MARCH 14 LENT III	15	16	17	18	19	20
21 LENT IV	22	23	24	25	26	27
28 LENT V	29	30	31	APRIL 1	2	3
4 LENT VI	5	6	7	8	PASCHAL THREE DAYS 9	PASCHAL THREE DAYS 10
APRIL PASCHAL THREE DAYS 11	12	13	14	15	16	17
18 EASTERTIME I	19	20	21	22	23	24
25 EASTERTIME II	26	27	28	29	30	MAY 1
2 EASTERTIME III	3	4	5	6	7	8
9 EASTERTIME IV	10	11	12	13	14	15
MAY 16 EASTERTIME V	17	18	19	20	21	22
23 EASTERTIME VI	24	25	26	27	28	29
30 EASTERTIME VII	The family could note special events on such a parish calendar.					

KEEPING THE CHRISTMAS CYCLE

Jesus, promised star of God; age 5.

darkness''

Chapter 5
CHRISTMAS-EPIPHANY SEASON

The child welcomes the light and love of Jesus at Christmas; age 4½.

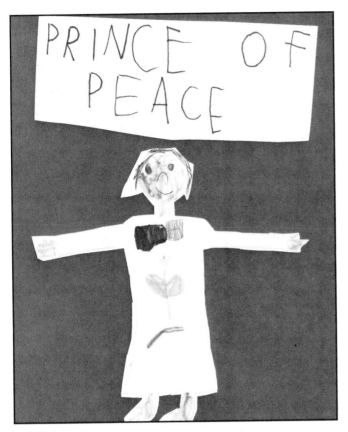

Christmas drawing; age 4½.

Origins and Spirit of Christmas-Epiphany

In the midst of the winter's darkness in our northern hemisphere, we delight in Christmas as the feast of light. Even though our culture has appropriated the lights and other symbols of this season, heaping on tinsel and diluting spiritual meaning, the season's Christian roots are, nevertheless, quite evident. Christmas is the feast of Jesus the Light, celebration of the Risen Sun of God, time of the splendid glory of the Lord!

Christmas is a rather late arrival on the Church's calendar, compared to the original weekly feastday, the Sunday, and the annual paschal cycle celebrations. In the Western Church, our first record of a day honoring the incarnation and nativity of Christ dates from A.D. 336. The Christmas date of December 25 is commonly considered to be related—either in origin or by later association—to a Roman sun festival at the time of the winter solstice. Even as the pagan world celebrated the unconquered light of the sun, Christians kept a feast of Christ the Light who overpowers the darkness (John 1:4-5). The proximity of Christmas to the "unconquered sun" festivity prompted these comments in a fifth-century sermon by Maximus of Turin: "The people are quite right, in a way, when they call this birthday of the Lord 'the new sun'. . . . We gladly accept the name, because at the coming of the savior not only is humankind saved but the very light of the sun is renewed."[1]

In the Eastern centers of Christianity, those clustered around Constantinople rather than Rome, January 6 became the feastday celebrating Christ's manifestation to the world, particularly through his baptism in the Jordan. The Western Church adopted this feast of Epiphany (in Greek, *epiphaneia* or *manifestation*), and gradually shifted the focus of the celebration in the West to the visit of the Magi. The two dates of December 25 and January 6 came to be the framework for the Twelve days of Christmas, a time period known to most of us only from the charming song of the same name. (Today, in Canada, Epiphany is transferred from January 6 to the nearest Sunday between January 2 and 8.)

What we celebrate in the season of Christmas-Epiphany is simply that in the darkness of our human condition, the love of God has shone upon us in Christ Jesus. The coming of a *messiah* (this Hebrew word is translated into Greek as *christos*, "anointed one") had long been promised to the people of Israel. Throughout Advent, the promise is heard again and again in the readings from the Hebrew Scriptures. Now, at the Christmas season, the proclamation is made that "the people that walked in darkness has seen a great light; on those who live in a land of deep shadow a light has shone . . . for there is a child born for us, a son given to us" (Isa 9:1-5). The promise of old is fulfilled. The Word of God which we have heard is now among us as the Word, Christ himself, the embodiment of the love and compassion, the power and the wisdom which is God.

Christmas, then, puts before God-with-us, Emmanuel; he is God among us, God visible, a God-man. This is an adult Christ, a king and ruler with "dominion laid on his shoulders" and whose name is "Wonder-Counselor . . . Eternal-Father, Prince-of Peace" (Isa 9:5). In this text as in many others, although the Scriptures speak of a child born this day, they juxtapose that image with one of the Lord as Ruler and King.

Interestingly, the Latin word for child— *puer*—also connotes servant. *Puer natus est nobis,* the Church has sung for centuries in its Christmas liturgy, "a child/servant is born for us." The image of servant in the Scriptures is most clearly etched in the Servant Songs of

Isaiah (Isa 42:1-9; 49:1-6; 50:4-9; 52:13—53:12), which are traditionally used in the paschal triduum liturgies. The Servant of God is the beloved of God, faithful one by contrast to Adam, suffering one who chooses the way of obedience to God. Is this not the paschal mystery already present to us at Christmas?

Indeed, the Jesus whom we celebrate during the Christmas season is the Risen Lord whose life we share by baptism. Once a child, he is now Lord of glory, the one we meet in the liturgy, the one we welcome into our hearts and homes, the one whose life in-spirits us to works of peace and justice, the one whose coming we await as we sing, "Dying you destroyed our death; rising you restored our life; Lord Jesus, come in glory!"

Patristic writings have consistently seen Christmas in the context of the paschal mystery. For instance, Leo the Great wrote of Christmas as the birthday of life when "our Lord, victor over sin and death, finding no one free of sin, came to free us all." In the same sermon, he continues: "Beloved, let us give thanks to God the Father, through his Son, in the Holy Spirit, because in his great love for us he took pity on us, 'and when we were dead in our sins he brought us to life with Christ,' so that in him we might be a new creation."[2]

The liturgical texts of the season themselves have a paschal/eschatological character. Over and over, the Lord's birth is linked to our salvation and to its completion in the end time. We celebrate the Redeemer who once came among us, is present to us now, and will come again in glory. There is a kind of telescoping of past, present, and future into a Christological totality which is the content of the liturgical celebration of Christmas.

The victorious Sun—Jesus, Risen Son of God—and not the birth at Bethlehem, is the object of our Christmas feast. While the crib should not be rejected, neither should it be extolled as the central aspect of the celebration. As one author puts it, "[Jesus'] birth at Bethlehem is rather the occasion than the object of the feast. The object is the total mystery of redemption, the already announced paschal mystery."[3]

One week, or in the liturgy, an "octave" after Christmas Day, we celebrate the oldest Marian feast of the Western Church—Mary, Mother of God. Other aspects are appended to January 1, namely, the civic New Year and prayer for world peace, but its liturgical wellspring is the festivity honoring Jesus' mother. Mary, whose relationship to her son is sung in icons,

frescoes, patristic writings, and the poetry of the Church, is naturally praised at this season as mother of him whose coming brings us gladness and light. The liturgical texts of this feast are summed up well by the entrance antiphon of the day's Mass: "Hail, holy Mother! The child to whom you gave birth is king of heaven and earth forever."

Epiphany centers on the manifestation of Christ the Incarnate Word to the world. With its origins in the East, where it was kept primarily as the feast of the baptism of Jesus, Epiphany's traditional themes include the visit of the Magi to the Lord and the wedding at Cana. In these mysteries of Jesus' life, he is revealed to all peoples as king of kings, Son and Servant; the one who, on the third day, changes water into wine at a wedding and manifests his glory—a profound prefiguration of paschal mystery.

On this day of Epiphany, a grand eschatological panorama opens before us: "Arise, shine out," cries the prophet, "for your light has come, the glory of the Lord is rising on you . . . the nations come to your light and kings to your dawning brightness" (Isa 60:1-3, First Reading for Mass of Epiphany). There is cosmic breadth now in God's manifestation of himself, for his light reaches out to all nations. It is the Magi who embody the ideal response of humankind. "In the persons of the magi," wrote Leo the Great, "let all people adore the creator of the universe; let God be known . . . in the whole world."[4] On Epiphany, God's people, along with the wise of all the ages and the whole of pilgrim humanity, are journeying to the eternal wedding, to the Lord who is himself the beloved Son and Bridegroom, the Star risen from Jacob (Num 24:17), Morning Star which never sets (*Exsultet*, Easter Vigil of the Roman Rite).

When the liturgy was revised following the Second Vatican Council, would it have been possible and ecumenically felicitous to have reincorporated the baptism of Jesus celebration fully into the Western Church's Epiphany day? As it is, a distinct feast is set aside, kept one week after the Epiphany Sunday (except when Epiphany falls on January 7 or 8 and the baptism of Jesus is not observed as a special feastday). The theme of the God-given mission of Jesus and the paschal overtones make the baptism of Jesus a fitting conclusion of the incarnation festivity and provide a suitable transition to the paschal cycle which is already on the horizon, but admittedly the *day* (not the mystery!) is somewhat anticlimactic as an end of the Christmas-Epiphany season. Nevertheless, the separate celebration of the Lord's baptism highlights one aspect of Emmanuel, that Jesus appears before us as God's anointed one—*messiah*, our hope and salvation.

Christmas-Epiphany in the Parish

There are texts for three Eucharistic liturgies of Christmas. These texts as a group are perhaps not altogether familiar to us, since in the past decades, indeed centuries, parishes have tended to emphasize the midnight service. More recently, some places have encouraged one or more premidnight liturgies for the children, although it may be observed that an extraordinary number of adults *sans* children are often in attendance! (In the following remarks on the Eucharistic liturgies of Christmas, the terminology "Eucharist," used elsewhere in this book, will be replaced by "Mass," as the latter is the accustomed manner of speaking about the Christmastime Eucharistic celebrations.)

It is instructive to know that the Daytime or Third Mass of Christmas is the oldest in origin and was long the principal liturgical service of this solemn feast day. The gospel of this liturgy is John 1:1-14, the beautiful text in praise of Christ the Word, the Light shining in the darkness. The Dawn Mass, Second Mass of Christmas, is known as the Shepherds' Mass because of the Lukan gospel of the shepherds receiving the news of Christ's birth. Christmas Midnight Mass is full of darkness/light imagery and tends more toward marking Christ's historical birth than to theological aspects of the incarnation.

Bearing in mind that the richest and oldest theology of Christmas is enshrined in the Daytime Mass, parish planners could try to enhance and encourage participation in that celebration. All too frequently, energies are concentrated on the Midnight Mass and perhaps on premidnight services, with the result that, for instance, sometimes scarcely a musician can be found to lead the song on the most song-full of days, Christmas Day itself. In a curious kind of liturgical turnabout, we as parishes seem to insist on the priority of the rather more devotional Midnight Mass over the powerful Christmas Day Mass, and we come to the former in droves; during the Paschal Three Days, however, we tend to bypass the late-night Paschal Vigil and show up instead at the Easter morning liturgies! While liturgical books have been rewritten since the Second Vatican Council, we parishioners have not always responded to the challenge to renew our understanding and our practice.

In many parishes, the question of which Christmas liturgies to highlight is complicated by the practice of anticipating Christmas Eucharist on the evening of December 24. Familial expectations, cultural customs, and the relative ease of taking young children to a premidnight Christmas service combine to make these liturgies very popular. Yet the tension created by anticipating the feast and diluting the festive day itself remains unresolved, here at Christmas as for the Sunday of every week.

Still it is a fact that early evening is a good time for families with little children to gather for the Christmas liturgy. Some also maintain that placing the Church's celebration ahead of the rest of the family festivities could in itself be regarded as a statement of priorities.

Whatever Christmas liturgy the family participates in, the parish might ask children in advance to bring along any Advent-Christmas symbol or drawing to be presented at the time of gathering gifts (and eventually to be hung in the place of welcome or social center for the Christmas season). Children might bring the Advent "sharing boxes," in which their families have collected money for others, and present these at the altar during the preparation of the gifts. Or perhaps each child could be invited to bring a bell to use at worship (the bells could be rung at the Glory, the Alleluia processional, the Holy, Holy, Holy, and the acclamations at the Eucharistic Prayer).

During the initial Christmas liturgy, and during the whole Christmas-Epiphany season, what of the baby Jesus? While the crib has taken its place in piety, it is important that the Christmastime festivity not be regarded as a historical birthday time during which we pretend Jesus is an infant, sing him lullabies at liturgy, or give him a birthday cake at Eucharist. (I witnessed this once; aside from the inappropriateness of the gesture, the children present were enormously disappointed to be given a cracker to eat because the cake had to be saved intact for the following liturgies!)

How vital it is for all of us to realize that Jesus is now with us as Risen Lord of glory. He once was an infant, and we gratefully remember that. But now, today, there is no baby Jesus. As we do not sing to other adults, "Happy Birthday, baby N.," we cannot sing to the resurrected Christ-among-us, "Happy Birthday, baby Jesus."

A crib display, part of our Christmas custom for many centuries, is probably a permanent fixture in the parish decor and in parishioners' hearts. It could be placed toward the side or back of the church (our parish puts it in the place of welcome) rather than under or in front of, beside or behind the altar, where it easily draws attention away from the Eucharistic action and risks narrowing the scope of celebration from Jesus, Lord and King, to the baby of Bethlehem. A parish could consider leaving the manger of the crib scene empty, even as the crib's originator, St. Francis of Assisi, is said to have done; this obliges us to search for the Lord where he is now, today.

Artists of the parish might be invited to review their efforts in the light of the best theology of the Christmas-Epiphany season. In decor, no clutter and confusion but noble strong simplicity befitting the Servant-King Jesus; in art, nothing tawdry but only pieces of artistic merit. Rather than having a great collection of trees in the assembly space, one huge tree could be decorated with fruits; in our parish we decorate a twenty-foot-high tree with shining red apples—visually stunning and fruit-fragrant besides. It is the Lord's tree which, unlike the tree of Eden, brings us the fruits of salvation. Or the one tree could be filled with white lights, sign of the pure Light of Lights. In honor of Jesus the King, royal gold might be given a prominent place in the decor of the Christmas-Epiphany season; for instance, gold on the Gospel-book cover, gold on processional banners, gold in the streamers over the assembly called together as the Lord's kingly people.

Musicians need to examine their Christmas-Epiphany liturgy repertoire from time to time, looking for texts that proclaim the essence of Christmas and eliminating saccharine tunes and words that reflect only Jesus' babyhood. Actually, many of our best-known Christmas carols have texts which are scripturally based and theologically oriented to the resurrected Lord Jesus. We sing, "Joy to the world! The Lord is come"; "He hath op'd the heavenly door and we are blessed forevermore"; "Hail the heav'n-born prince of peace! Hail, the sun of righteousness! Light and life to all he brings, ris'n with healing in his wings," to cite only a few familiar lines.

This is the season to pay special honor to the Word of God in Scripture, for this is the time we honor the Word of God made flesh. One way this might be done in the liturgical ritual is with a children's processional dance around the gospel book. An example of such a dance can be seen in the Weyman-Deiss videotape, *Liturgical Dance* (Phoenix: North American Liturgy Resources, 1984).

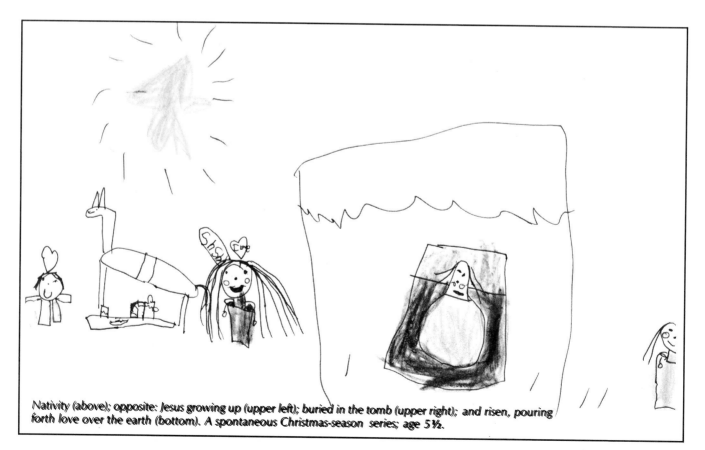

Nativity (above); opposite: Jesus growing up (upper left); buried in the tomb (upper right); and risen, pouring forth love over the earth (bottom). A spontaneous Christmas-season series; age 5½.

The Sundays and the feasts of Christmas-Epiphany basically continue our reflection on the mystery of the incarnation. Although the First Sunday after Christmas has in recent years become Holy Family Sunday, it is well for the parish community to remember that like Christmas season as a whole, this day is less a search for historical detail or an expression of sentimentality than a celebration of the divine gift given us in Jesus of Nazareth.

January 1, feast of Mary, Mother of God, is an opportunity for Marian celebration in our parishes. There is much lovely Marian music in both the traditional chant and polyphonic repertoire as well as in popular carols. This could be a time to decorate the Marian shrine in the parish church; it is an opportunity to have a Marian procession, with a true icon, perhaps, or with the parish representation of Mary—a representation that is in good taste and thus supportive of the faith of the community.

The exuberant imagery of the feast of Epiphany calls for a grand parish feast, with no less decor, no fewer trumpets, no decreased zeal in proclaiming the Word than at Christmas! This is a day for incense, gold, and light in lavish abundance—and a hospitality hour after each liturgy so that all people who have come seeking Christ's light may continue to have the opportunity to find it in one another. On Epiphany, as well as on the feast of the Baptism of Jesus, there might be special attention to the baptismal font and water, with the consciousness that in Jesus at the Jordan, God continues to manifest himself even as at the incarnation, summoning all nations to behold the beloved Son who is both Servant and King of glory.

Christmas-Epiphany in the Home

One of the first things a family can do in its approach to this season is commit itself to the whole time, December 25 onward to Epiphany Sunday, and insofar as is possible, also to the feast of the Baptism of Jesus. After our society has attempted to saturate us with a surfeit of carols and secular events during the weeks of Advent, on December 25 the commercial world returns to normal—but for the Church, December 25 is when "we've only just begun!" A household can offset a pre-Christmas immersion by keeping Advent well; then the Christmas season is fresh and new as it should be when it arrives, and is not really difficult to sustain during a two-to-three-week period. For the entire season, keep the decorations up, keep the table settings festive, continue lighting your Christmas candles; let the music play, and let everyone sing the songs of Christmas; if you have a videocassette recorder, you might want to collect tapes of fine Christmas music, dance, art, and drama to replay for your family during this and future Christmas seasons. The sense of good will, giving, and concern for others needs to continue, both in our attitudes as expressed in conversation and prayer, and in whatever personal contact and visiting or sharing the household can arrange for this time. Even in the ongoing enjoyment of Christmas gifts and cards, parents can nurture in their children a spirit of gratitude toward those who have remembered the family.

In presenting to young children the meaning of Christmas, the gospel infancy narratives could be prayerfully read by parent and child. Probably the Lukan account (Luke 2:1-20) could be used consistently for the early years, as it is the one children will hear proclaimed at worship. It might be helpful to note for ourselves some points regarding the Four Gospels. Neither Mark nor John gives an account of the Lord's nativity, and Matthew and Luke's versions differ from one another in many details. From this we can only conclude that the infancy narratives are primarily theological statements and not meticulous reports intended to be historically factual. What we hear about Jesus from the infancy accounts is that he is the anointed one of God, who was promised of old; he is Son of God, Lord, and Savior. The evangelists invite us to rejoice in the saving presence of God in Jesus.

For the very young child, placing principal emphasis on the crib scene—for instance, by activities such as filling the crib with straw throughout Advent in preparation for Jesus' coming at Christmas—seems overly historical in orientation. Instead of focusing primarily on baby Jesus, it is possible to draw upon the scriptural/liturgical "light" theme of this season and speak often of Christmas as the time of Jesus the Light. Cavalletti describes convincingly the young child's affinity for and receptivity to the light symbol: "Light has an immediate effect on the sense and it is psychologically gratifying and reassuring," she writes; "thus the child associates the image of Christ the Light with the Good Shepherd and consequently the effect of the former image is reinforced."[5] As lights and candles surround us on every side during this season, it is an easy thing to take the opportunity many times to point out how lovely the light is, showing us the beauty of Jesus the Light. Sunrise and sunset, our natural light itself, afford a further pedagogical chance every day.

In its origins the Christmas tree was associated with the medieval plays of Adam and Eve and so was first decorated with apples. When the tree took its place in the Christmas festivity, apples and other fruits, and later sweets and cookies were used to decorate it. From the ancient signficant tree of human history, the tree of Eden, humankind received only the fruits of death and darkness; but from the new tree, the tree of the cross of Christ (which the Christmas tree somehow prefigures), we have received the fruits of life and light, the fruits of salvation. This imagery, found frequently in the writings of the Fathers of the Church, has provided our household with the theological inspiration for decorating our tree with apples, and for setting apples among the pine boughs on our dining table. Putting lights on the Christmas tree is a custom reaching back to Martin Luther, according to popular belief; inspired by the twinkling stars, he is said to have added candles to the tree in honor of Jesus the Light.

One issue which parents of very young children need to address is the question of Santa Claus. While positive things can be said of the symbolic value of Santa as a generous gift-giver who seeks nothing in return, some negative aspects tend to outweigh the good.[6] A major difficulty with the figure of Santa Claus is that it tends to usurp the central place in the Christmas celebration of a young child. Cheered on by television, shopping malls, and parades, as well as by well-meaning grandparents and friends, the jolly present-bearer gives overwhelming competition to the little child's Jesus-focus. Some attempts are occasionally made at integrating the Santa and Jesus images by, for instance, depicting Santa in adoration of the Christ child; such solutions can be regarded as quite contrived at best.

It seems that other cultures have dealt with the Christmas gift-giving figure more successfully than many North Americans. In central Europe there is the St. Nicholas feast on December 6, separated from Christmas by a fair space of time; in Italy, on January 6, Old Befana appears, a kindly woman ever searching for the Christ child and bringing gifts to all children as she journeys. Whether as a revival of their ethnic heritage or for Santa-replacement reasons, some families have restored the celebration of one of the above traditions in order to free Christmas for Christ.[7]

Another solution to the Santa Claus question might be to avoid drawing attention to Santa at all in the earliest years. In our home we managed by careful speech

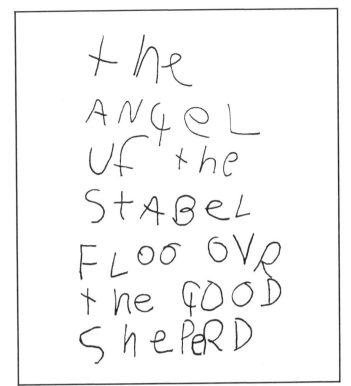

A fusion of the child's understanding of Christmas and Easter, for the one of whom angels sing is Jesus the Good Shepherd; age 4½.

and by strict television supervision to dodge Santa altogether until our daughter was four years old. Later, when she attended a preschool and heard of Santa from her peers, we spoke of him as a delivery person of the season, one specially designated to take gifts to people, usually gifts from other persons.

It has been our family's experience that activities and songs and family time together can enrich the Christmas celebration for a child so amply that Santa Claus is not really missed at all. For example, as December 25 draws near, our family anticipates Christmas Eve customs with eager excitement. We have re-adopted the East European tradition of a ritual Christmas Eve meal which both ends the fast of the vigil day and begins the feast of Christmas. The preparation of food and table (including the setting of an extra place at table for the stranger who might happen by), the family's bathing and dressing up in Christmas best, and above all, the children's watching for the first star to signal the onset of evening and the new day—all these keep the attention of the day focused until we gather around the table to bless the food and share in unleavened bread together, wishing each other "Blessed Christmas! Happy feast of Jesus, the Light!"

Resources for Christmas-Epiphany

1. Morning and Evening Prayer for Christmas-Epiphany

Call to Prayer

> (SONG 27)
> Praise, O Jesus, Emmanuel,
> Your light shatters the darkness!

Psalm for Christmas-Epiphany: Ps 97[98]

> (SONG 28)
> Refrain: All the ends of the earth
> have seen the saving power of God.
>
> Verse: Sing a new song to the Lord
> for he has worked wonders.
> His right hand and his holy arm
> have brought salvation.

Scripture Reading: a seasonal gospel passage or selected verses (see Appendix B)

Canticle: for morning, Song of Zechariah (*Benedictus*), p. 153, especially appropriate for the Christmas season:

> (SONG 29)
> Refrain: The rising sun has come to give light,
> to guide our feet in the way of peace.
>
> Verse: Blessed be the Lord, the God of Israel,
> for he has visited his people and set them free.
> He has raised up for us a Savior
> from the house of his servant, David.
>
> For evening, Song of Mary (*Magnificat*), see p. 155

Intercessions

Our Father

Blessing

2. Songs for Christmas-Epiphany

Christmas season music is so plentiful that no additional songs are given here except for a litany text.

Some or all of the litany could be used at various times, either all sung or all spoken, or with only the "Amen" response sung:

(SONG 30) A Christmas Season Litany
Blest are you Lord God.

(Response for each line: Amen)
Holy is your name.
You have sent your Son to be one of us.
You love your people with deepest love.
You have sent your Son to save us from sin.
Great is your mercy for your people.
You fill your children with joy.
You call us to praise your name.
Look with love upon your holy Church.
Send the spirit of your Son into our hearts.
Let us bring glory and praise to your name.
Through Jesus Christ your Son
And in the love of your Holy Spirit.

Uniting the cross with the Christmas image of "Jesus the Light;" age 4½.

3. Activities for "The Twelve Days of Christmas"

ADVENT-CHRISTMAS WREATH

The Advent wreath may be adapted for the Christmas season by adding a large white candle in the middle and lighting all five candles whenever a prayer gathering is held around the wreath. There are no wreath services during this season, but the wreath may serve as a candelabrum to be lighted for prayer times.

A REFLECTION TIME

A child who has come to know the paschal presence of Jesus as Risen Lord generally has little difficulty in understanding that now Jesus is an adult. The preschooler is quite conscious of age, and is convinced that he or she is "not a baby any more." This personal awareness increases the child's receptivity to the fact that while we celebrate Jesus' birth, he, too, is no longer an infant.

With a Bible and a candle on hand, the parent may speak to the child about Christmas in the following or similar words:

"For a long, long time, people were waiting in darkness for the light to come. When Jesus was born, the true light began to shine. Now, at Christmas, we remember how Jesus' light fills the whole world and sends away the darkness. Can you think of some things around us that remind us of the wonderful light of Jesus? (The child can list some of the light symbols of the season.)

"We know that Jesus is always with us now and his light is in our hearts. But long ago, he came into the world as a little baby. We can listen together to the word that tells us about Jesus' birth in Bethlehem." (The adult lights the candle and reads from the Scriptures, Luke 2:1-20.)

DECEMBER 25

Even after a household has kept a richly liturgical Advent, it is possible that Christmas day will still be claimed by the forces of consumerism, simply by the presence of a multitude of gifts, which always threaten to become the real meaning of Christmas. Some families have tried to offset the gift deluge by saving one gift for each of the Twelve Days of Christmas, making up any difference in numbers by adding family gifts such as bags of nuts, popcorn, or dried fruits, books, or small items of clothing. The household might choose to participate in the Christmas morning liturgy at the parish as a way of strongly affirming the centrality of the Lord in this day.

Other ways of keeping the Christ-orientation of this day are easily at hand:

- Candles in abundance, lights on the tree; these can always be pointed out even to the youngest children as signs of Jesus the Light.

- Music of Christmas, which includes some based on the scriptural texts familiar to the household from Advent, for example, the Advent-Christmas sections of Handel's *Messiah;* in our family, when our daughter was three, the infectious baroque rhythm of "For unto us a Child is Born" summoned us all to a Christmas morning dance throughout the house—bells, drums, nightclothes and all!

- Meal prayers for Christmas might be the singing of "Joy to the World," an excellent Lordship-of-Christ song for this season; or another carol, or the litany above.

- Evening prayer after the Christmas dinner, following the usual structure except with Christmas texts (see "Resources" p. 100) and with the Advent-Christmas wreath used as a gathering place.

DECEMBER 26, ST. STEPHEN

The feast of St. Stephen, deacon and first Christian martyr (Acts 6–7), offers us another opportunity to reflect on service and witness in our lives. For young children, one can emphasize the aspect of giving which surrounds this day when, according to British custom, parish alms boxes were opened and the money distributed to the poor. It is also said that people boxed some of their own gifts and foods for the less fortunate (hence the name, "boxing" day). The family's Advent sharing box might be delivered to its destination on the feast of St. Stephen; even young children can go along to the soup kitchen or friendship center for such a delivery and meet some of the people for whom they have been praying and sharing.

The carol "Good King Wenceslas" is a fine one for today, with its references to St. Stephen and to the service of the poor. The text is easily divided to give sung roles to the king and the page, with all others narrating.

A short refrain which may be used sometime this day is:

> (SONG 21) A Trinity Song
> May the gift of God the Spirit keep us as one family.

DECEMBER 27, ST. JOHN THE APOSTLE AND EVANGELIST

St. John, to whom the Fourth Gospel and three Letters in the Christian Scriptures have been attributed, is sometimes called the apostle of love. Proclaiming that God is light, God is love, the First Letter of John equates light and love in our lives: "Anyone who loves his brother is living in the light" (1 John 2:10).

A legend tells us that John drank poisoned wine and was not harmed; associated with that story, a tradition has grown up over the centuries that wine is blessed this day. Wine can be set out on the dinner table and blessed by a parent or by all, with hands outstretched:

> Blessed are you, O Lord our God,
> you have given us this wine in your goodness.
> (All) Blessed be God forever!

A brief song which may be used at some time today, perhaps as a response to the Johannine reading at evening prayer, is:

> (SONG 21) A Trinity Song
> May the love of God our Father be in all our homes today.

DECEMBER 28, HOLY INNOCENTS

Matthew 2:13-18 tells of the little children of Bethlehem said to have been killed by Herod in his attempt to destroy Jesus. Whatever the historical accuracy of this account, the Church has long celebrated the Holy Innocents on this day as a sign of all those who have given their lives for Christ. This feast is a reminder in the midst of our Christmas celebration that paschal mystery, death and resurrection, is ever with us at the heart of our Christian living and celebrating.

To keep this feast with very young children, it is not necessary to present them with Matthew's gospel account; it is sufficient to speak of all people, especially children and youth, who have been full of the light of Christ. A mealtime ceremony could take up this theme. After the table-center candles are lit, each child could receive its own lighted candle with a reminder that as Jesus is light for us, we are to be a light for others.

(SONG 21) A Trinity Song
May the light of Christ our Savior shine in us for all to see.

DECEMBER 29 AND 30

Engaging children in the life of the whole household can be part of the continuing festive celebration. Thank-you cards need to be sent, guests are coming and going, and regular household work like baking and cooking has to be done.

Writing thank-you cards can be a protracted task if you wish to involve your children in the valued experience of expressing gratefulness for someone's thoughtfulness, time, and generosity in selecting or making gifts for the family. We try to make a fun project of it by making our own cards. One can use the potato-stamp technique (see "Resources for Advent," p. 124); or cut-and-paste, using the season's best Christmas cards and prefolded card paper as available from a print shop; or if the number of cards needed is large, a hand-penned design on white 8½" x 11" (21.5 x 28 cm) bond, which has been folded in half, then half again to make a card, and which is then photocopied as needed (the child need only add its own "signature" or a tiny message and a splash of color!).

At evening prayer on thank-you card day, we pray for each person who remembered us in gift-giving, ensuring that we also include those who have given us the gifts of their time, prayer, hospitality, friendship, and care.

Guests are part of the holiday excitement in most homes, and receiving them with love and honor can be part of children's growing awareness of Christian hospitality. The moving story "Where Love Is, God Is" by Leo Tolstoy describes how a cobbler unawares welcomes the Lord by receiving a motley assortment of ordinary people into his home; the story is made very accessible for children in the book, *Martin the Cobbler* (New York: Harper and Row, 1982) and in the film of the same name.

If visitors are coming to the home during these days, children can prepare something special for them, like a game to share, music to sing or play, a piece of art to give, or placecards if the guests will be with the family for a meal. At our home, if visitors are present during what is our usual prayertime, we invite them to join us in that prayer.

SUNDAY AFTER CHRISTMAS, ALSO THE FEAST OF THE HOLY FAMILY

This is a good day for a common family blessing, and for beginning—if it is not already your custom—a bedtime and a departure blessing within your household. The following text is adapted from a liturgical blessing of the Roman Rite:

May God keep you from all harm and bless you with every good gift.
May God's Word be in your heart and give you joy.
May you walk in God's ways and know his peace.

At mealtime today, all may join hands and say the above prayer together.

On this occasion, our family uses the venerable Judeo-Christian blessing of Numbers 6:24-26 (see page 4).

DECEMBER 31, LAST DAY OF THE YEAR AND NEW YEAR'S EVE

While understanding large blocks of time such as a year (or a week or sometimes even a day!) is not natural to the very young child, a ritual of remembering and thanks can still be part of this day. All family members could choose a photo of, or write about, or draw, what they are thankful for this day and this year. The individual pieces could be brought separately or as a collage to the family's evening prayer, where all could give their thanksgiving before singing "Mary's Song," the *Magnificat*.

There are numerous possibilities for a family-oriented New Year's Eve. Several families might join together for their year-end celebration of thanks. In a French-Canadian custom, the grandmother hosts a New Year's Eve gathering for her extended family. Our parish has often sponsored a family party on this evening, a potluck followed by songs, games, and dancing—all children are welcome.

JANUARY 1, FEAST OF MARY, MOTHER OF GOD, AND NEW YEAR'S DAY

Besides the parish liturgy honoring Mary, the family can have its own Marian rituals on this day. An icon or another fine artistic representation of Mary with Jesus may already be in the family's possession; if not, it would be a good time to invest in one for this and other Marian feasts. (Most Marian icons make a strong theological statement, as they show Mary holding her little son not as a helpless baby but as a young king, already Lord of all.) Whatever Marian representation is chosen, it is important that Jesus also be depicted, for the presence of the son with the Mother is the oldest and truest image of Mary and the source of authentic Marian devotion.

The icon or other representation can be enshrined in a prominent place this day and surrounded with vigil lights. At a suitable time, the family gathers there to sing a song such as the *Magnificat* from the family's evening prayer.

On New Year's Day in many cultures, parents and grandparents are specially honored. (Is this only a coincidental link with the liturgical honoring of Mary, mother of the Lord?) A British custom is that a child and its godparents visit on this day; the godparents offer the child a blessing and a "godcake," a sweet pastry. Inspired by this practice, a household might wish to welcome the godparents of its child(ren) to a come-and-go tea or other event.

On January 1 in our home, we invite each child's godparents and their family (altogether referred to as the "godfamily") for afternoon visiting, supper, and evening prayer. We prepare for the occasion by placing near our Marian icon a candle representing each set of godparents. As the godfamily arrives, their candle is lighted, a sign of their light in our lives. Later on, there will be photos taken of each child with its godparents or godfamily, and at departure time there is the presentation of freshly baked muffins (our version of "godcakes") to each family from its godchild.

DAYS FROM JANUARY 2 UNTIL EPIPHANY SUNDAY

Depending on when the Sunday falls in a given year, this segment of the Christmas season may continue until January 8 or may conclude as early as January 2. The suggestions for seasonal activities and crafts found later in this section can be used as necessary.

EPIPHANY

On this day which concludes the Twelve Days of Christmas, there is a sense of fullness and completion of the season. After the finale of today's liturgy and home customs, it is possible to take down the tree and household decorations (even though, at present, the feast of the Baptism of Jesus, yet to come a week or so later, is the official end of the season).

Home Blessing

The custom of blessing homes on this day seems to be linked to the gospel read at the Eucharistic gathering: "and going into the house they saw the child with his mother Mary, and falling to their knees they did him homage" (Matt 2:11).

Children love processions, and here is a wonderful opportunity to have one. With everyone carrying something—a cross or icon, candles (for safety with children, candles enclosed in a lantern or glass vigil-light holder are best), a Bible, incense, and a glass bowl or pitcher of blessed water from the parish baptistry—the procession can move from room to room. At each place, a brief blessing may be said:

> Leader: Peace be to this house.
> All: And to all who live in it.

> Leader (or another), with such words as: May this dining room be blessed for our family's meals . . .
> May this family room be filled with happiness . . .
> May this bedroom be a place of quiet rest . . .

At the end of the procession, all might sing a carol.

Two or three families may want to do their home blessings together, beginning at one home with the procession and prayers, then moving on to the other home(s). A party or potluck supper might take place in the last home.

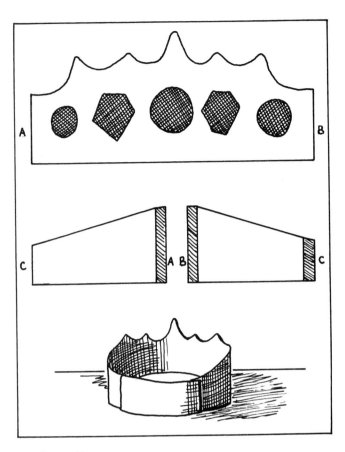

Epiphany Party

For even very small children, this day's festive gathering can be a memorable way to conclude the Christmas season.

As they arrive at the host home, children can be given paper crowns to wear (easily made with construction paper and gummed stickers of bright colors or foil; we leave the crowns laid open until the guests arrive and can be individually fitted). A parent might tell or read the gospel story of the Magi, and in keeping with the full tradition of this day, also of the baptism of Jesus and of the wedding at Cana. Simple games and activities follow. One highly successful activity we have used is body-tracing, when each child lies down on a large paper to be traced—crown and all—then cuts out and decorates the paper figure with crayons, markers, or stickers.

Left: Stars and hearts symbolize the light and love the child receives in the Lord Jesus; age 4½.

Epiphany Cake

At some point on this day, the customary dessert of Epiphany cake can be served. This is simply a high fancy cake which may be decorated to look like a crown (colorful gumdrops make quite dazzling "jewels," and the children love to help with the jeweling). Inside are the usual three beans or large nuts—we add many more to ensure that each child receives one—and every finder is then declared to be among the royal ones, the Magi. Regal vestments (colorful old curtains, silky scarves, and costume jewelry) may be donned at this point and for the rest of the party/day, the royal ones rule; they preside over activities and songs and may demand favors from their subjects.

EASTERN RITE CHRISTMAS

In our locality, where there are many Eastern Rite Christians who follow the Julian calendar (Christmas falls on January 7), our family tries to be conscious of the prayer and celebration of Eastern Rite friends. As children grow older and can share in lengthier worship services, participating in an Eastern Rite Christmas Eucharist would be a fitting celebration near the end of the Christmas season.

BAPTISM OF JESUS

For the feast of Jesus' baptism, Christmas songs and prayers can be used one last time. This is also the day family members can bless one another with baptismal water brought from the church.

4. Other Activities for Christmas-Epiphany

The following ideas may be used in place of some of those given above. Further suggestions are available in *Keeping Christmas* by Sandra Sorlien (Minneapolis, Minn.: Augsburg Publishing House, 1982).

BOOKS TO SHARE

Besides enjoying children's books of the nativity, families could search out, purchase, or borrow books of art featuring nativity events, such as *The Nativity in Stained Glass* (New York: Walker Publishing, and Pickering, Ont.: Beaverbooks, 1977) or *Nativity* (New York: Harper and Row, 1983). If scriptural texts are included in the art books, as is the case in both books above, these may be read aloud, slowly and prayerfully, to even the very young child.

CARDS AND GIFTS

All communications received for Christmas from relatives and friends can be enjoyed again during the season. Cards and letters can be read together and photos shared. As the family uses gifts that have been received, there are always opportunities to foster a spirit of gratitude to each person who made or bought a gift. Parents can draw their children's attention to how people have remembered the family, and with them can offer a short prayer of blessing for all who have shown love and care for the family in any manner.

SHARING

Even in small ways, young children can gradually be introduced to the social dimensions of living the gospel of Jesus the Light. Together, the family could think of someone to invite for a meal or an evening; it might be a single person, for whom this time of year is often lonely, or a university student far from home. Senior citizens or the handicapped in special-care homes generally appreciate visits when their residences are quieter, sometimes well-nigh deserted, after the pre-Christmas bustle.

Possibly each member of the family could set aside one toy or gift to give to the Salvation Army or another charitable group. A preschooler of any age can competently assist in packing and delivering a food hamper to someone unemployed or to a local soup kitchen.

MUSIC AND DANCE

This is a good time to relax with your children and listen to Christmas recordings, including the great seasonal classics.

Learn to sing a Christmas carol that is new to the children. One possibility would be "Good Christians All, Rejoice," which has a fine theological text incorporating nativity details with the meaning of Christ's coming as Savior, and which also has repetitious melodic patterns quite easy for little ones to learn.

Carols, which are in their origin a song-with-dance, provide young children with opportunities for free-movement dancing, perhaps with the use of simple rhythm instruments like tambourines or bells. Or if the children are ready for some choreography, find ideas on simple dance patterns in a book such as *Dancing Christmas Carols* (Saratoga, Calif.: Resource Publications, 1978).

The following suggestions for dancing the carol ''Angels We Have Heard on High'' are a loose composite inspired by the book cited above:

Angels we have heard on high,
Sweetly singing o'er the plains.
(All hold hands and circle to the right.)

And the mountains in reply,
Echoing their joyous strains.
(All circle to the left.)

Refrain:
Gloria in excelsis Deo.
Gloria in excelsis Deo.
(Releasing the circle, all spiral freely with arms extended upward and outward expressive of the joyous melodic turns and cascades of the refrain.)

ARTS AND CRAFTS

The following suggestions, chosen because they are easy for little children, represent only a smattering of the craft projects possible for the Christmas season. From the multitude of craft books available, one can select/adapt ideas suitable to the family's spiritual understanding of the season and to the capability of the children involved.

■ Pomanders: These make lovely little presents, and at this season their fragrance is reminiscent of the rare spices brought to Jesus by the Magi.

Materials: oranges or firm apples; a quantity of whole cloves; bright ribbon.

Activity: Insert the cloves securely into the fruit, covering the entire surface. Then tie on four sides with ribbon, leaving one end long for hanging the pomander.

■ Bookmarks:

Materials: colored construction paper (or felt) for background, about 2 x 6 inches (5 x 15 cm); paper star shapes, or nativity scenes from old Christmas cards (or, for felt background, other small pieces of felt to

cut into designs); glue; and, if the bookmarks are to be of paper, clear contact paper.

Activity: have the child choose the decorations desired and glue them onto the bookmark background; to ensure flatness, press bookmarks under a large, heavy book until thoroughly dry; if desired, paper bookmarks may be covered in front and back with clear contact paper to increase their durability.

■ A Christmas joy mural

Materials: a sheet of bristol board or a large piece of brown wrapping paper, glue, and that inevitable box of unsorted wrapping paper and ribbons left over from Christmas gifts.

Activity: for a family art project, each person can choose papers and cut out light-shapes, such as stars, suns, candles, glory-bursts, or heart shapes for Jesus' love. All these can be pasted into a collage. Ribbons and yarn add a merry touch to a mural honoring Jesus who brings us joy.

CHRISTMAS FOOD

Festive foods are already part of the holiday custom in many households, originating either from the family's ethnic traditions or from the many books and magazines available for Christmas cookery. In our home we have made an effort to keep festive food at least somewhat healthy and nutritious, which helps everyone's spirit both in the making and in the subsequent mood of eaters, especially children!

Bethlehem, which means "house of bread," has prompted Christian peoples of all lands to have unique breads for this season. Some specific ingredients also have religious significance at this time. Dates and figs, for example, are linked with the land of Jesus' birth; and spices symbolize the Magi and their gifts.

The following two breads are not the elegant kind which require an expert hand and which might grace the breakfast table of the high feast. Rather, these are nutritious snack breads with ingredients significant to the season, breads which can be made as a family project.

DATE LOAF

1¼ tsp	Baking soda	6 ml
½ cup	Boiling water	125 ml
¾ cup	Dates, finely chopped	175 ml
1	Large egg, well beaten	1
½ cup	Brown sugar	125 ml
½ tsp	Vanilla	2 ml
½ tsp	Salt	2 ml
½ cup	Salad oil or melted butter	125 ml
1¼ cup	Flour, sifted	300 ml
1½ cup	Bran	375 ml
½ cup	Chopped walnuts	125 ml
½ cup	Ripe mashed bananas	125 ml
⅓ cup	Crushed pineapple, drained	75 ml
⅓ cup	Glazed cherries, red and green, chopped	75 ml

Dissolve soda in boiling water, and pour over finely cut-up dates; cool. Combine with cooled date mixture, egg, brown sugar, vanilla, salt, and oil or melted butter. Add the remaining ingredients in order given, stirring only until combined: flour, bran, walnuts, bananas, pineapple, and cherries. Spread into greased, paper-lined loaf pan. Allow to stand 20 minutes, then bake at 350 degrees F (180 C) for about 1 hour. If using pyrex loaf pan, bake at 325 F (160 C).

A QUICK BREAD: SPICY CARROT MUFFINS

These muffins are flavorful and crunchy in texture. We present these instead of sweet pastry "godcakes" to our godfamilies at a festive gathering on January 1 (see above, p. 104).

2 cups	Flour	500 ml
1¼ cups	Sugar	300 ml
2 tsp	Baking soda	10 ml
2 tsp	Cinnamon	10 ml
½ tsp	Salt	2 ml
2 cups	Grated carrots	500 ml
½ cup	Raisins	125 ml
½ cup	Chopped nuts	125 ml
½ cup	Coconut	125 ml
1	Apple, peeled, cored, and grated	1
3	Eggs	3
1 cup	Salad oil	250 ml
1½-2 tsp	Vanilla	7-10 ml

Preheat oven to 350 degrees F (180 C). Mix together flour, sugar, soda, cinnamon, and salt. Stir in carrots, raisins, chopped nuts, coconut, and apple. In another bowl, beat eggs with salad oil and vanilla. Stir egg mixture into the flour mixture until the batter is just combined. Spoon batter into well-greased muffin tins, filling nearly to top. Bake for 35 minutes. Makes 18 muffins.

GAMES, OUTDOOR ACTIVITIES

In the season when we celebrate the Prince of Peace, it is most fitting to encourage family activities that are cooperative and peaceful rather than intensely competitive.

- It is useful to have on hand a cooperative games book such as Jim Deacove's *Games Manual*. "Skills," in a form adapted from that valuable little volume, is an easy and quick game in which even very small children can share: all participants line up and show others a skill or action they can do. Each person has to be shown how to do the skill or action until all know it. In this way everyone learns something new and also learns how to teach someone else. Can you somersault? Stand on one foot? Sing a Christmas song? Make a peace sign? Hop? Dance? Wiggle your fingers like a twinkling star?

- Family outdoor walks are specially memorable at sunset or by starlight and offer another chance to speak of the beauty of Jesus the Light. During a daytime walk, draw family "portraits" in the snow or make snow angels to keep little ones harmoniously busy.

- A project for both indoors and outdoors is providing birds with Christmas treats, a European custom in honor of the birds which legend says were present at Christ's birth. Children can help string garlands of popcorn and cranberries for a colorful addition to their birdfeeder or to a tree or hedge, and the family can enjoy the outdoor decorating together. (For more detailed birdfood suggestions, see "Resources for Advent," p. 121.)

Chapter 6

ADVENT

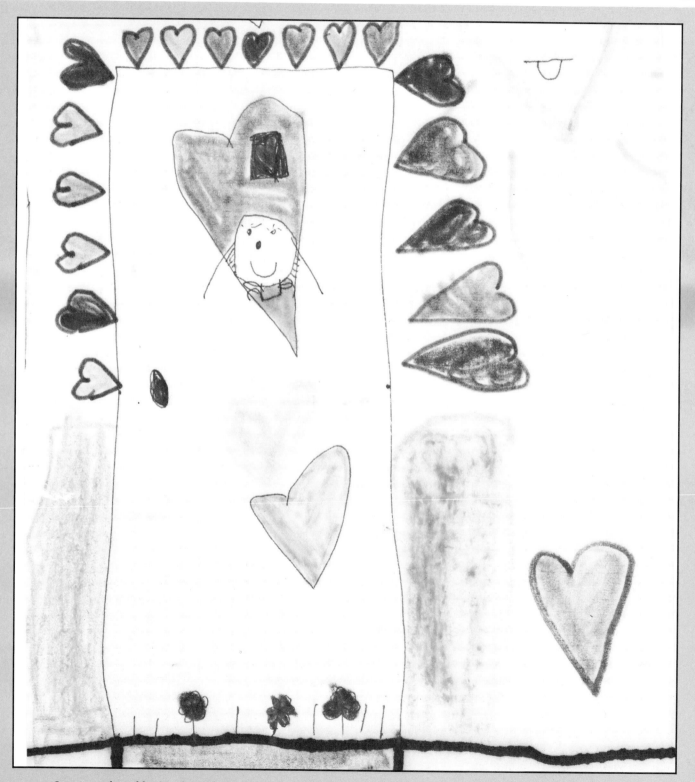

Segment of a table-size drawing in which the child depicts herself in her own home, looking east and awaiting the coming of "Love, the Lord"; age 5½.

The rising sun, coming to give light to the world; collage, age 5.

Origins and Spirit of Advent

Advent seems to touch each of us closely because it crystallizes into one season all our personal and communal rhythms of darkness and longing for light. Christmas, as we have seen, is the feast of the true Light who is Christ; Advent, its preparatory season, is a time of awareness of the darkness in our lives and of waiting for the rising Sun to shine on us.

In the history of the liturgical year and its major seasons, Advent is *the* latecomer! Although Christmas is known to us from the early fourth century, it was then a single festal day and not yet a season, much less with a preparation period of its own. Liturgical records of the later fourth century indicate that some kind of prefestal time had come into existence in Spain and Gaul. In the sixth century, first monastics and then the laity in certain Franco-Germanic regions were ordered to fast several times weekly during a lengthy pre-Christmas period. Later, the penitential aspects of Advent grew still stronger as the season came to accent the coming of the Lord on the last day, the day of judgment. Liturgical vestiges of the penitential strata of Advent are with us to this day in the use of purple

vestments and in the omission of the "Glory" at Sunday Eucharist during Advent (although the latter practice is now interpreted as a "saving" of that hymn text for the season to which it truly belongs—Christmastime).

The Roman Church did not originally regard Advent as a penitential time (even though there was fasting in Rome during the prenativity period, it seems to have been linked with the Ember Days, which were related to the agricultural cycle). Rather, the Advent liturgy of Rome described in the seventh century focused on the incarnation of Christ and prepared for its liturgical celebration. The duration of Advent, quite long in some places, was confined in Rome to the several Sundays prior to Christmas; our present-day Advent, which encompasses four Sundays, is heir to this tradition.

The very name Advent, from the Latin *adventus,* or "coming," illumines and unites the two primary foundation blocks of the season, the first and second comings of Christ. In a text like the following from Cyril of Jerusalem, we see that the Lord's two comings, far from being opposed to one another, can be fused into one spiritual tapestry:

> We proclaim the coming of Christ—not just a first coming but another as well that will be far more glorious than the first. The first took place under the sign of patient suffering; the second, on the contrary, will see Christ wearing the crown of God's kingdom. . . . We hailed him at his first coming with the words, "Blessed is he who comes in the Lord's name!" and shall hail him in the same way at his second coming. For we shall go out to meet the Lord and his angels, and, prostrating ourselves before him, we shall cry, "Blessed is he who comes in the Lord's name!"[1]

The Advent aspects so eloquently described above are the very ones highlighted in the recent *General Norms for the Liturgical Year and the Calendar:*

> The season of Advent has a twofold character. It is a time of preparation for Christmas when the first coming of God's Son is recalled. It is also a season when minds are directed by this memorial to Christ's second coming at the end of time. It is thus a season of joyful and spiritual expectation (no. 39).

In the Christian Scriptures the thought of the Lord's coming on the last day is very prominent. The Synoptic Gospels, for instance, paint a vivid picture of the end of time, using such images as signs in the heavens

(Matt 24:29-31; Mark 13:24-27; Luke 21:25-27); or parables of the wedding banquet (Matt 22:1-14), or of the great harvest at the close of this age (Matt 13:36-43) or of the Son of Man separating the sheep from the goats (Matt 25:31-46). Christians are to be vigilant, alert, and ready at all times, for the Son of Man will appear among us suddenly, unexpectedly! Meanwhile, as we wait and long for his appearance, we are to conduct ourselves in a holy and saintly manner (2 Pet 3:11-12, reading for the Second Sunday of Advent). Advent, then, summons us to a spirit of watchfulness and reminds us of how we are to live as we await the day of the Lord's final coming.

Throughout the season, the rich spiritual imagery and marvelous poetry of Isaiah keep the vision of the last age before us. We hear of the coming messianic kingdom of peace and justice where "the wolf lives with the lamb, the panther lies down with the kid . . . for the country is filled with the knowledge of the Lord" (Isa 11:6, 9); of the desert springing into blossom, and of the day when the blind shall see, the deaf hear (Isa 35:5). All these are the gifts of the promised one, of the stem springing forth from the root of Jesse, the one who will rule with the Spirit of God and who will bring us justice and peace (Isa 11:1-9); his name will be Emmanuel, God-with-us (Isa 7:14).

Ancient prophecies which speak of the coming Savior, the promised king of David's line, advance more and more into the forefront of the Advent liturgy as the season progresses. With the prophets, we turn our eyes to Bethlehem (Mic 5:1), and to the maiden who is with child (Isa 7:14). We are invited to prepare spiritually for Christmas, to ready ourselves for celebration of the historical coming of the Messiah. As we look forward to the incarnation feast, Advent offers us the opportunity to recall our need for God, to give voice to our yearning for the presence of God, to renew our trust in God's Word that his promise will indeed be fulfilled. In Advent, with Israel of old, we call to our God to come and save us.

Another prophet stands on the horizon of our Advent lives, crying out "Prepare a way for the Lord!" (Matt 3:1-3). John the Baptist, one of Advent's great figures, calls us to make ready our hearts for the One who is to come. When asked to be more precise about what this preparation, this readiness for the Lord means, John answers in a manner that echoes prophetic concerns throughout the Hebrew Scriptures: we are to act justly, with integrity, with compassion like that of the God whose compassion we seek. "If

anyone has two tunics he must share with the man who has none," declares the Baptist, "and the one with something to eat must do the same" (Luke 3:11).

While fasting and ritual have their place, they alone are insufficient as a way to welcome the Lord into our lives. In the end, what we need is the willingness to recognize and live out the full implication of John the Baptist's proclamation that the Lord must grow greater in us, even as we grow smaller (John 3:30).

The Baptist expresses the spiritual truth which was the hallmark of the *anawim*, God's poor, namely, that our human condition is one of complete dependence on our God. Insofar as we recognize our need, our weakness, God's presence fills us. The *anawim* of Israel sought refuge in God and hoped in God alone; they emptied themselves of all selfish desires to provide a space into which God might come. For us as for them, there is the assurance that those who wait for the Lord will not be disappointed, that his salvation is very near.

Of all God's *anawim*, Mary, mother of Jesus, was the poor one par excellence. She relied on God, waited for God's presence and gift, the Divine Word. As Leo the Great writes, "[Mary conceives the Lord] in her soul before she conceives him in her body."[2] The *Magnificat* or "Song of Mary," sung daily at evening prayer of the Church's Liturgy of the Hours, captures the spirit of the *anawim* and sums up Advent: "My soul proclaims the greatness of the Lord . . . he has exalted the lowly. The hungry he has filled with good things . . . . He has come to the help of Israel his servant, mindful of his mercy to Abraham and to his descendants forever" (Luke 1:46-55). Mary and her song can be our Advent tutors as we wait in joy for the coming of the Lord Jesus Christ.

For us, as for Mary, a paradox of our life in God is that what we await, we already possess! For us Christians, the Lord has already come, not only historically, of course, but to each of us in our baptism, in the gift of his Spirit poured out within us, in the taste of his eternal banquet in each Eucharist. The kingdom is already present wherever the breath of God is at work fashioning a new creation of beauty and truth, of justice and peace. In the midst of the ongoing aspirations and struggles of humanity and of all creation, however, we recognize that salvation is not yet complete. The tension between the presence of God-already-with-us and our continuing need until the final coming—this is at the heart of Advent and this compels us to sing with one breath, "Rejoice!" and "O come, O come, Emmanuel."

Advent in the Parish

The liturgies of the four Sundays of Advent represent a progression from an eschatological emphasis in the first Sunday—prophetic calls to prepare for and recognize the Lord's salvation—to the fourth Sunday, with its Marian overtones and its focus on Jesus' historical coming. From the themes of the Advent readings, prayers, and songs, we can see that this season is not predominantly penitential in tone; for instance, a joyful "alleluia" concludes many of the antiphons of the Liturgy of the Hours. Advent is marked by a crescendo of glad hope which binds seemingly disparate liturgical images into one: staying awake for the Bridegroom's arrival, the exalting of mountain and valley as he comes, the cry of the Baptist announcing the Lord, and the voice of Mary welcoming God's Word.

It is a venerable tradition that throughout Advent, the community of the Church stands near Mary, mother of Jesus. Mary's spirit of waiting for the Lord's Word to come into her heart and her life, her courage in accepting the ramification of God's gift to her, her gratitude for the marvels God has wrought for her—all these are a model for our own spirituality.

The parish would do well to remind itself that Advent is the Church's prime season for honoring Mary. This is when we say with God's messenger, "Rejoice, so highly favoured! The Lord is with you" (Luke 1:28); this is when we say with the whole Church, "Blessed are you, O Virgin Mary, for your great faith; all that the Lord promised you will come to pass through you, alleluia" (Evening Prayer, Second Sunday of Advent, Liturgy of the Hours of the Roman Rite). Those parishes which search for Marian "months of devotion"

Mary, mother of Jesus, shown in collage of warm colors and with a golden "womb area;" age 4½.

113

at other times of the year may well have overlooked the best opportunity for the veneration of Mary, that presented by the Advent liturgy and crowned by the Christmas season feast on January 1, the solemnity of Mary, Mother of God. (In our parish, there is but one Advent banner, and it features the flowering stem of Jesse [representing Jesus] surrounded by a crown of twelve stars [representing Mary], all on background colors of plum, dusty lavender, and deep rose.)

The light/darkness imagery that underpins the Advent-Christmas cycle recurs throughout the Sunday liturgies of the season. "O House of Jacob, come," says the prophet, "let us walk in the light of the Lord" (Isa 2:5, First Sunday of Advent). We hear the news that "a man came, sent by God . . . as a witness to speak for the light" (John 1:6-7, Third Sunday of Advent). At the threshold of Christmas, our prayer is the traditional psalm of the Advent season. "God of hosts, bring us back; let your face shine on us and we shall be saved" (Ps 79[80], Fourth Sunday of Advent).

One of the strongest Advent symbols for both our parishes and our homes, and one which carries the light theme most vividly for Advent-Christmas, is the wreath. Of Germanic orgin, the Advent wreath is actually a domestic custom which has frequently found its way into the liturgical setting. If used in the parish church, the Advent wreath should be given significant proportions and bold placement. It could be on a large stand in the place of welcome or even the center of the church or suspended from the ceiling. Those elements which constitute the symbolism of the wreath— evergreens in a circular form, a sign of eternity, fidelity, hope; and the candles, progressive light in the darkness—should be displayed with uncluttered prominence. A memorable Advent wreath in the church can be an excellent supportive link with a family's Advent wreath customs at home.

As part of their Advent decor, some parishes have a Jesse tree. Using important symbols from the Hebrew Scriptures, such as the tablets of the Ten Commandments or the Star of Jacob, the parish adds decorations to its tree each week until it is fully adorned for Christmas. There is considerable merit to this practice, especially if families help to make the symbolic decorations and come to understand their meaning; however, it is difficult to do sufficient scriptural catechesis so that the whole parish can find the Jesse tree spiritually meaningful. Little children below the age of seven or so are not really ready to grasp the theological truth which lies behind the colorful de-

tail of many of the stories of the Hebrew Scriptures, and their involvement in a Jesse tree project is better saved until later years.

Aside from the Advent wreath and the Jesse tree, parishes often have a hodgepodge of other Advent activities and decor, some influenced more by secular practices than by the liturgy. A community might do well to define for itself what Advent is, a time of preparation, hope, waiting; a time of empty-handedness and open-heartedness, a time not of saturation but of emptiness. For a parish to give consistent expression to the real meaning of Advent, there may have to be radical surgery, such as postponing parish parties to the Christmas season or to January, ruthlessly weeding out vapid decorative elements inspired by commercial displays, or reorienting seasonal music concerts from exclusively Christmas content to programs that include a strong Advent representation. There is wonderful Advent music, both centuries-old and contemporary. In our city, a secular choir has discovered this music and performs it as an Advent program on the first Sunday of the season; meanwhile, some Church organizations continue to sponsor pre-Christmas caroling in a round of concerts during Advent!

As for music in the liturgy, it is actually possible that musicians outdo themselves needlessly in Advent. Liturgical awareness of the unity of the season suggests once again that all acclamations for the celebration of the Eucharist (Alleluia; Holy, Holy, Holy; acclamation of faith; Amen; and the doxology after the Our Father) be kept the same for the four Sundays of Advent. Pastoral sensitivity requires that not only should Advent music be used where possible, but that at least some of it be used repeatedly during this short liturgical period. Many parishes accomplish the dubious feat of never letting the community repeat one song during the entire time of Advent! One could hardly recommend this as a way of handing on to the assembly— and especially to the children—the aural tradition of this season.

At this season of good will, the community can make a concerted effort to forge the generosity of its members into acts of justice and mercy. The parish could begin a long-term project of support for the underprivileged at home and abroad; attempt to educate parishioners on the devastating effects of militarism; encourage any home-oriented peace effort, such as a boycott of military toys in this season of peace; or sponsor local initiatives on behalf of the needy, not only to provide them with a Christmas hamper but to help change the system which keeps them from sharing in basic necessities of life.

The involvement of little children in larger projects for justice and peace may not be possible or suitable. However, the parish might invite its young members to save some money and, in conjunction with their families, purchase a gift for an underprivileged child (one parish specified particular needs, e.g., sleepwear for a two-year-old girl, crayons for five-year-olds, etc.). These could be presented by the children at the Eucharist, possibly on the Third Sunday of Advent, and passed on by the parish social action committee to appropriate recipients.

Advent in the Home

For a family planning its Advent, perhaps *the* main point to remember is that Advent, like Lent, is a secondary season, because it is a preparatory time. As such, it is a less significant time than Christmas-Epiphany, just as an engagement period is less important than the time of marriage itself. While all this may seem obvious, our behavior often gives little evidence that the perspective is clear to us. Advent is frequently littered with the pre-Christmas excesses of our culture; or alternately, we mount a vigorous family campaign to stave off that commercial influence, and we fill Advent with activities, prayers, and biblical stories. The latter effort is fine, even commendable . . . except that we often abandon our efforts from December 25 on to the end of the Christmas-Epiphany season. In a word, we exhaust our energies on Advent and then do not keep the Christmastime!

Advent, as a season of spiritual longing and joyful anticipation of the Lord, needs to be a simple calm time. The goal of Advent is to empty the vessel which will be filled by the Lord's coming in our lives, to ready ourselves for prompt response when the Master arrives. A quietness marks the time of waiting, of emptiness before fulfillment.

A household with young children, even while engaged in the family activities of Advent, can create an atmosphere of seasonal silence, for instance, by reducing television fare to an absolute minimum (or replacing it altogether with fine videocassette recordings suitable for Advent-Christmas), avoiding frenzied shopping trips to tinseled and noisy stores, and bypassing Santa Claus parades. All this can free the impressionable mind of the very young child for a spiritual receptivity.

This kind of freedom from a sensorial deluge can be paralleled in the realm of giving and receiving gifts, a subject which is thrust into center stage in many children's minds during the time the Church celebrates Advent. "Creative deprivation" is the suggestion offered by one author as a substitute for the practice of commercialized Christmas gift-giving.[3] To creatively deprive children is to keep their senses and emotions and minds clear from an overwhelming onslaught of material goods. Refusing to participate in the materialistic smothering of our children liberates them to keep their imaginations and spirits fresh and teaches them as well that life is frequently defined by limits. Parents of very young children know that the child's interest in nature, in time together, in simple pleasures can either be nurtured or be dulled by the intrusion of flashy television shows, glittering gimmicks, spiritless toys that absorb attention for a short while, then lead to a bored surfeit. Making a deliberate option for simplicity is much easier when children are tiny, for they have few expectations except for our love and our time, and their first experiences of Advent-Christmas are what we adults make of them. That is the time to lay foundations, to set the precedent to establish a firm pattern that, it is hoped, the inevitable influences of later years cannot erode.

With an Advent of stillness, of sensorial and material deprivation, what is left? Is this not a kill-joy preparation for Christmas? It can be quite the contrary. Instead of maintaining a frantic pace and an enslavement to societal expectations, the family with young children can prepare itself in many ways for the feast of Jesus the Light with tranquility and wonder.

As always, family prayer in common will be one of the major sources of the season's spirit and spirituality. A daily service around the Advent wreath is possible; or a family might wish to use its wreath as the gathering point for evening prayer, with the lighting of the appropriate number of candles at the opening acclamation. Unless it is too large, the Advent wreath could also be used at the family table, a principal focal point in the home.

The Hebrew Scriptures play a preeminent role in the liturgy of Advent, but as we have noted, young children are not generally capable of comprehending their theological significance. Cavalletti suggests that children under six be presented with only a few short prophetic passages during Advent; it is her experience that these biblical segments are among those which the child can understand deeply because of their vivid and striking imagery.[4] Cavalletti proposes that the first Advent passage to be given should be, "The people that walked in darkness has seen a great light" (Isa 9:1). Other prophetic or gospel passages can be presented to the child later in Advent or in subsequent years (see the list given in conjunction with the Advent wreath service, "Resources," p. 119). In these passages, the children find images and expressions which they can readily understand and which furnish them with a language of prayer.

Advent, as we have noted, is a season interwoven with the spirituality of Mary, mother of the Lord. It would be appropriate for a parent to present the older preschool child with a brief Marian prayer during Advent, simply the text: "Hail Mary, full of grace, the Lord is with you" (based on Luke 1:28). While speaking with the child about Mary, the parent may find an opportune moment to comment on pregnancy, both that of Mary and of other women: how precious a time this is for both mother and the unborn baby, how the mother looks forward to the birth of her baby, and so forth. Children especially like to hear about their own stay in their mother's womb and about how welcome and loved they were there, near their mother's heart. (If the child is not particularly intrigued by the topic at this time, there will certainly be a day when he or she is, and the parent might then be ready to include in the discussion a sensitive allusion to Mary as mother of Jesus.)

A household's normal preparations for Christmas can be incorporated into Advent spirituality, and children are eager to share in them. The best of activities in crafts, arts, baking, the enjoyment of nature at this season—all these can be part of celebrating the Lord's feast. While very young children cannot manage many gift-making projects all that successfully, they can make delightful giftwrapping even in their early years. In successive Advents our preschool daughter made wrapping paper with potato-stamp stars, then peace doves, then suns and hearts—all for Jesus the Light, the Prince of Peace who loves us. Creating Christmas cards, window transparencies, collages, and so on, provides an opportunity for the child to explore and express the meaning of Jesus the Lord, the Light.

Many parents of young children, even in those homes with two careers, still try to do some special food preparations for the Christmas season. Instead of making Santa Claus heads or candy canes, why not make star cookies, or tree cookies to decorate with "lights," or bells of joy; why not beautiful decorated bread or a spice-and-fruit cake for Epiphany in remembrance of the gifts of rare spices brought by the Magi to Jesus? The child of two or three (with considerable guidance and much parental patience!) can help to pour premeasured ingredients into a bowl; slightly older children love to mix, knead, cut, decorate . . . all the while, in these activities, there is opportunity to listen to music of Advent, chat about the spiritual meaning of the project at hand, and finish with an informal prayer, something like: "Lord Jesus, our Shepherd, our Light, we are happy that you come to us and are with us. We make these (breads) to show our happiness in you and to thank you."

And thus we have come full circle in this section on Advent in the home. We began by emphasizing Advent's subordinate relationship to the feast and season of Christmas; we contrasted Advent's stillness with the pre-Christmas extravaganza that our society would impose on us. Yet we have seen that this season is not impoverished but profoundly rich as it moves forward to the feast of Christ, Word, Everlasting Light. For ourselves and our children, this time of waiting need be neither frantic nor stagnant. It can be life-giving and fruitful, replete with prayer and the praises of the work of our hands.

Resources for Advent

1. Morning and Evening Prayer for Advent

Call to Prayer

(SONG 31)

Leader: You are light in darkness;
  All: Come, O Lord, and save us.

  or

(SONG 32)

Leader: Arise, for the dawn is coming!
  All: Awake, for the Lord is near!

Psalm for Advent: Psalm 79[80]

(SONG 33)

Refrain: Lord, make us turn to you,
  let us see your face and we shall be saved.

  Verse: O shepherd of Israel, hear us,
  Shine forth from your cherubim throne.
  O Lord, rouse up your might,
  O Lord, come to our help.

Scripture Reading: the Sunday gospel passage or selected verses (see Appendix B)

Canticle: for morning, Song of Zechariah *(Benedictus)*, see p. 153
  for evening, Song of Mary *(Magnificat)*, page 155, especially appropriate for the Advent season:

(SONG 34)

  All: My soul gives glory to the Lord, my God,
  My spirit rejoices in God.

Leader: The Lord has done wonders for me;
  holy is his name.

  The loving kindness of God
  lasts from age to age.

Intercessions

Our Father

Blessing

---

2. A Marian Song for Advent-Christmas

(SONG 35) A Rose Has Come

Leader: A rose has come from Jesse's stem,
All: Let us praise the Lord;

Leader: The promised king of David's house,
All: Let us praise the Lord.

Leader: And you, O Mary, Mother of God,
Be our Mother too.
Show your Son to us this day.
All: Let us praise the Lord.

3. Activities for Advent

AN ADVENT-CHRISTMAS CALENDAR

Advent activities are best planned as a unit with those of Christmastime so that there is a suitable balance and proportion between Advent, the preparatory season, and Christmas, the festal season. A unified plan also makes clearer for children the inseparable link between the two seasons.

A modest calendar such as the one at the end of this section (see p. 127) might be hung on the family bulletin board for the entire Advent-Christmas cycle. The calendar is an example of how a predominant theme—Light, based on the scriptural image of Jesus the Light—can be developed for a household with very young children. We keep the format spartan to provide a sharp contrast with the highly visual posterboard calendars of the paschal cycle, for the child should be able to see, touch, and experience which of the two annual cycles has priority.

Our household does not use commercial Advent calendars with a little "door" to be opened each of the days until Christmas, because they seem to narrow the child's Advent preoccupation to a countdown, and because they deflect attention from the Christmas season in its entirety.

The activities suggested on the calendar are described in more detail below.

THE ADVENT WREATH

Even little children will be delighted to assist or accompany parents in buying or cutting tree boughs for the wreath. The greens are secured with fine wire to a commercially purchased frame or to an inexpensive circular form made of coat hangers. Greens can be sustained for the season by providing each stem with water from tiny plastic floral vials. For the longest-lasting wreath, purchase a florists' sponge wreath form (sometimes called an "oasis wreath"); the greens need only be inserted into the sponge and the wreath can then be kept well watered.

Four natural-colored candles are as suitable as the customary three purple and one pink. In fact, the natural color is more versatile, as it is appropriate for Christmastime as well as Advent; one can buy a fifth candle and set it in the center of the wreath as a Christ candle once the Christmas season has begun. (If desired, the colors of the seasons can be represented by a ribbon or bow for each candle, purple/pink for Advent, to be replaced with white/gold or another festive color for Christmas-Epiphany.) If a homemade wreath frame is being used, attaching the candles securely is difficult; the candles may simply stand in sturdy holders on the inside edges of the wreath.

The Advent wreath may be used as a table centerpiece or as the candelabrum for evening prayer or as part of the household's prayer corner.

The Advent wreath service may take place Saturday evenings. We found that this time worked very well for our household, as it oriented the children toward the Sunday Advent liturgy at the parish.

Presenting selected Advent texts to the very young child can be ideally done in the Advent wreath set-

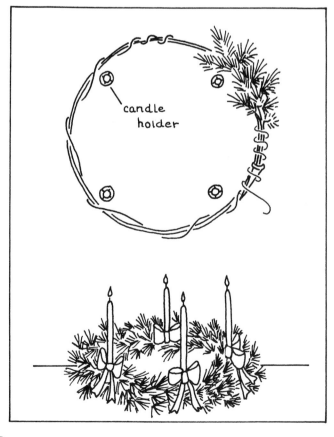

candle holder

ting. The usual format for the presentation of scriptural texts (see p. 25 above) could become the structure for the Advent wreath ceremony. Due to children's age-spread in the family, judicious flexibility will guide the choice of scriptural texts; choices should probably favor the younger child(ren). The following suggestions for a simple Advent wreath service are inspired largely by the practice of Cavalletti.

ADVENT WREATH SERVICE

Introduction (given by a parent in these or similar words:)

"We are in the season of waiting and hoping. Our Advent wreath reminds us of our waiting, because each week we wait for a greater and greater light. The prophets (on the fourth Sunday: gospel writers) are very special friends of God. They tell us God's word to help us know the wonderful things happening for us." (In his or her own words, a parent could recount simply one of the Scripture passages listed below, and its meaning.)

Lighting of the Candle(s)

(One candle for the first Sunday, an additional one each following Sunday)

Scripture Reading

> First week, Isa 9:1 (with very young children, one can repeat this
> passage during all of Advent)
> Second week, Isa 9:5-6
> Third week, Mic 5:1
> Fourth week, Luke 1:26-38

Response

(may include silence, song, spontaneous comment, and brief prayers)

Blessing

May our loving God bless us,
Father, Son, and Holy Spirit. Amen.
(All may share a sign of peace and love.)

MUSIC

While music suited to Advent is quite abundant, it is less well known than it deserves to be, largely because Christmas music has tended to usurp its place.

For the very young, learning one or two songs well in an Advent Season is sufficient achievement. A song like "People Look East" with its lilting dance-like tune and its text firmly rooted in the ancient tradition of regarding the east as source of light—east is also the direction from which Christ is to come again—this song is a fine choice for children. One verse may serve as the mealtime prayer, even with some easy gestures that children love to do.

Of all the beloved traditional Advent hymns, one of the best with a powerful "light" text is "Wake, Awake, for Night is Dying," a four-hundred-year-old Reformation classic which has only recently reached the repertoire of the Roman tradition. Its strong soaring melody and scripturally rich text are well worth the longer time it will take to learn the piece.

Besides singing the music of Advent, hearing it on recordings is an excellent way of establishing the sound of Advent in the home. Of the classic repertoire, obvious choices are Bach's Cantata No. 140, *Wachet auf,* which makes extensive use of the hymn-tune "Wake, Awake, for Night is Dying"; and segments of Handel's *Messiah,* particularly the aria "The People that walked in Darkness"; and the following chorus "For unto us a Child is Born" (the latter two selections are based on Isaiah 9, the very text Cavalletti recommends for young children and the text suggested above in connection with the Advent wreath service).

SHARING

Social action projects in response to the prophetic call of Advent do not fully correspond to the receptivity and capabilities of the very young child (see "Resources for Lent," p. 76). Nevertheless, it is important at this season—as throughout the year—that social awareness and acts of giving be fostered as a first step toward later involvement on a fuller scale. Further, the household's witness to simplicity and responsible stewardship during what can be a time of commercialized excess is vital to the child. That witness becomes a foundation for understanding not only the Advent-Christmas season but also the totality of Christian living, namely, that keeping religious festivals without working toward peace and justice is futile.

A Sharing Box

Very near the beginning of Advent, our family makes a sharing box to which we all contribute during the season. Its contents may be given to a charitable group just before Christmas, or the box may be broken open on December 26, St. Stephen's Day, for Christmas sharing with someone in need or with a local charity. A small box with a money slit made in the top suffices well (see drawing, p. 86). Young children might help select pictures of others in need to cover the box; the four- and five-year-olds can help cut and paste such pictures and may even want to draw their own. When our child was five and a half years old, she illustrated an Advent box with a house, food, and clothing, and then added to the bottom of the box a drawing of the world.

In the season when we remember God's gracious gift to us, Jesus the Light, we think of others and want to help bring happiness to everyone. Older children will better comprehend how sharing is like being a light to others, and will be interested in learning about people in the developing countries who are in need—see magazines such as *New Internationalist* (175 Carlton St., Toronto, Ont. M5A 2K3; and P.O. Box 1143, Lewiston, N.Y. 14092) or news photos. In the year of the disastrous Colombian mudslide, our child begged to send our Advent collection to a Colombian relief group.

Being of Service

Of course, a still better way to become sensitized to others is by direct contact and action. The older preschooler could accompany a parent to a work shift at the local food bank or in a clothing depot (although it is advisable to check in advance with the agency, for sometimes regulations or policies prevent such an enterprise). Best yet, the family could make the acquaintance of a refugee family or some other household in need of support and friendship. This is the most time consuming but also probably the most consistent and rewarding way to help children take an active part in responding to the needs of others.

IN TUNE WITH NATURE

Sunrise-watching

As the Christmas festival is related to the time when light begins its ascendancy over darkness, the link of the celebration with nature's cycles can be easily made for children. During Advent, our family often watches the sunrise dispelling darkness, noting that its light comes from the east, the place of Jesus' return in glory. Our daughter at five and a half, after sunrise-watching for several Advents, once spontaneously exclaimed at the sight of an exceptionally radiant dawn, "Beautiful sunrise! It must be like Jesus the Light!"

Starlight Walks

Starlight walks are especially appropriate in Advent. They are more easily done at this season, for the evening falls very early, and even tiny children can "get to see stars" before their bedtime. Everyone looks for light in the darkness!

Feeding the Birds

A charming north European custom of the sixteenth century honored birds, who were said to be present at the birth of Christ. Having children prepare food for winter birds can be not only a reminder of the Lord's coming but also a step toward learning to live in harmony with all his creatures. Once birds find your food supply, they may come to depend on it, so the Advent-Christmas treats should continue for the remainder of winter.

For a feeding center, choose a tree clearly visible from your window so children can enjoy watching their feathered guests. If the goodies are attached with colorful strings and ribbons, the tree will be a pretty, festive decoration for your yard. In the absence of a tree, even a pole or broomstick adorned with pegs and attached to a balcony would do nicely.

Some bird treats might include:

- Peanut butter pine cones: spread pine cones with peanut butter, roll in birdseed and bread crumbs, and fasten to a tree with wire.

- Suet cakes: purchase suet (available at most grocery counters), birdseed, raisins, sunflower seeds, and grit (made of granite particles and ground oyster shells); line muffin tins with paper liners; melt suet in a heavy saucepan and stir in remaining ingredients, then pour into muffin tins and chill in refrigerator overnight; wire the cakes to a tree (any extra cakes may be stored in freezer).

- Garlands: using heavy nylon or buttonhole thread, string popcorn, fresh cranberries, diced apple, chunks of stale bread, and car-

Dancing for joy, for the Lord is coming; age 6.

rot slices ¼″ to ½″ (6 to 12 mm) in thickness (for ground feeders, a similar assortment of treats, along with birdseed and sunflower seeds, can be sprinkled around the tree's base).

FOOD FOR ADVENT

Advent's preparatory character seems to pervade the kitchen as well as the liturgy during this season, as most of the activity in baking and cooking points toward Christmas!

In our household, we keep the Advent daily meals very simple, in the spirit of the season. This frees us to do our other Advent-Christmas projects, which include culinary ones for gifts or for our own Christmastime use.

As there are cookbooks in abundance for the Advent-Christmas season, this book offers recipes to be used at only two of Advent's significant moments: a plum pudding to "stir up" on the First Sunday of Advent and a Polish butter cookie, which our family uses at the ritual Christmas Eve meal that ends Advent and begins Christmas in the East European tradition.

Keeping the Christmas Cycle

The "Stir-up" Pudding (First Sunday of Advent)

For families who like to have the traditional English plum pudding at Christmas, readying it at the beginning of Advent can have a liturgical connotation as well as the practical value of an early start for Christmastime desserts. The following suggestion of associating the plum pudding with an Advent text, thus capitalizing on a pun, appears in Helen McLoughlin's *Family Advent Customs* (Collegeville, Minn.: The Liturgical Press, 1954; reprint ed., 1979).

Filled with delectable good things, the plum pudding at Christmas represents all the goodness brought into our world by Christ. Now, at the very beginning of Advent, stirring the pudding can call to mind the rousing cry of the classic Advent prayer: "Stir up your power, O Lord; come and save us!".

The family can assemble/chop/measure ingredients for the pudding on this day. At one of the Sunday meals, the pudding is passed around for family and guests to stir before it is steamed and then stored for Christmastime.

Of the many plum pudding recipes available, the following is not very sweet and is made without sugar-laden candied peel.

PLUM PUDDING

2 cups	Chopped dates	500 ml
1 cup	Chopped dried apricots	250 ml
½ cup	Raisins	125 ml
½ cup	Chopped almonds	125 ml
2 Tbsp	Grated lemon rind	30 ml
½ cup	Soft butter	125 ml
2	Eggs	2
1 cup	Brown sugar	250 ml
¾ cup	Grated raw carrot	175 ml
¾ cup	Grated raw potato	175 ml
⅓ cup	Milk	75 ml
1 cup	Sifted flour	250 ml
1½ tsp	Baking powder	7 ml
1 tsp	Baking soda	5 ml
1 tsp	Salt	5 ml
¼ tsp	Mace	1 ml
¼ tsp	Ginger	1 ml
¼ tsp	Cloves	1 ml

Combine the first five ingredients. Beat together the butter, eggs, sugar. Stir carrots, potato, and milk into the fruit-nut mixture. Blend in sifted dry ingredients. Mix thoroughly and pour into a well-greased bowl or mold, leaving space at the top for expansion. Cover with well-buttered waxed paper and tie with string. Steam for at least 1½ hours. Cool and store in the refrigerator or freezer. Resteam 1½ hours at Christmas, and serve with butterscotch ripple or vanilla ice cream and caramel sauce.

At our home the following have become known as "star" cookies, for we make them only in star shapes both to remind us of Jesus the Light, and to represent the first star of Christmas Eve, signaling the beginning of the feast. Children can assist in mixing, cutting shapes, and decorating.

BUTTER COOKIES

1 cup	Unsalted butter	250 ml
¾ cup	Granulated sugar	175 ml
1 tsp	Vanilla	5 ml
½ tsp	Grated lemon rind	2 ml
5	Hard-cooked egg yolks	5
2 cups	Flour	500 ml
½ tsp	Salt	2 ml
	Egg glaze	
	Poppy seeds	

Cream together butter and sugar. Stir in vanilla and lemon rind. Press egg yolks through a sieve and add to creamed mixture along with flour and salt; mix well. Shape into ball; wrap in plastic wrap and chill until firm enough to roll, about 1 hour.

Roll out dough to ¼" (6 mm) thickness; cut into small shapes. Arrange on greased baking sheets.

Egg glaze: Whisk together 1 egg white and 1 tsp (5 ml) water. Brush glaze onto each cookie and sprinkle lightly with poppy seeds. Bake in 350 degree F (180 C) oven for 10 minutes or until lightly browned. Makes about 60 cookies.

MAKING CARDS FOR CHRISTMAS

Writing Christmas cards is one of the larger projects that many households do during the Advent weeks. If sending cards is a meaningless, routine exercise involving expensive cards that have no spiritual significance or beauty, possibly the family should reevaluate the practice. Some people send cards only to those to whom they write letters as well; others print a greeting in a newspaper, or send no cards at all and donate the money saved to charity.[5]

In our home, we value the opportunity to exchange Christmas greetings and family news with friends and relatives at a distance. By designing and making our Christmas cards, we send not only our good wishes but also a small part of ourselves, that is, our very understanding and celebration of this season. Our children share in the card-making, and in putting on stamps and return-address labels. When the message writing is done and the cards ready to mail, we offer for those to whom we are sending cards a prayer of thanks and blessing.

Using the image of Jesus the Light, lovely cards can be made in various techniques simple enough to involve children.

■ Potato-stamp cards:

Materials: a large oval potato and a smaller one, red and yellow tempera paints, and prefolded blank cards of medium-weight paper (often available for a small price at print shops).

Activity: slice the potatoes in half lengthwise; the large oval one can be hollowed out in the middle and frayed or grated on the edges to form a glory-burst; the smaller potato can be cut into a star-shaped stamp;

an adult or older child can print the glory-burst on the card surface, and the younger child can add the star in the center. (Inside, one could later handprint the Advent prophecy, "A star shall rise from Jacob," Num 24:17).

■ Gummed-paper cards:

Materials: gummed paper shapes commercially pre-cut into rectangles approx. 2-3" x ½" (5-8 x 1 cm), into small diamonds and large circles; prefolded blank cards of medium-weight paper.

Activity: two or three rectangles can be pasted on the card vertically, overlapping to form a candle shape; top with the large circle and superimpose a diamond shape for the candle flame. (Inside, one could later hand-print a line adapted from the gospel of the Christmas Daytime Mass, "Jesus . . . a light that shines in the darkness," John 1:4).

■ Stenciled cards:

Materials: firm cardboards slightly larger than the card surface, an X-Acto knife or sharp scissors (an adult will do the work with these tools); either tempera paint, bright water colors, markers, *or* poster paint, in metal-lic gold if desired; prefolded blank cards of medium-weight paper.

Activity: have the child draw on the cardboard a bold sun surrounded by rays, or a half-sun with rays as in sunrise; with knife or scissors cut out a stencil based on the drawing; place stencil over card surface and apply color to card with sponge, brush, or marker. (Inside, one could later handprint the opening line of the first reading of Christmas Midnight Mass, "The people that walked in darkness has seen a great light," Isa 9:1).

PREPARING GIFTS FOR CHRISTMAS

Giving gifts at Christmas, like sending cards, can be a costly and time-consuming formality or a thoughtful creative sharing of self, or perhaps something combining elements of both these extremes. How can one live up to the ideals of Christian simplicity and of generosity directed primarily toward the poor and at the same time respect the feelings of others and acknowledge that which is worthy in the custom of exchanging gifts?

Rather than give material gifts to friends and relatives, some people choose to send money to charity

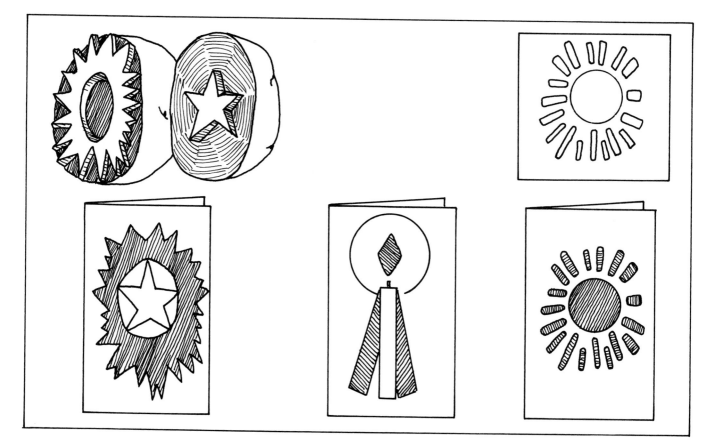

in the name of their friends and relatives. Others give only items they have made: handicrafts, baking, preserves, artwork, and so on.

For some people, particularly the elderly who often have all they need in material possessions, vouchers for personal services are a wonderful gift. For Granny, there might be a promise to shovel/sweep the walk every weekend; for a young family, three nights of free babysitting at times of their choice; for one's own children, a pledge of "ten times of skating with you before the ice melts."

Having the family make Christmas gifts, especially for grandparents and godparents, can be a fun experience, as well as an integral part of the religious celebration of Advent-Christmas. Making candles in honor of Jesus the Light or decorating paper placemats or coasters (cover them with clear contact paper) with nativity scenes or cutting out star shapes for tree decorations —all these can help the child express the meaning of Christmas for others. Home baking is always a popular possibility both with children-helpers and with recipients. Even a simple building project could have memorable results: two of the gifts our daughter has prized the most in her young life are a cedar birdhouse and a leaf-press made for her by little friends and their families.

If our family is purchasing gifts, we try to shop early (often during the fall months) for items that we hope will suit the recipient and also express our own values. Some gifts we have given are books, including Cavalletti's *The Religious Potential of the Child* and the McGinnis' book, *Parenting for Peace and Justice*; recordings, plants, pottery, or other handcrafted articles, magazine subscriptions, cooperative games, and religious art such as icons.

When selecting a gift, one might well remember that not only the item itself but also its source speaks of a set of values. Care might be taken to obtain locally made gifts, thus supporting local artists and craftspeople. Or one could elect to support artisans of the developing countries by purchasing Christmas gifts at a store which distributes their handmade goods.

In any case, if gift-giving is important to a family as part of its Advent-Christmas, it can be done in such a way that even the very young child can learn that a gift is a symbol of the loving sharing of self.

For giftwrapping, we have in the past several years used only the homemade variety created by our children. Several suggestions follow for giftwrapping with Jesus-the-Light symbols. All use lightweight, white art

Music to welcome Jesus; age 7.

paper or the good quality tablecovering available in rolls (for best results the paper should not be very absorbent).

■ Potato-stamp gift wrap

This is the easiest for young children . . . a few stray color splotches on the paper will add to artistic interest!

Materials: potato halves designed to stamp star shapes or sunbursts, tempera or poster paints.

Activity: N.B. Theoretically, this is a dip-and-stamp activity, but very young children often get their potato stamps saturated with so much paint that they can scarcely proceed. We find it good to have nearby a helping adult with paintbrush in hand, so the potato stamp can be quickly brushed with paint for the child.

Let your child freely fill the giftwrapping paper. Set sheets aside for thorough drying before use.

■ Paint-roller giftwrapping

While a bit more complicated to organize, this method is very efficient and an older preschooler of four and a half or more can produce a considerable amount of giftwrapping in a relatively short time.

Materials: small-size rollers which will be easy for the child to maneuver (the less ''furry'' the roller, the better); perforated sponge insoles as available in shoe stores; contact cement (for the adult's use only); tempera or poster paints.

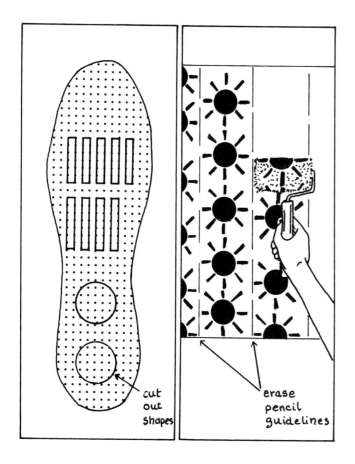

cut out shapes

erase pencil guidelines

Activity: have the child draw its own designs of sun, stars, other suitable Advent-Christmas shapes; trace the design onto the sponge insole and cut out, pasting onto the roller with contact cement (it is best to have a continuous line of designs around the roller to produce a fully decorated giftwrapping); when the glue is dry, let the child dip the roller into paint and simply roll it lengthwise down the paper (we first draw a series of light pencil-lines on each giftwrapping paper to provide guidelines for the child to follow with its roller).

■ Marker-design giftwrapping

This variety is best done after the gift is wrapped in plain white art paper. Using broad-tipped felt markers in brilliant colors, the child can freely interpret Advent-Christmas ideas.

ARTS AND CRAFTS

There are many simple art projects which children can do as part of their Advent experience, such as:

—drawings of the annunciation.

—collage of darkness and light (using magazines, old Christmas cards, and so on).

—tabletop cover or placemats illustrating an Advent song (use large white sheets, cover with clear contact paper for permanence).

—candle-making: of many creative possibilities, the simplest is to melt old candles and add some wax crayon pieces for color; pour into small molds—tiny tin cans, etc.—and insert string wicks, available in craft shops.

Many books of arts and crafts for children are readily available and the ideas can be easily adapted to the spiritual meaning of the season.

126

A Sample Calendar For Advent—Christmas—Epiphany

NOV 27 Advent I "Stir-up" pudding Advent wreath service	**28** Prepare sharing box to be opened Dec. 26	**29** Talk about how sharing is being like a light	**30** Sing/hear "Wake, Awake" (J.S. Bach)	**DEC. 1** Make cards with light theme.	**2** Stamp cards using Christmas postage stamps	**3** Finish cards Pray for the persons to whom sent
4 Advent II Advent wreath service	**5** "People, Look East" - sing/talk about the meaning of 'east'	**6** Watch the sun rise, set Talk about light/darkness	**7** Make gift wrap with star theme	**8** Buy/make last gifts - include a needy person or family	**9** Wrap gifts Make tags with light theme	**10** Wrap gifts Make seals with light theme
11 Advent III Advent wreath service	**12** Set up bird-feeder tree outside	**13** Make bird treats for feeder tree	**14** Make a star collage Talk about Jesus the Light	**15** As a family go for a star light walk	**16** Listen to "The People that walked in Darkness" (Messiah)	**17** Make window transparencies one for an older friend
18 Advent IV Advent wreath service	**19** Read the Christmas story	**20** Talk about Mary, Mother of God	**21** Bake cookies, Christmas stars	**22** Make an annunciation or nativity painting	**23** look at a book of the nativity in stained glass	**24** Watch for first star Fast-day Supper Tree up
25 Christmas Daytime mass Sing carols	**26 St. Stephen** Open/give away sharing box Evening- carols	**27 St. John** Make/write thank yous St. John's wine and song	**28 Holy Innocents** Candle ceremony at supper - use yesterday's song	**29** Guests visit Read Tolstoy's "Martin the Cobbler"	**30** Grandparents' visit Make them a Christmas picture	**31** Short prayer service of thanks Family party
JAN. 1 Mary, Mother of God Open house for godparents	**2** Have as a guest some- one alone or away from home	**3** Look at nativity art, icons	**4** Tell the story of a carol — "Silent Night"	**5** Take a carolling party to a senior citizens' home	**6** Share in an Eastern rite liturgy	**7** Make a joy- mural with wrappings, etc of the season
8 Epiphany Blessing of house Epiphany party and cake	This is an example of how a predominant theme — <u>Light</u>, based on the Scriptural image of Jesus the Light — can be developed for a household with young children.					

Appendix A

A Postscript: Lifestyle and Gospel Values

Our family has tried to identify some lifestyles areas which constantly need examination from the viewpoint of the faith formation of our children. Our inquiry into lifestyle choices was much aided by the ideas of Kathleen and James McGinnis in *Parenting for Peace and Justice* and by the work of Milo Shannon-Thornberry, particularly in his publication *The Alternative Celebrations Catalogue*. The following thoughts reflect our family's ongoing aspiration to let gospel values shape our lives.

In a consumer society, simplicity of lifestyle is always a goal to establish more securely, a vision to live more generously. The family can work continuously toward a greater concern with people and relationships and toward an accompanying decrease in preoccupation with possessions and objects. Ways to implement this ideal with young children include the fostering of creativity and new skills rather than reliance on passive entertainment and expensive toys: for instance, an adult might spend an afternoon baking muffins or planting a garden with a little child instead of giving him or her the newest "talking bear" or a few hours under the care of television. "Fewer possessions!" has become my husband's motto; and in lieu of all these "things," we have tried inventing our own games, sharing skills and insights, composing our own verses and songs, and fostering mutual cooperation through common projects. Freeing ourselves from preoccupation with possessions opens the possibility of nurturing inner resources and spiritual receptivity.

Greater simplicity in the family's use of food and clothing is not merely an economic measure but also an educational tool for the household, encouraging more modest expectations than society and advertising do, and engendering a generally appreciative attitude in each person. Food choices can stress nutrition; if possible, food purchases can support local growers or cooperative food producing ventures; possibly the family could grow even a small garden to supply some of its food. As for clothing, an excellent concept to introduce early is that of sharing, not only sibling to sibling, but family to family, or by buying through second-hand shops (which in our house have come to be known as "sharing stores").

Through a family's other options and activities, we are finding that children can gradually learn sharing and stewardship on a broader scale. The household may be able to make its living space available for gatherings—meetings or other activities of community groups; perhaps the home might become a haven for someone in need—a troubled teenager, an immigrant, a foster child, an elderly person. Family goods—toys, books, records, and so on—might be shared with others. As the family uses community recreational/cultural facilities (parks, swimming pools, libraries, museums), parents can easily convey to children an attitude of care and respect for common property. Appreciation of the natural environment is something which even very young children can develop; and the most simple beginnings, such as curiosity about plants and fascination with bugs, can be nurtured into a lifetime of wonder and ecological responsibility.

In the home itself, the family can always strive for a more peaceful and harmonious environment (without despairing over the many days that miss the mark!). Efforts to emphasize positive behavior, to consciously affirm, to express affection, to listen and to share, to resolve conflict in nonviolent ways—all these are part of the ongoing agenda of the young family trying to lay a firm basis for explicit religious formation later in life. There is much excellent literature available on the subjects of parenting and family relationships, and the reader is referred to these for a specific discussion of family living.

Formation of attitudes connected with major social issues of our day also begins at home in early childhood. In our household, my husband and I try to keep alive some questions that can challenge us, remind us of our responsibility for shaping the future. We want our children to accept a wide range of differences in people: Does our network of family friends include persons of more than one race, of all ages, of varying physical and mental abilities? (One of our friends, a young man confined to a wheelchair, who is a resident of a special-abilities home, has helped our young children to glimpse the challenges facing the handicapped.) Do we encourage the positive appreciation of other cultures by taking our children to ethnic festivals, multi-cultural events? We want our children to learn nonsexist language and behavior: in our home, does everyone share serving roles? Do we provide children's literature which avoids sex-stereotyping? Do we esteem the contribution of women and men equally? And do we fully encourage the interests and talents of each person, whether male or female? We want our children to become people of peace: Do we give them a living model of peaceable relationships? Do we fill their young years with toys and activities that teach cooperation and nonviolence, or with war toys and highly competitive games?

As for the family's direct involvement with social justice issues, often the commitment inolved in caring for small children precludes the expenditure of much time in working for social change in the world (although my son came with me to peace meetings for the first twelve months of his life, and the McGinnis family, in *Parenting for Peace and Justice*, documents a most impressive record of their young children's presence in direct action for peace and justice). If the family decides to become involved in projects for social change, it is important that parents exercise discretion about their young children's in-

volvement, for as the McGinnises write, "exposing children to situations for which they have neither the intellectual nor emotional capacity may do more harm than good" (*Parenting*, p. 100). It is useful to note the distinction between working for justice and works of mercy. The former is a long-term effort in changing political, economic, and cultural structures that oppress people anywhere in the world; the latter is direct service to persons at hand—feeding the hungry, visiting the sick, and so on.

For young children, the works of mercy seem to us a more appropriate place to begin awareness of social responsibility. Some suggestions are included in this book in connection with various liturgical seasons. Eventually, as children are older, integration of works for justice and mercy becomes an attainable goal.

Appendix B
Scriptural Readings for Sundays and Feasts

References for the readings are given as they appear in the Jerusalem Bible translation, and, for the most part, as they are used in the liturgy. Occasionally, the listing below omits some verses as does the Lectionary; but sometimes the listing has additional verses, included here for the sake of simplicity in reading a scriptural passage.

While all the readings of each Sunday and feast are indicated, the Gospel is generally the preferred text

for the young child. Parents should feel free to adapt the length of any Gospel, even to select only one or two appropriate verses. Normally, the Sunday Gospel continues to be read during the course of the week following a given Sunday.

The two numbers given for the psalms are the Greek Septuagint and Hebrew enumeration, respectively. The Grail translation of the psalms used in this book is indicated by the first (smaller) number.

Sunday	First Reading	Second Reading	Gospel
Advent Readings			
1 Advent-A			
Psalm 121 [122]	Isa 2:1-5	Rom 13:11-14	Matt 24:37-44
1 Advent-B			
Psalm 79 [80]	Isa 63:16-17; 64:3-7	1 Cor 1:3-9	Mark 13:33-37
1 Advent-C			
Psalm 24 [25]	Jer 33:14-16	1 Thess 3:12–4:2	Luke 21:25-28, 34-36
2 Advent-A			
Psalm 71 [72]	Isa 11:1-10	Rom 15:4-9	Matt 3:1-12
2 Advent-B			
Psalm 84 [85]	Isa 40:1-5, 9-11	2 Pet 3:8-14	Mark 1:1-8
2 Advent-C			
Psalm 125 [126]	Bar 5:1-9	Phil 1:4-6, 8-11	Luke 3:1-6
3 Advent-A			
Psalm 145 [146]	Isa 35:1-6, 10	Jas 5:7-10	Matt 11:2-11

Sunday	First Reading	Second Reading	Gospel
3 Advent-B Luke 1:46-55	Isa 61:1-2, 10-11	1 Thess 5:16-24	John 1:6-8, 19-28
3 Advent-C Isa 12:2-6	Zeph 3:14-18	Phil 4:4-7	Luke 3:10-18
4 Advent-A Psalm 23 [24]	Isa 7:10-14	Rom 1:1-7	Matt 1:18-24
4 Advent-B Psalm 88 [89]	2 Sam 7:1-5, 8-11, 14, 16	Rom 16:25-27	Luke 1:26-38
4 Advent-C Psalm 79 [80]	Mic 5:1-4	Heb 10:5-10	Luke 1:39-45

Christmas-Epiphany Readings

Sunday	First Reading	Second Reading	Gospel
Midnight Psalm 95 [96]	Isa 9:1-3, 5-6	Titus 2:11-14	Luke 2:1-14
Dawn Psalm 96 [97]	Isa 62:11-12	Titus 3:4-7	Luke 2:15-20
Day Psalm 97 [98]	Isa 52:7-10	Heb 1:1-6	John 1:1-18
Holy Family-A Psalm 127 [128]	Sir 3:2-6, 12-14	Col 3:12-21	Matt 2:13-15, 19-23
Holy Family-B Psalm 104 [105]	Gen 15:1-6; 21:1-7	Heb 11:8-12, 17-19	Luke 2:22-40
Holy Family-C Psalm 83 [84]	Isa 1:24-28	1 John 3:1-2, 21-24	Luke 2:41-52
Mary, Mother of God Psalm 66 [67]	Num 6:22-27	Gal 4:4-7	Luke 2:16-21
2nd Sunday after Christmas Psalm 147	Sir 24:1-2, 8-12	Eph 1:3-6, 15-18	John 1:1-18
Epiphany Psalm 71 [72]	Isa 60:1-6	Eph 3:2-6	Matt 2:1-12
Baptism of the Lord-A Psalm 28 [29]	Isa 42:1-7	Acts 10:34-38	Matt 3:13-17
Baptism of the Lord-B Isa 12	Isa 55:1-11	1 John 5:1-9	Mark 1:7-11
Baptism of the Lord-C Psalm 103 [104]	Isa 40:1-5, 9-11	Titus 2:11-14; 3:4-7	Luke 3:15-16, 21-22

Lenten Readings

Sunday	First Reading	Second Reading	Gospel
Ash Wednesday Psalm 50 [51]	Joel 2:12-18	2 Cor 5:20–6:2	Matt 6:1-6, 16-18
1 Lent-A Psalm 50 [51]	Gen 2:7-9; 3:1-7	Rom 5:12-19	Matt 4:1-11
1 Lent-B Psalm 24 [25]	Gen 9:8-15	1 Pet 3:18-22	Mark 1:12-15
1 Lent-C Psalm 90 [91]	Deut 26:4-10	Rom 10:8-13	Luke 4:1-13
2 Lent-A Psalm 32 [33]	Gen 12:1-4	2 Tim 1:8-10	Matt 17:1-9

Sunday	First Reading	Second Reading	Gospel
2 Lent-B Psalm 115 [116]	Gen 22:1-2, 9-18	Rom 8:31-34	Mark 9:2-10
2 Lent-C Psalm 26 [27]	Gen 15:5-12, 17-18	Phil 3:17–4:1	Luke 9:28-36
3 Lent-A Psalm 94 [95]	Exod 17:3-7	Rom 5:1-2, 5-8	John 4:5–42
3 Lent-B Psalm 18 [19]	Exod 20:1-17	1 Cor 1:22-25	John 2:13-25 (or readings for 3 Lent-A
3 Lent-C Psalm 102 [103]	Exod 3:1-8, 13-15	1 Cor 10:1-6, 10-12	Luke 13:1-9 (or read- ings for 3 Lent-A)
4 Lent-A Psalm 22 [23]	1 Sam 16:1, 6-7, 10-13	Eph 5:8-14	John 9:1-41
4 Lent-B Psalm 136 [137]	2 Chr 36:14-16, 19-23	Eph 2:4-10	John 3:14-21 (or read- ings for 4 Lent-A)
4 Lent-C Psalm 33 [34]	Josh 5:9-12	2 Cor 5:17-21	Luke 15:1-3, 11-32 (or readings for 4 Lent-A)
5 Lent-A Psalm 129 [130]	Ezek 37:12-14	Rom 8:8-11	John 11:1-45
5 Lent-B Psalm 50 [51]	Jer 31:31-34	Heb 5:7-9	John 12:20-33 (or read- ings for 5 Lent-A)
5 Lent-C Psalm 125 [126]	Isa 43:16-21	Phil 3:8-14	John 8:1-11 (or read- ings for 5 Lent-A)
Passion Sunday-A Psalm 21 [22]	Isa 50:4-7	Phil 2:6-11	Matt 26:14–27:66
Passion Sunday-B Psalm 21 [22]	Isa 50:4-7	Phil 2:6-11	Mark 14:1–15:47
Passion Sunday-C Psalm 21 [22]	Isa 50:4-7	Phil 2:6-11	Luke 22:14–23:56

Paschal Three Days Readings

Holy Thursday Lord's Supper Psalm 115 [116]	Exod 12:1-8, 11-14	1 Cor 11:23-26	John 13:1-15
Good Friday Psalm 30 [31]	Isa 52:13–53:12	Heb 4:14-16; 5:7-9	John 18:1–19:42
Easter Vigil Psalm 103 [104] or 32 [33]	Gen 1:1–2:2	Rom 6:3-11	A:Matt 28:1-10
Psalm 15 [16]	Gen 22:1-18		B:Mark 16:1-8
Exod 15	Exod 14:15–15:1		C:Luke 24:1-12
Psalm 29 [30]	Isa 54:5-14		
Isa 12	Isa 55:1-11		
Psalm 18 [19]	Bar 3:9-15, 32–4:4		

Sunday	First Reading	Second Reading	Gospel
Psalm 41-42 [42-43] or Isa 12 or Ps 50 [51]	Ezek 36:16-28		

Easter Readings

Sunday	First Reading	Second Reading	Gospel
Easter Sunday Psalm 117 [118]	Acts 10:34, 37-43	Col 3:1-4 (or 1 Cor 5:6-8)	John 20:1-9 (or Luke 24:13-35)
2 Easter-A Psalm 117 [118]	Acts 2:42-47	1 Pet 1:3-9	John 20:19-31
2 Easter-B Psalm 117 [118]	Acts 4:32-35	1 John 5:1-6	John 20:19-31
2 Easter-C Psalm 117 [118]	Acts 5:12-16	Rev 1:9-13, 17-19	John 20:19-31
3 Easter-A Psalm 15[16]	Acts 2:14, 22-28	1 Pet 1:17-21	Luke 24:13-35
3 Easter-B Psalm 4	Acts 3:13-19	1 John 2:1-5	Luke 24:35-48
3 Easter-C Psalm 29 [30]	Acts 5:27-32, 40-41	Rev 5:11-14	John 21:1-19
4 Easter-A Psalm 22 [23]	Acts 2:14, 36-41	1 Pet 2:20-25	John 10:1-10
4 Easter-B Psalm 117 [118]	Acts 4:8-12	1 John 3:1-2	John 10:11-18
4 Easter-C Psalm 99 [100]	Acts 13:14, 43-52	Rev 7:9, 14-17	John 10:27-30
5 Easter-A Psalm 32 [33]	Acts 6:1-7	1 Pet 2:4-9	John 14:1-12
5 Easter-B Psalm 21 [22]	Acts 9:26-31	1 John 3:18-24	John 15:1-8
5 Easter-C Psalm 144 [145]	Acts 14:21-27	Rev 21:1-5	John 13:31-35
6 Easter-A Psalm 65 [66]	Acts 8:5-8, 14-17	1 Pet 3:15-18	John 14:15-21
6 Easter-B Psalm 97 [98]	Acts 10:25-26, 34-35, 44-48	1 John 4:7-10	John 15:9-17
6 Easter-C Psalm 66 [67]	Acts 15:1-2, 22-29	Rev 21:10-14, 22-23	John 14:23-29
Ascension-A Psalm 46 [47]	Acts 1:1-11	Eph 1:17-23	Matt 28:16-20
Ascension-B Psalm 46 [47]	Acts 1:1-11	Eph 4:1-13	Mark 16:15-20
Ascension-C Psalm 46 [47]	Acts 1:1-11	Heb 9:24-28; 10:19-23	Luke 24:46-53
7 Easter-A Psalm 26 [27]	Acts 1:12-14	1 Pet 4:13-16	John 17:1-11
7 Easter-B Psalm 102 [103]	Acts 1:15-17, 20-26	1 John 4:11-16	John 17:11-19
7 Easter-C Psalm 96 [97]	Acts 7:55-60	Rev 22:12-14, 16-17, 20	John 17:20-26

Sunday	First Reading	Second Reading	Gospel
8 Easter, Pentecost Psalm 103 [104]	Acts 2:1-11	1 Cor 12:3-7, 12-13	John 20:19-23

Ordinary Time Readings

Sunday	First Reading	Second Reading	Gospel
Trinity Sunday-A Dan 3	Exod 34:4-9	2 Cor 13:11-13	John 3:16-18
Trinity Sunday-B Psalm 32 [33]	Deut 4:32-34, 39-40	Rom 8:14-17	Matt 28:16-20
Trinity Sunday-C Psalm 8	Prov 8:22-31	Rom 5:1-5	John 16:12-15
Corpus Christi-A Psalm 147	Deut 8:2-3, 14-16	1 Cor 10:16-17	John 6:51-59
Corpus Christi-B Psalm 115 [116]	Exod 24:3-8	Heb 9:11-15	Mark 14:12-16, 22-26
Corpus Christi-C Psalm 109 [110]	Gen 14:18-20	1 Cor 11:23-26	Luke 9:11-17
2 Ordinary Time-A Psalm 39 [40]	Isa 49:3-6	1 Cor 1:1-3	John 1:29-34
2 Ordinary Time-B Psalm 39 [40]	1 Sam 3:3-10, 19	1 Cor 6:13-20	John 1:35-42
2 Ordinary Time-C Psalm 95 [96]	Isa 62:1-5	1 Cor 12:4-11	John 2:1-12
3 Ordinary Time-A Psalm 26 [27]	Isa 8:23–9:3	1 Cor 1:10-13, 17	Matt 4:12-23
3 Ordinary Time-B Psalm 24 [25]	Jonah 3:1-5, 10	1 Cor 7:29-31	Mark 1:14-20
3 Ordinary Time-C Psalm 18 [19]	Neh 8:2-10	1 Cor 12:12-30	Luke 1:1-4; 4:14-21
4 Ordinary Time-A Psalm 145 [146]	Zeph 2:3; 3:12-13	1 Cor 1:26-31	Matt 5:1-12
4 Ordinary Time-B Psalm 94 [95]	Deut 18:15-20	1 Cor 7:32-35	Mark 1:21-28
4 Ordinary Time-C Psalm 70 [71]	Jer 1:4-5, 17-19	1 Cor 12:31–13:13	Luke 4:21-30
5 Ordinary Time-A Psalm 111 [112]	Isa 58:7-10	1 Cor 2:1-5	Matt 5:13-16
5 Ordinary Time-B Psalm 146 [147]	Job 7:1-7	1 Cor 9:16-19, 22-23	Mark 1:29-39
5 Ordinary Time-C Psalm 137 [138]	Isa 6:1-8	1 Cor 15:1-11	Luke 5:1-11
6 Ordinary Time-A Psalm 118 [119]	Sir 15:15-20	1 Cor 2:6-10	Matt 5:17-37
6 Ordinary Time-B Psalm 31 [32]	Lev 13:1-2, 45-46	1 Cor 10:31–11:1	Mark 1:40-45
6 Ordinary Time-C Psalm 1 [2]	Jer 17:5-8	1 Cor 15:12, 16-20	Luke 6:17, 20-26
7 Ordinary Time-A Psalm 102 [103]	Lev 19:1-2, 17-18	1 Cor 3:16-23	Matt 5:38-48
7 Ordinary Time-B Psalm 40 [41]	Isa 43:18-25	2 Cor 1:18-22	Mark 2:1-12

Sunday	First Reading	Second Reading	Gospel
7 Ordinary Time-C Psalm 102 [103]	1 Sam 26:2, 7-13, 22-23	1 Cor 15:45-49	Luke 6:27-38
8 Ordinary Time-A Psalm 61 [62]	Isa 49:14-15	1 Cor 4:1-5	Matt 6:24-34
8 Ordinary Time-B Psalm 102 [103]	Hos 2:16-17, 21-22	2 Cor 3:1-6	Mark 2:18-22
8 Ordinary Time-C Psalm 91 [92]	Sir 27:4-7	1 Cor 15:54-58	Luke 6:39-45
9 Ordinary Time-A Psalm 30 [31]	Deut 11:18, 26-28	Rom 3:21-25, 28	Matt 7:21-27
9 Ordinary Time-B Psalm 80 [81]	Deut 5:12-15	2 Cor 4:6-11	Mark 2:23–3:6
9 Ordinary Time-C Psalm 116 [117]	1 Kgs 8:41-43	Gal 1:1-2, 6-10	Luke 7:1-10
10 Ordinary Time-A Psalm 49 [50]	Hos 6:3-6	Rom 4:18-25	Matt 9:9-13
10 Ordinary Time-B Psalm 129 [130]	Gen 3:9-15	2 Cor 4:13–5:1	Mark 3:20-35
10 Ordinary Time-C Psalm 29 [30]	1 Kgs 17:17-24	Gal 1:11-19	Luke 7:11-17
11 Ordinary Time-A Psalm 99 [100]	Exod 19:2-6	Rom 5:6-11	Matt 9:36–10:8
11 Ordinary Time-B Psalm 91 [92]	Ezek 17:22-24	2 Cor 5:6-10	Mark 4:26-34
11 Ordinary Time-C Psalm 31 [32]	2 Sam 12:7-10, 13	Gal 2:16, 19-21	Luke 7:36–8:3
12 Ordinary Time-A Psalm 68 [69]	Jer 20:10-13	Rom 5:12-15	Matt 10:26-33
12 Ordinary Time-B Psalm 106 [107]	Job 38:1, 8-11	2 Cor 5:14-17	Mark 4:35-41
12 Ordinary Time-C Psalm 62 [63]	Zech 12:10-11	Gal 3:26-29	Luke 9:18-24
13 Ordinary Time-A Psalm 88 [89]	2 Kgs 4:8-16	Rom 6:3-4, 8-11	Matt 10:37-42
13 Ordinary Time-B Psalm 29 [30]	Wis 1:13-15; 2:23-24	2 Cor 8:7-9, 13-15	Mark 5:21-43
13 Ordinary Time-C Psalm 15 [16]	1 Kgs 19:16, 19-21	Gal 5:1, 13-18	Luke 9:51-62
14 Ordinary Time-A Psalm 144 [145]	Zech 9:9-10	Rom 8:9-13	Matt 11:25-30
14 Ordinary Time-B Psalm 122 [123]	Ezek 2:2-5	2 Cor 12:7-10	Mark 6:1-6
14 Ordinary Time-C Psalm 65 [66]	Isa 66:10-14	Gal 6:14-18	Luke 10:1-12, 17-20
15 Ordinary Time-A Psalm 64 [65]	Isa 55:10-11	Rom 8:18-23	Matt 13:1-23
15 Ordinary Time-B Psalm 84 [85]	Amos 7:12-15	Eph 1:3-14	Mark 6:7-13

Sunday	First Reading	Second Reading	Gospel
15 Ordinary Time-C Psalm 68 [69]	Deut 30:10-14	Col 1:15-20	Luke 10:25-37
16 Ordinary Time-A Psalm 85 [86]	Wis 12:13, 16-19	Rom 8:26-27	Matt 13:24-43
16 Ordinary Time-B Psalm 22 [23]	Jer 23:1-6	Eph 2:13-18	Mark 6:30-34
16 Ordinary Time-C Psalm 14 [15]	Gen 18:1-10	Col 1:24-28	Luke 10:38-42
17 Ordinary Time-A Psalm 118 [119]	1 Kgs 3:5-12	Rom 8:28-30	Matt 13:44-52
17 Ordinary Time-B Psalm 144 [145]	2 Kgs 4:42-44	Eph 4:1-6	John 6:1-15
17 Ordinary Time-C Psalm 137 [138]	Gen 18:20-32	Col 2:12-14	Luke 11:1-13
18 Ordinary Time-A Psalm 144 [145]	Isa 55:1-3	Rom 8:35-39	Matt 14:13-21
18 Ordinary Time-B Psalm 77 [78]	Exod 16:2-4, 12-15	Eph 4:17, 20-24	John 6:24-35
18 Ordinary Time-C Psalm 94 [95]	Eccl 1:2; 2:21-23	Col 3:1-5, 9-11	Luke 12:13-21
19 Ordinary Time-A Psalm 84 [85]	1 Kgs 19: 9, 11-13	Rom 9:1-5	Matt 14:22-33
19 Ordinary Time-B Psalm 33 [34]	1 Kgs 19:4-8	Eph 4:30–5:2	John 6:41-51
19 Ordinary Time-C Psalm 32 [33]	Wis 18:6-9	Heb 11:1-2, 8-19	Luke 12:32-48
20 Ordinary Time-A Psalm 66 [67]	Isa 56:1, 6-7	Rom 11:13-15, 29-32	Matt 15:21-28
20 Ordinary Time-B Psalm 33 [34]	Prov 9:1-6	Eph 5:15-20	John 6:51-58
20 Ordinary Time-C Psalm 39 [40]	Jer 38:4-10	Heb 12:1-4	Luke 12:49-53
21 Ordinary Time-A Psalm 137 [138]	Isa 22:19-23	Rom 11:33-36	Matt 16:13-20
21 Ordinary Time-B Psalm 33 [34]	Josh 24:1-2, 15-18	Eph 5:21-32	John 6:60-69
21 Ordinary Time-C Psalm 116 [117]	Isa 66:18-21	Heb 12:5-7, 11-13	Luke 13:22-30
22 Ordinary Time-A Psalm 62 [63]	Jer 20:7-9	Rom 12:1-2	Matt 16:21-27
22 Ordinary Time-B Psalm 14 [15]	Deut 4:1-2, 6-8	Jas 1:17-18, 21-22, 27	Mark 7:1-8, 14-15, 21-23
22 Ordinary Time-C Psalm 67 [68]	Sir 3:17-20, 28-29	Heb 12:18-19, 22-24	Luke 14:1, 7-14
23 Ordinary Time-A Psalm 94 [95]	Ezek 33:7-9	Rom 13:8-10	Matt 18:15-20
23 Ordinary Time-B Psalm 145 [146]	Isa 35:4-7	Jas 2:1-5	Mark 7:31-37

Sunday	First Reading	Second Reading	Gospel
23 Ordinary Time-C Psalm 89 [90]	Wis 9:13-18	Phlm 9-17	Luke 14:25-33
24 Ordinary Time-A Psalm 102 [103]	Sir 27:30–28:7	Rom 14:7-9	Matt 18:21-35
24 Ordinary Time-B Psalm 114–115 [116]	Isa 50:5-9	Jas 2:14-18	Mark 8:27-35
24 Ordinary Time-C Psalm 50 [51]	Exod 32:7-11, 13-14	1 Tim 1:12-17	Luke 15:1-32
25 Ordinary Time-A Psalm 144 [145]	Isa 55:6-9	Phil 1:20-24, 27	Matt 20:1-16
25 Ordinary Time-B Psalm 53 [54]	Wis 2:12, 17-20	Jas 3:16–4:3	Mark 9:30-37
25 Ordinary Time-C Psalm 112 [113]	Amos 8:4-7	1 Tim 2:1-8	Luke 16:1-13
26 Ordinary Time-A Psalm 24 [25]	Ezek 18:25-28	Phil 2:1-11	Matt 21:28-32
26 Ordinary Time-B Psalm 18 [19]	Num 11:25-29	Jas 5:1-6	Mark 9:38-41
26 Ordinary Time-C Psalm 145 [146]	Amos 6:1, 4-7	1 Tim 6:11-16	Luke 16:19-31
27 Ordinary Time-A Psalm 79 [80]	Isa 5:1-7	Phil 4:6-9	Matt 21:33-43
27 Ordinary Time-B Psalm 127 [128]	Gen 2:18-24	Heb 2:9-11	Mark 10:2-16
27 Ordinary Time-C Psalm 94 [95]	Hab 1:2-3; 2:2-4	2 Tim 1:6-8, 13-14	Luke 17:5-10
28 Ordinary Time-A Psalm 22 [23]	Isa 25:6-10	Phil 4:12-14, 19-20	Matt 22:1-14
28 Ordinary Time-B Psalm 89 [90]	Wis 7:7-11	Heb 4:12-13	Mark 10:17-30
28 Ordinary TIme-C Psalm 97 [98]	2 Kgs 5:14-17	2 Tim 2:8-13	Luke 17:11-19
29 Ordinary Time-A Psalm 95 [96]	Isa 45:1, 4-6	1 Thess 1:1-5	Matt 22:15-21
29 Ordinary Time-B Psalm 32 [33]	Isa 53:10-11	Heb 4:14-16	Mark 10:35-45
29 Ordinary Time-C Psalm 120 [121]	Exod 17:8-13	2 Tim 3:14–4:2	Luke 18:1-8
30 Ordinary Time-A Psalm 17 [18]	Exod 22:20-26	1 Thess 1:5-10	Matt 22:34-40
30 Ordinary Time-B Psalm 125 [126]	Jer 31:7-9	Heb 5:1-6	Mark 10:46-52
30 Ordinary Time-C Psalm 33 [34]	Sir 35:12-18	2 Tim 4:6-9, 16-18	Luke 18:9-14
31 Ordinary Time-A Psalm 130 [131]	Mal 1:14–2:2, 8-10	1 Thess 2:7-9, 13	Matt 23:1-12
31 Ordinary Time-B Psalm 17 [18]	Deut 6:2-6	Heb 7:23-28	Mark 12:28-34
31 Ordinary Time-C Psalm 144 [145]	Wis 11:22–12:2	2 Thess 1:11–2:2	Luke 19:1-10

Sunday	First Reading	Second Reading	Gospel
32 Ordinary Time-A Psalm 62 [63]	Wis 6:12-16	1 Thess 4:13-18	Matt 25:1-13
32 Ordinary Time-B Psalm 145 [146]	1 Kgs 17:10-16	Heb 9:24-28	Mark 12:38-44
32 Ordinary Time-C Psalm 16 [17]	2 Macc 7:1-2, 9-14	2 Thess 2:16–3:5	Luke 20:27-38
33 Ordinary Time-A Psalm 127 [128]	Prov 31:10-13, 19-20, 30-31	1 Thess 5:1-6	Matt 25:14-30
33 Ordinary Time-B Psalm 15 [16]	Dan 12:1-3	Heb 10:11-14, 18	Mark 13:24-32
33 Ordinary Time-C Psalm 97 [98]	Mal 4:1-2	2 Thess 3:7-12	Luke 21:5-19
Christ the King-A Psalm 22 [23]	Ezek 34:11-12, 15-17	1 Cor 15:20-26, 28	Matt 25:31-46
Christ the King-B Psalm 92 [93]	Dan 7:13-14	Rev 1:5-8	John 18:33-37
Christ the King-C Psalm 121 [122]	2 Sam 5:1-3	Col 1:12-20	Luke 23:35-43

Appendix C

Music

Much of the music in this section presumes an adult leader who can sing in dialogue with small children. Taking such a cantor role is actually quite easy, even if one does not consider oneself a musician, for children have refreshingly few expectations about correct vocal style and the like!

The musical settings here are for the most part fairly simple. Often they use the traditional intervals and stepwise melodic movement of Church chant, which is a purely vocal type of music and thus eminently singable. The psalm arrangements emulate the chant practice of using sparse notation for the stanza or verses so that the text is of primary significance to singer and hearer alike. Accompaniment is not at all necessary.

It is important to bear in mind a point made earlier in this book and which I will reiterate here: if fine liturgical antiphons, psalms, and songs are in use in one's parish, it is preferable to choose those for home use (and I might add, school use) in order to reinforce and unify children's experience of the Church's feasts and seasons.

Sunday

SONG 1.   A Call to Prayer

SONG 2.   Psalm 121 [122], A Psalm to Welcome the Sunday

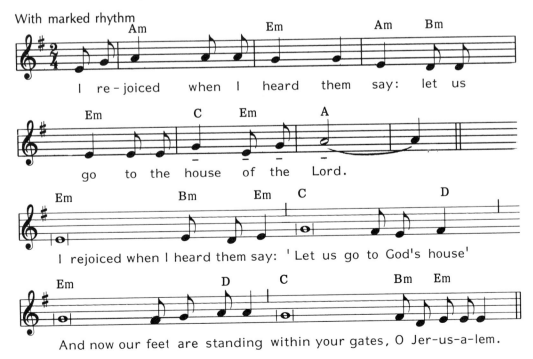

SONG 3. Song of Mary *(Magnificat)*

My soul glo-ri-fies the Lord. Ho - ly is his name.

My spir-it re-joi - ces. Ho - ly is his name.

In God my Sa - vior Ho - ly is his name.

© Alphonse M. Gerwing, 1970
Used with permission

SONG 4. Prayers for a Sunday-Welcoming Meal

Leader: (at the lighting of the candle)

Blessed are you, O God, who give us this pasch - al light,

light that shines in the darkness and brings us joy.

All:

Bless - ed be God for - ev - er!   (brief pause in silence)

Leader:

May the light of Christ fill our hearts on this day of re - sur - rec - tion,

And may his peaceful light shine up - on all peo - ples.

All:

A - men, a - men!

Song 4—continued
Leader: (holding up the bread)

Blessed are you, O God, for your gift of bread, many grains made one,

bread which nourishes our life and our un - i - ty.

All:

Bless - ed be God for - ev - er! (all consume a small piece of bread)

Leader: (holding up the cup of wine)

Blessed are you, O God, for your gift of wine, fruit of the vine,

this cup which we share in thanksgiv - ing and in glad - ness.

All:

Bless - ed be God for - ev - er! (all drink of the cup)

SONG 5.   This Is the Day

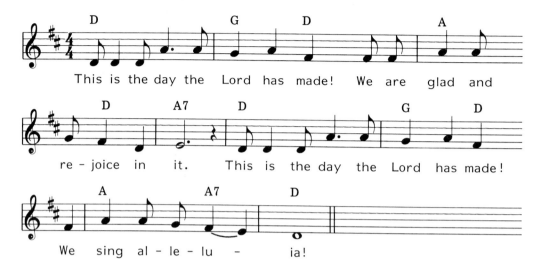

This is the day the Lord has made! We are glad and

re - joice in it. This is the day the Lord has made!

We sing al - le - lu - ia!

SONG 6.   The Lord's Day

Vigorously
Leader:

The Lord's day is our day to sing,

All:

Praise the Lord for - ev - er.

Leader:

Clap your hands for the Ris-en King!

All:

Praise the Lord for - ev - er.

Leader:

Earth and sky and sun so bright,

Leader:

Dance in res - ur - rec - tion light.

Clap your hands for the Ris-en King!

Praise the Lord for - ev - er.

Paschal Three Days

SONG 7. A Call to Prayer

Text based on Phil 2:6-11

Leader: / All:
O Je - sus Christ, O Je - sus Christ.

Leader: / All:
Shep - herd Lord, Shep - herd Lord,

Leader:
You showed your love by death on a cross.

All:
You showed your love by death on a cross. (Friday: stop here)

Leader:
Raise us up to new life with you.

All:
Raise us up to new life with you. (Saturday: stop here)

Leader: / All:
Al - le - lu - ia! Al - le - lu - ia! (Sunday)

SONG 8.   Psalm 15 [16]

Keep me safe, O God; you are my hope.

My heart rejoices, my soul is glad;

Even my body shall rest in safe - ty.

For you will not leave my soul a - mong the dead,

Nor let your beloved know de - cay.

SONG 9.   Song of the Cross

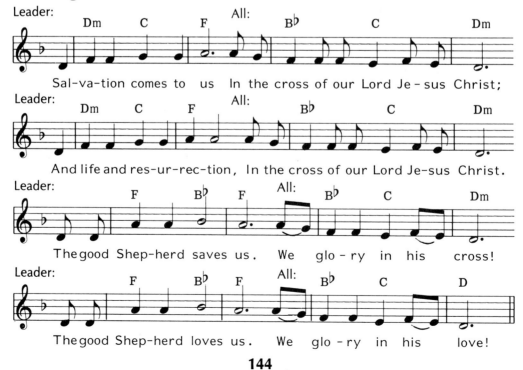

Sal-va-tion comes to us In the cross of our Lord Je-sus Christ;

And life and res-ur-rec-tion, In the cross of our Lord Je-sus Christ.

The good Shep-herd saves us.   We glo-ry in his cross!

The good Shep-herd loves us.   We glo-ry in his love!

SONG 10.   We Adore You, Christ

Leader:
We a - dore you, Christ, and we bless you,

All:
By your cross you have saved the world.

SONG 11.   We Worship You, O Lord

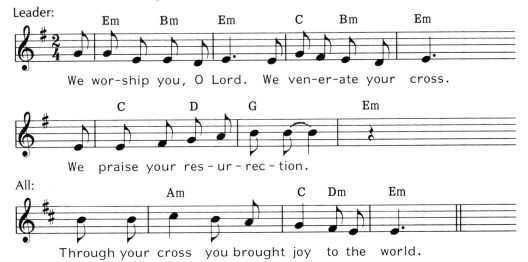

Leader:
We wor-ship you, O Lord. We ven-er-ate your cross.

We praise your res - ur - rec - tion.

All:
Through your cross you brought joy to the world.

50 Days of Easter

SONG 12.   A Call to Prayer

Leader sings each line first, all repeat
Je - sus is our light,

Light of the world,

Al - le - lu - ia.

SONG 13.   Psalm 22 [23]

The Lord is my shep-herd; there is noth-ing I shall want.

The Lord is my shepherd; there is noth-ing I shall want.

Fresh and green are the pas-tures where he gives me re-pose.

Near restful wa-ters he leads me,

To revive my droop-ing spir-it.

SONG 14.   Our Shepherd Lord Is Ris'n

Our Shep-herd Lord is ris'n, Al-le-lu, al-le-lu – ia.

O let our voi-ces ring! Al-le-lu, al-le-lu – ia.

His light shines in our hearts, Al-le-lu, al-le-lu – ia.

For fif-ty days we sing Al-le-lu, al-le-lu – ia.

146

SONG 15. Alleluia Clapping Song

Al-le-lu – ia   al -le-lu – ia   al -le – lu – ia_____

Al-le-lu – ia   al -le-lu – ia   al -le – lu – ia_____

Al-le-lu – ia   al -le-lu – ia   al -le – lu – ia_____

SONG 16. Milk and Honey Song

We've come to the land of milk and hon-ey,   Hal-le-lu –

ia! We've come to the land where it's al - ways sun-ny,

Hal-le-lu – ia!   And now   we   see   the

tree of   life, and the Shep-herd Lord who   is   our   light. We've

come to the land of milk and hon-ey,   Hal-le-lu – ia!

SONG 17.   O Light of Christ

O light of Christ,   shine in our hearts.

Won-der-ful light,   shine in our hearts.

Be with us al-ways,   shine, shine in our hearts.

SONG 18.   The Lord Is My Shepherd

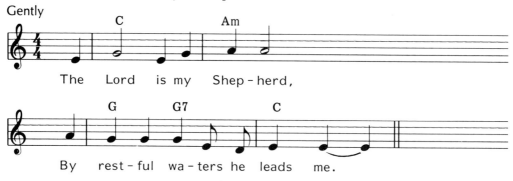

The Lord is my Shep-herd,

By rest-ful wa-ters he leads me.

SONG 19.   Jesus

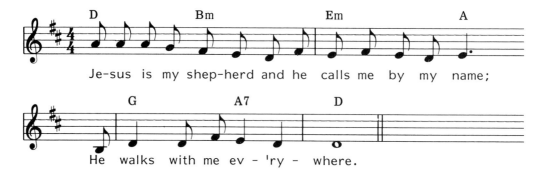

Je-sus is my shep-herd and he calls me by my name;

He walks with me ev - 'ry - where.

SONG 20. Lift High the Cross

With conviction

Lift high the cross, Lift high the cross of Christ!

All peo - ple, come, a - dore and praise his ho – ly name.

SONG 21. A Trinity Song

Hungarian traditional melody

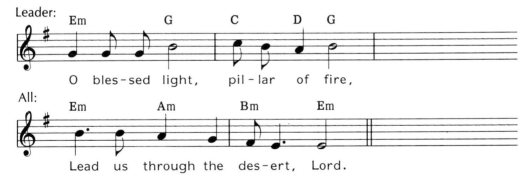

1. May the love of God our Fa -ther be in all our homes to - day.
2. May the light of Christ our Sa -vior shine in us for all to see.
3. May the gift of God the Spi- rit keep us as one fam - i - ly.

Lent

SONG 22. A Call to Prayer

Leader:

O bles -sed light, pil - lar of fire,

All:

Lead us through the des -ert, Lord.

SONG 23. Psalm 129 [130]

With the Lord there is mer-cy, and full-ness of re-demp-tion.

My soul is waiting   for the Lord,

I count   on his word.

My soul is longing for the Lord

More than watch - men for day-break.

SONG 24. Song of the Forty Days

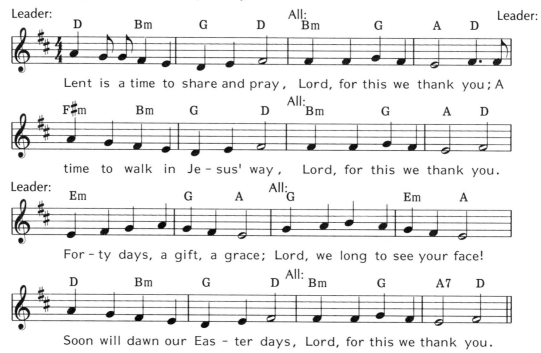

Lent is a time to share and pray, Lord, for this we thank you; A

time to walk in Je - sus' way,   Lord, for this we thank you.

For - ty days, a gift, a grace; Lord, we long to see your face!

Soon will dawn our Eas - ter days, Lord, for this we thank you.

SONG 25.   Lenten Journey Song

At a walking pace

Je-sus, Lord, we walk with you on our Len-ten jour-ney.

Your word shows us what to do on our Len-ten jour-ney.

Shep-herd, Lord, you give us light, liv-ing wa-ters and new life.

Je-sus, Lord, we walk with you on our Len-ten jour-ney.

SONG 26.   Prayers from the Gospel

Je-sus, I am thirs-ty. Give me liv-ing wa-ter.

Je-sus, I am blind. Let me see a-gain.

Leader: 2nd time, All:

Raise me up to live with you.

Christmas

SONG 27.   A Call to Prayer

Rhythmically (Sing three times, moving from soft to loud.)

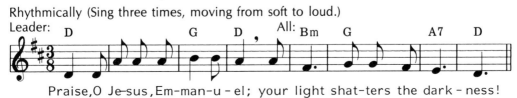

Praise, O Je-sus, Em-man-u-el; your light shat-ters the dark-ness!

SONG 28. Psalm 97 [98]

Lilting and joyful

All the ends of the earth have seen the sav-ing pow-er of God.

Sing a new song to the Lord

for he has worked won - ders.

His right hand and his ho - ly arm

have brought sal - va - tion.

SONG 29. Song of Zechariah *(Benedictus)*

Em	Am	Em	Am

The ris - ing sun has come to give light, to

Dm7	Em	F	G	A

guide our feet in the way of peace.

Am   Dm

1. Blessed be the Lord, the God of Is - ra - el,
2. He has raised up for us a Sav - ior

Em   Am

1. for he has visited his people and set them free.
2. from the house of his ser - vant Da - vid.

SONG 30. A Christmas Season Litany

Leader: G   C   G   All: Bm Em

Blest	are	you Lord	God.	A-men! A-men!
Ho-	ly	is your	name.	
You	have	sent your Son to be		
		one of	us.	
You	love	your people with deep-		
		est	love.	
You	have	sent your Son		
		to save us from	sin.	
Great is	your	mercy for your	peo-ple.	
You	fill	your children with	joy.	
You	call	us to praise your	name.	
Look	with	love upon your holy	Church.	
Send	the	Spirit of your Son		
		into our	hearts.	
Let	us	bring glory and		
		praise to your	name.	
Through Je-		sus Christ your	Son	
And	in	the love of your Holy	Spi-rit.	

Advent

SONG 31.   A Call to Prayer

You are light in dark-ness; Come, O Lord, and save us.

SONG 32.   A Call to Prayer

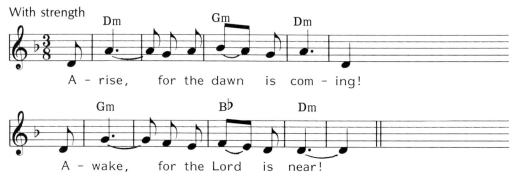

A - rise, for the dawn is com - ing!

A - wake, for the Lord is near!

SONG 33.   Psalm 79 [80]

Lord, make us turn to you, let us see your face and we shall be saved.

O shepherd of Is - ra - el, hear us,

shine forth from your che - ru - bim throne.

O Lord, rouse up your might,

O Lord, come to our help.

SONG 34.   Song of Mary (*Magnificat*)

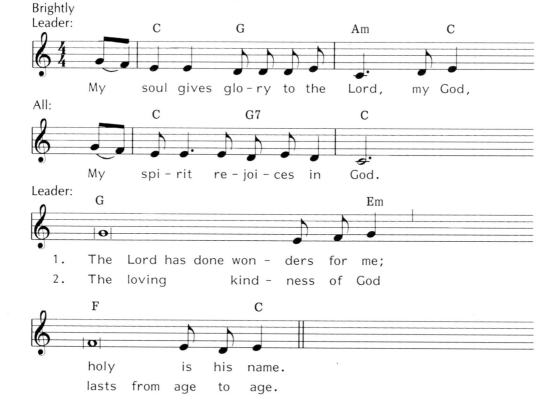

Brightly

Leader:
My soul gives glo-ry to the Lord, my God,

All:
My spi-rit re-joi-ces in God.

Leader:
1. The Lord has done won-ders for me;
2. The loving kind-ness of God

holy is his name.
lasts from age to age.

SONG 35.   A Rose Has Come

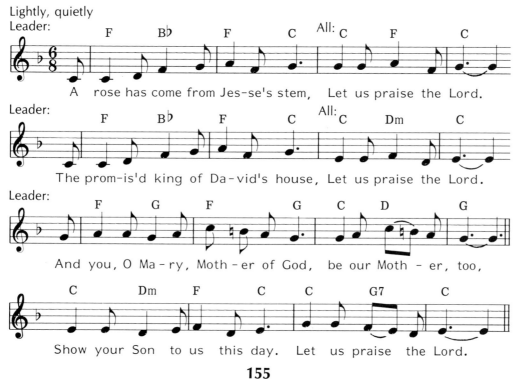

Lightly, quietly

Leader:
A rose has come from Jes-se's stem, Let us praise the Lord.

Leader:
The prom-is'd king of Da-vid's house, Let us praise the Lord.

Leader:
And you, O Ma-ry, Moth-er of God, be our Moth-er, too,

Show your Son to us this day. Let us praise the Lord.

General Use

SONG 36. Song of Thanks

Anonymous

O give thanks, O give thanks, O give thanks un-to the Lord

O give thanks, O give thanks, O give thanks un-to the Lord.

SONG 37. Song for a Mealtime

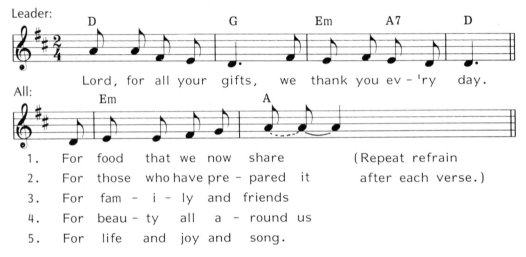

Lord, for all your gifts, we thank you ev – 'ry day.

1. For food that we now share (Repeat refrain
2. For those who have pre – pared it after each verse.)
3. For fam – i – ly and friends
4. For beau – ty all a – round us
5. For life and joy and song.

SONG 38. Psalm 116 [117], A Psalm of Praise

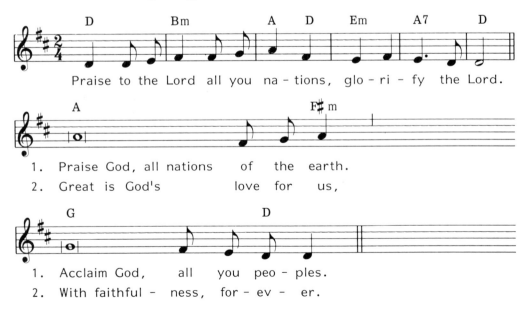

Praise to the Lord all you na – tions, glo – ri – fy the Lord.

1. Praise God, all nations of the earth.
2. Great is God's love for us,

1. Acclaim God, all you peo – ples.
2. With faithful – ness, for – ev – er.

Notes

Introduction

1. Sofia Cavalletti, *The Religious Potential of the Child,* trans. Patricia M. Coulter and Julie M. Coulter (New York: Paulist Press, 1983) 30f.
2. These comments on the spirituality of children reflect the insights of Cavalletti as presented during a summer course, "The Religious Potential of Young Children," St. Joseph's College, Toronto, 1986. I am indebted to Dr. Cavalletti and her co-catechists for wisdom generously shared.
3. Gail Ramshaw Schmidt, "Readiness for Liturgy: The Formation of Christian Children," *Assembly* 9 (1982) 190.
4. Josef Pieper, *Leisure the Basis of Culture,* (London: Faber and Faber, 1952) 78.
5. Robert Hamma, "Adapting to Children: A Commentary on the DMC," *Assembly* 9 (1982) 188.
6. Those interested in integrating religious themes and music education based on the Kodaly Choral Method will find an invaluable collection of graded material for young children in Alphonse M. Gerwing's *Twenty Centuries of Christian Song* (Muenster, Sask.: St. Peter's Press, 1981).
7. Cavalletti, in private conversation, Toronto, July 22, 1986.

Sunday

1. Justin, *Apol.* 1:67, trans. Lucien Deiss, *Early Sources of the Liturgy* (Collegeville, Minn.: The Liturgical Press, 1967) 25.
2. *Passio SS. Dativi, Saturnini Presbyteri et al.,* in P. F. de Cavalieri, *Note agiografiche,* fasc. 8 (Rome, 1935) 449.
3. Justin, *Apol.* 1:67, *Early Sources,* 26.
4. Jerome, *In die dominicae Paschae homilia* in G. Morin (ed.), *Anecdota Maredsolana* 3:2 (1897) 418.
5. Canadian Conference of Catholic Bishops, "The Meaning of Sunday in a Pluralistic Society," (Ottawa, 1986) 24.
6. *General Norms for the Liturgical Year and Calendar* (1969) 43. Actually, this quotation refers to the whole of Ordinary Time; it is the Sundays of this part of the Church Year that seem to be most vulnerable to "theming."
7. I am aware particularly of the valuable work of Christiane Brusselmans and others, who are preparing a book of Scripture readings and responsorial psalms for the use of groups of children in the Liturgy of the Word.
8. Gail Ramshaw Schmidt, "The Pre-schooler in the Liturgy," *The Sacred Play of Children,* ed., Diane Apostolos-Cappadona (New York: Seabury Press, 1983) 116.
9. Louis Weil, "Children and Worship," in *The Sacred Play of Children,* 58.
10. Joseph Gelineau, "Reflections: Children and Symbols and Five Years after the *Directory for Masses with Children,*" in *The Sacred Play of Children,* 28.
11. It is possible that our understanding of children as "Church, here and now" may be clouded partly by the manner in which we conduct children's initiation, with the sacraments of baptism, confirmation, and Eucharist separated from one another by several years. Baptized children who have not yet celebrated confirmation and Eucharist may in fact seem *not* to be fully Church! This raises the question of the manner and theology of infants' and children's initiation, but that intriguing topic must remain outside the scope of this book.
12. Louis Weil, "Children," 55–59, offers an insightful reflection on the intuitive quality of children's participation in worship.
13. Ramshaw Schmidt, "Readiness," 191.
14. Eugene A. Walsh, *Giving Life: The Ministry of the Parish Sunday Assembly* (Daytona Beach, Fla: Pastoral Arts Associates of North America, 1985) 22f.

The Paschal Three Days

1. Throughout his book, references to texts from both the Sacramentary and Lectionary will be given as for the Roman Rite, although other communions presently use many of the same texts in worship.
2. Ambrose, *Letter 23,* 13, trans. Mary Melchoir Beyenka in *The Fathers of the Church* 26: 194.
3. Leo the Great, *Sermon 72,* 3, trans. Charles Lett Feltoe in *Nicene and Post-Nicene Fathers,* Second Series, 12: 185.
4. In the *General Norms for the Liturgical Year and Calendar,* the term *triduum paschale* of the Latin original is translated "Easter triduum." Because the English-language word "Easter" connotes primarily resurrection, the translation rendered is less inclusive than would be a literal translation as "paschal triduum." Since the latter is more explicitly comprehensive of the Lord's suffering, dying, and rising, many liturgical writers prefer to use the term paschal triduum, or literally, the Paschal Three Days. For a more ample discussion of this matter, see Patrick Regan, "The Three Days and the Forty Days," *Worship* 54:1 (1980) 16–17. I gratefully acknowledge Patrick Regan's enduring influence on my work.
5. Venantius Fortunatus, *Vexilla Regis,* trans. John Mason Neale, *The Collected Hymns, Sequences*

Notes

and Carols of John Mason Neale (London: Hodder and Stoughton, 1914) 9–10.

6. *Pange lingua gloriosi, Collected Hymns,* 7–9.
7. A rubric to this effect is given in the Roman Sacramentary for Good Friday (note 1). In spite of its clarity, this rubric is generally ignored.

The Fifty Days of Easter

1. Tertullian, *On Prayer* 23, 2, trans. S. Thelwall in *The Ante-Nicene Fathers* 3:689.
2. Tertullian, *On Baptism* 19,2, *Patrologia Latina* (PL), ed. J. P. Migne 1:1222.
3. Basil the Great, *On the Spirit* 27, 66, trans. Blomfield Jackson in *Nicene and Post-Nicene Fathers, second series,* 8:42.
4. Augustine, *Sermon 243,* 9, trans. Mary Sarah Muldowney in *The Fathers of the Church* 38:278.
5. Augustine, *Sermon 252,* 9, *Fathers,* 333.
6. Cavalletti, *Religious Potential,* 62f.
7. Andrew of Crete, *Oratio 10, Patrologia Graeca (PG),* 97:1020.
8. For ideas on content in the reflections for parents and children during several of the Easter weeks, I am indebted to Dr. Sofia Cavalletti and her team of international catechists who presented similar material at the seminar, "The Religious Potential of Children," St. Joseph's College, Toronto, July 21—August 8, 1986. I have also adapted some material from Cavalletti's book, *Religious Potential.*
9. Doug Adams, "Dancing Carols: An Introduction to Dance in Worship," in Doug Adams, ed., *Dancing Christmas Carols,* (Saratoga, Calif.: Resource Publications, 1978) 12.
10. Justin, *Apol. 1:61,* trans. Cyril C. Richardson, *Early Christian Fathers* (New York: Macmillan, 1970) 283.
11. Cavalletti, *Religious Potential,* 98f.

Lent

1. *Egeria's Travels to the Holy Land* trans. John Wilkinson, (Jerusalem: Ariel Publishing House, 1981), 45,2–4.
2. Leo the Great, *Sermon 39,3,* trans. Charles Lett Feltoe in *Nicene and Post-Nicene Fathers, second series,* 12: 152.
3. Augustine, *Sermon 210,4-5, Fathers,* 102.
4. Augustine, *Sermon 243,9, Fathers,* 278.
5. Augustine, *Sermon 206,3, Fathers,* 89.
6. Leo the Great, *Sermon 40,4,* PL 54:270.
7. Leo the Great, *Sermon 49,6,* PL 54:305.
8. Leo the Great, *Sermon 42,2,* PL 54:276.
9. Gabe Huck, "Introduction to the Seasons," in *Parish Path through Lent and Eastertime,* ed., Mary

Ann Simcoe, second edition (Chicago: Liturgy Training Publications, 1985) 10. This small book is representative of the excellent and comprehensive liturgical materials from Liturgy Training Publications for parish celebration of feasts and seasons.

10. *The Canadian Catechism* series is written and produced by the National Office of Religious Education of the Canadian Conference of Catholic Bishops, Ottawa, Canada.
11. Cavalletti, *Religious Potential,* 151f.
12. Cavalletti, *Religious Potential,* 62f.
13. Cavalletti, *Religious Potential* 67f.
14. The presentation of the Good Shepherd parable is given in this manner by Cavalletti.

Christmas-Epiphany

1. Maximus of Turin, *Sermo 62:1, Corpus Christianorum, Series Latina* 23:261.
2. Leo the Great, *Sermo 21 in Nativitate Domini, 1, 3* PL 54:192.
3. H. Jenny, *The Paschal Mystery in the Christian Year* trans. A. Stehling and J. Lundberg (Notre Dame: University of Notre Dame Press, 1962) 32.
4. Leo the Great, *Sermo 33 in Epiphania Domini, 3, 3* PL 54:242.
5. Cavalletti, *Religious Potential,* 98.
6. Gertrud Mueller Nelson, in her recent book, *To Dance with God* (New York: Paulist Press, 1986) 75f, presents a vigorous case for the retention of Santa Claus on the basis that he is, potentially, a powerful sainted father figure. She acknowledges, if somewhat unenthusiastically, the viability of the position on Santa Claus taken in this book. Milo Shannon-Thornberry in *Let Jesus Come, Let Santa Go,* three-volume cassette (Kansas City, Mo.: National Catholic Reporter Publishing, 1983) is definitely a Santa abolitionist!
7. For one family's account of establishing its own December 6 custom, see Kathe and Michael Sherer's "Good-bye Santa, Hello St. Nicholas," in Milo Shannon-Thornberry, *The Alternate Celebrations Catalogue* (New York: Pilgrim Press, 1982) 104–105.

Advent

1. Cyril of Jerusalem, *Catechesis 15, 1,* PG 33:869.
2. Leo the Great, *Sermo 21 In Nativitate Domini, 1, 1, PL* 54:191.
3. Shannon-Thornberry, *Alternate,* 113-4.
4. Cavalletti, *Religious Potential,* 106–7.
5. For more details on this suggestion, see Shannon-Thornberry, *Alternate,* 92.

158

Bibliography

Select Bibliography

Apostolos-Cappadona, Diane, ed. *The Sacred Play of Children.* New York: Seabury Press, 1983

Beginning the Journey: From Infant Baptism to First Eucharist. Washington, D.C.: United States Catholic Conference, 1994

Cavalletti, Sofia. *The Religious Potential of the Child.* Trans. Patricia M. Coulter and Julie M. Coulter. New York: Paulist Press, 1983

Cavalletti, Sofia, et al. *The Good Shepherd and the Child: A Joyful Journey.* New Rochelle, N.Y.: Don Bosco Multimedia, 1994

Coles, Robert. *The Spiritual Life of Children.* Boston: Houghton Mifflin, 1990

Directory for Masses with Children. Congregation for Divine Worship, 1973

Huck, Gabe. *A Book of Family Prayer.* New York: Seabury Press, 1979

McGinnis, Kathleen and James. *Parenting for Peace and Justice.* Maryknoll, N.Y.: Orbis Books, 1981; revised edition, *Parenting for Peace and Justice: Ten Years Later,* 1990

National Bulletin on Liturgy. Ottawa, Ontario: Canadian Conference of Catholic Bishops. ''Children and Liturgy,'' 63 (1978); ''Children Learn to Celebrate,'' 89 (1983); ''Children and Liturgy,'' 121 (1990)

Shannon-Thornberry, Milo. *The Alternative Celebrations Catalogue.* New York: Pilgrim Press, 1982

Liturgical Year

Baker, J. Robert, Evelyn Kaehler, and Peter Mazar, eds. *A Lent Sourcebook: The Forty Days.* 2 vols. Chicago: Liturgy Training Publications, 1990

Days of the Lord: The Liturgical Year. 7 vols. Collegeville, Minn.: The Liturgical Press, 1991–94

Easter's Fifty Days. Journal of the Liturgical Conference, 3 (1982)

Halmo, Joan, Frank Henderson, and Peter Mazar, eds. *A Triduum Sourcebook,* revised edition, 3 vols. Chicago: Liturgy Training Publications, 1996

Huck, Gabe. *The Three Days: Parish Prayer in the Paschal Triduum.* Revised edition. Chicago: Liturgy Training Publications, 1992

Huck, Gabe, Gail Ramshaw, and Gordon Lathrop, eds. *An Easter Sourcebook: The Fifty Days.* Chicago: Liturgy Training Publications, 1988

Nocent, Adrian. *The Liturgical Year.* Trans. Matthew J. O'Connell. 4 vols. Collegeville: The Liturgical Press, 1977

O'Gorman, Thomas, ed. *An Advent Sourcebook.* Chicago: Liturgy Training Publications, 1988

Simcoe, Mary Ann, ed. *A Christmas Sourcebook.* Chicago: Liturgy Training Publications, 1984

Walsh, Eugene A. *Giving Life: The Ministry of the Parish Sunday Assembly.* Daytona Beach, Fla.: Pastoral Arts Associates of North America, 1985

Various Resources

Adams, Doug, ed. *Dancing Christmas Carols.* Saratoga, Calif.: Resource Publications, 1978

Assembly. Notre Dame: Center for Pastoral Liturgy. ''The Child and the Liturgy,'' 9 (1982)

Cronin, Gaynell. *Sunday Throughout the Week.* Notre Dame: Ave Maria Press, 1981

Deacove, Jim. *Games Manual.* Perth, Ont.: Family Pastimes, 1974

Deiss, Lucien and Weyman, Gloria Gabriel. *Liturgical Dance* (book and videotape). Phoenix: North American Liturgy Resources, 1984

Family Book of Prayer. Ottawa: Canadian Conference of Catholic Bishops, 1983

Gerwing, Alphonse M. *Twenty Centuries of Christian Song.* Muenster, Sask.: St. Peter's Press, 1981

Hays, Edward. *Prayers for the Domestic Church.* Easton, Kansas: Forest of Peace Books, 1979

Nelson, Gertrud Mueller. *To Dance with God.* New York: Paulist Press, 1986

Ramshaw, Elaine. *The Godparent Book.* Chicago: Liturgy Training Publications, 1993

Ramshaw, Gail. *Sunday Morning.* Chicago: Liturgy Training Publications, 1993

Shannon-Thornberry, Milo, and Grissom, Harriette. *Let Jesus Come, Let Santa Go* (3 vol. audio-cassette). Kansas City: National Catholic Reporter Publishing, 1983

Sorlien, Sandra. *Keeping Christmas.* Minneapolis: Augsburg Publishing, 1982

Tharlet, Eve. *The Little Cooks: Recipes from around the world for boys and girls.* New York: UNICEF, 1988

Vitz, Evelyn Birge. *A Continual Feast.* New York: Harper and Row, and Toronto: Fitzhenry and Whiteside, 1985

Voth, Norma Jost. *Festive Breads of Easter.* Scottdale, Pa.: Herald Press, 1980